DATE DUE

APR 16 2012	

BRODART, CO.   Cat. No. 23-221-003

EYEWITNESS PACIFIC THEATER

EYEWITNESS PACIFIC THEATER

Firsthand Accounts of the War in the Pacific from Pearl Harbor to the Atomic Bombs

JOHN T. KUEHN, COMMANDER, USN (RETIRED)
with D.M. GIANGRECO
Foreword by ERIC M. BERGERUD

STERLING
New York / London
www.sterlingpublishing.com

Published by Sterling Publishing Co., Inc.
387 Park Avenue South, New York, NY 10016

Text © 2008 by John T. Kuehn and D. M. Giangreco

Distributed in Canada by Sterling Publishing
c/o Canadian Manda Group, 165 Dufferin Street
Toronto, Ontario, Canada M6K 3H6

Distributed in the United Kingdom by GMC
Distribution Services
Castle Place, 166 High Street, Lewes, East
Sussex, England BN7 1XU

Distributed in Australia by Capricorn Link
(Australia) Pty. Ltd.
P.O. Box 704, Windsor, NSW 2756, Australia

ISBN-13: 978-1-4027-6215-4

Printed in China

10 9 8 7 6 5 4 3 2 1

For more information about custom editions,
special sales, premium and corporate
purchases, please contact Sterling Special
Sales Department at 800-805-5489 or
specialsales@sterlingpub.com

Acknowledgments

HALF-TITLE PAGE: A Nakajima B6N "Jill" torpedo bomber, flies through a storm of antiaircraft fire in a futile effort to sink an American warship near Ulithi anchorage on January 31, 1945.

TITLE PAGE: A diver glides silently over the eerie ghost of a Mitsubishi F1M2 "Pete" observation seaplane that crashed or was shot down near the New Guinea coast more than sixty years ago.

BELOW: Antiaircraft gunners aboard the USS *Iowa* put a 20-mm Oerlikon through its paces during the battleship's shakedown cruise in 1943.

CONTENTS PAGES: One of several Marine M4A2 Sherman tanks and amtracs that were destroyed during the June 1944 invasion of Saipan. The waterproof wading trunks attached to its exhaust and air intake systems have long since been removed.

END PAPERS: Mount Suribachi on Iwo Jima, Japan.

Any project like this has a very large cast of characters who are critical to its completion. First, the authors extend their gratitude to all the professionals at Barnes & Noble, whose tireless efforts contributed to making this book a quality product. The authors would like to gratefully acknowledge the support of their families, in particular. In addition, the authors gratefully acknowledge the patience, support, and advice of their wives Kathryn Moore and Kimberlee Kuehn. They also extend thanks to the Air Force Historical Center, Naval Historical Center, Combined Arms Research Library at Fort Leavenworth, and United States Naval Institute for their help and assistance in the project and for granting access to their oral history collections. The authors also thank Andrea Giangreco, who was invaluable in correcting the text for final submission to the editors at Barnes & Noble. Finally, the most important are those soldiers, sailors, marines, and airmen who sacrificed so much—many of whose words grace the pages of this book. A staggering number of them gave their lives in the Pacific Theater in World War II. This debt can never be repaid, only honored. Hopefully this book, if it accomplishes anything, accomplishes that.

Contents

Foreword

It is ironic that Japan and the United States both entered the "Great Game" of Asian politics in the late nineteenth century. Japan showed its growing strength by military victories over China and drove the point home with a spectacular triumph over Russia in 1905 while the United States arrived on the scene due to the largely unexpected consequences of the Spanish-American War fought mainly in the Caribbean. As often pointed out, Japan's leaders in this period were only following a path long pioneered by European imperialist nations. However, with the incalculable advantage of hindsight, we can now see that Japan entered the imperial contest with extreme vigor at almost exactly the same time that many in Europe (and the United States) were beginning to doubt the value of game altogether.

Japanese imperial policy from the outset was more aggressive and comprehensive than was exhibited by the other competing powers. This was partially due to simple geography—Japan's initial imperial holdings in Korea, Formosa, and Manchuria were in Tokyo's backyard and included peoples Japan had long, and not always pleasant, contact with. More to the point, the Japanese government was deeply influenced by the "geopolitics" being taught and embraced in many nations such as Germany, Korea, Manchuria, and, to a lesser degree, Formosa. When Japan opportunistically joined the Allies during World War I, it showed vividly that Tokyo wished to create a client state out of China itself. This aim was thwarted in 1919, but dreams of the Greater East Asian Co-Prosperity Sphere were already evident.

America's role in Asia during the first forty years of the twentieth century was different from that of Japan. The United States was interested in the potential, although never realized, China Market and actively promoted equal access to China under the Open Door Policy. In the Philippines, American rule was largely benign and more than a little disorganized. Indeed, in the early 1930s the United States declared its intention of granting independence to Manila in a short period. A different picture, however, appeared when looking at naval affairs. To a remarkable degree, the American and Japanese navies defined themselves against each other. It is true that U.S. contingencies existed for naval operations against other nations, but the various "Orange" war plans, which posited a war against Japan, were the only ones taken seriously and they were taken very seriously indeed. The Japanese Navy returned the favor by viewing conflict with the U.S. Navy as the inevitable centerpiece of any future war in the Pacific. The result was a naval arms race between the two nations that began the day World War I ended.

As late as early 1939, however, war between the U.S. and Japan was still very much in the realm of the hypothetical. The Isolationist Congress had been kinder to the USN than to the Army, but the fact remained that America was not prepared for war. And, as long as a coalition between the USN, the Royal Navy, and perhaps the French Navy was a possibility, Japan was not strong enough fight a war alone. As it was, the war in China had gone very badly for Japan. Imperial forces won each major battle but simply lacked the manpower to occupy the enemy countryside. It is very difficult to speculate what Japan would have done in this situation had the world's political landscape not been changed by Adolph Hitler.

Having the Western powers stuck in a general war in Europe with no obvious end, was a kind of miracle for Tokyo. With their enemies in disarray, Tokyo moved quickly to take advantage of the situation diplomatically. In September 1940, Japan signed the Tripartite Pact with Italy and Nazi Germany. As many diplomatic historians have pointed out in the years since World War II, there was an oddly parasitic character to this agreement. Tokyo clearly hoped Hitler would keep Britain and the United States busy. Hitler, for his part, hoped Japan would give Roosevelt something to think about. Although defensive in theory, the spirit of the agreement was clearly aggressive as events were to prove.

The creation of the Axis completely changed American policy toward Japan. Regardless of rhetoric, Washington had previously done nothing to hinder Japanese expansion in China. After the fall of 1940, however, Washington believed that Berlin and Tokyo might be acting together. The issue was no longer China, but America's position in all of Asia. The Americans had good reason to worry. With Britain and France neutralized, the Japanese military was determined to take advantage of the diplomatic/military revolution caused by Hitler while the opportunity existed.

It was one of the amazing ironies of World War II: The day Japanese planes took off from their carriers toward Pearl Harbor, the Red Army launched a blistering counteroffensive against the Wehrmacht at the gates of Moscow. With Hitler's victory now in doubt, Japan faced calamity. Nazi dominance in Europe had been the bedrock of Japanese aggression. An Allied victory over Germany spelled doom for Japan. What was not clear, however, was how a war in the Pacific would play out and how large would be the cost to the Allies for victory.

Outnumbered, out-led, and fighting with inferior resources, the Japanese

Empire could only rely on the extraordinary courage and fanaticism of its servicemen. America had learned as early as Guadalcanal that Japanese forces would not surrender. That, however, was only part of the terrible chemistry. Japanese officers could, and did, assume their infantry would resist until the end, allowing deployments on islands like Iwo Jima and Okinawa that a "normal" army would not have considered. And so the Japanese soldiers proved most expert at making American soldiers bleed for every victory, despite the fact that the outcome was never in doubt during any of the island battles.

The Japanese attitude toward death and surrender bewildered American servicemen. Surrender in war is always a reciprocal relationship. In many cases, American intelligence went to great lengths to capture Japanese soldiers, but rarely succeeded. (The only area of the Pacific that showed large numbers of Japanese surrenders was the Southwest Pacific, which, by 1945, had been isolated for over two years. Tokyo simply assumed all of its men had perished. In fact, the Allies had created the war's largest POW camp with 250,000 bypassed and starving Japanese. Even in this area, however, organized surrender rarely took place.) Simply put, Allied

soldiers concluded that not only would Japanese soldiers not surrender, but that it was dangerous to attempt to take them prisoner. The result was a war with no quarter on the battlefield.

No matter how much the "kill ratio" favored Allied forces, American, Australian, and British soldiers were dying until the last day of the war. With no possibility of a negotiated peace, the Allies simply decided to destroy Japan. Some U.S. officers believed an air and naval blockade would do the trick. Others were convinced that rapid victory could only come by invasion of the Home Islands. In the back of American minds was the sobering realization that Nazi Germany had gone down in flames long after the possibility of anything less than complete capitulation. If Hitler would drag down Germany, what could be expected from a Japanese government that had made suicide a principal weapon of war by 1945?

Sobering but cruel logic dictated that the Pacific War end with atomic bombs. There was no hint that Tokyo was ready to surrender except under terms that prevented an American occupation; an alternative not considered by Washington. No matter what option had been followed without the bomb, the number of dead would have

continued to rise and the Allies were sick of losing thousands of men in a war whose violence almost defied imagination. Employing atomic bombs to shock the Japanese government into surrender was a harsh, but ultimately successful, tactic.

Between Pearl Harbor and the Japanese surrender in Tokyo Bay, there were thousands of engagements of all types, large and small. Everyone in the Pacific Theater faced conditions that were appalling. Indeed, mud, malaria, and dysentery were almost as dangerous to both sides as each other's soldiers. The men who fought this war showed courage, ingenuity, and remarkable tenacity. Their stories, ably organized by Commander John T. Kuehn and D.M. Giangreco, are grim, but the things of the highest drama.

—Eric M. Bergerud,
Author of *Fire in the Sky: The Air War in the South Pacific*; *Touched with Fire: The Land War in the South*; and *The Dynamics of Defeat: The Vietnam War in Hau Nghia Province*

BELOW: Lieutenant Colonel Howard Kurgis accepts the surrender of Captain Sakae Oba, Imperial Japanese Army on Saipan on December 1, 1945. Oba and his forty-five men hid in the island's hills and caves for nearly seventeen months after American forces declared Saipan secure.

Introduction

The war in Asia that America unwillingly "joined" in late 1941, after Japan's attack on Pearl Harbor had been set in motion almost ten years earlier with Japan's conquest of Manchuria and its re-designation as the Japanese puppet-state of Manchukuo. From that point on, Japanese conflict with the turbulent forces of nationalism and Communism inside China, as well as the Western nations with colonies in the Pacific, was almost guaranteed.

World War II in the Pacific, known in Japan as the Greater East Asian War, actually began in 1937 when insubordinate Japanese officers and militarists engineered an incident at the Marco Polo Bridge north of Beijing that resulted in Japan's invasion of China proper. Despite such incidents as the Rape of Nanking (with the Japanese army committing atrocities against both prisoners of war and civilians), the rest of the world only looked on in horror and did not intervene beyond diplomatic measures. Although the Japanese conquered most of North China and later moved south to subjugate much of central and coastal China, the country proved to be too big and turbulent to absorb into the Japanese Empire. Japan soon had an interminable quagmire on its hands with conventional forces led by the Nationalist Chinese under Chiang Kai-shek resisting in the south and Communists under Mao Zedong waging guerrilla war throughout many of the occupied areas and in bastions in the north from the remote province of Yenan. These forces, especially the Nationalists, received both the tacit and material support of the United States.

Japan's frustration only increased when its attempted expansion into Mongolian areas of the Soviet Union was thwarted by a resounding defeat at Nomonhan at the hands of Soviet General Georgy K. Zhukov in 1939. With the resources of Asia in question and an ongoing war in China, Japan turned its attentions south to an area rich in the natural resources that its strategic planners felt were necessary to acquire in order to prosecute "total war." This area was known as the Southern Resource Area and encompassed rubber, oil, tin, and other strategic materials found in Malaysia and the Dutch East Indies [Indonesia] as well as the "rice bowl" areas of Indochina that could feed Japan's hungry and expanding Empire.

However, between Japan's industrial base located in the home islands and the "promised land" to the south lay the American-owned Philippine Islands. Although prevented by treaty from building up the naval and airbases in the Philippines for most of the interwar period, the United States still maintained substantial air, ground, and naval forces in the Philippines. These would lay like a dagger across Japan's strategic sea lines of communication with any prospective conquests to the south. It was for this reason, and the fact the United States had recently cut off most of Japan's access to West Coast oil leases in response to Japanese aggression, that Japan's fateful decision was taken to attack the United States. This despite the fact that President Franklin D. Roosevelt had promised the American people in the latest election that he would, like his predecessor Woodrow Wilson, keep the United States out of the wars raging across the globe and instead serve as the "Arsenal for Democracy." That the United States would go to war to protect British, French, and Dutch colonial interests was not likely—but the Japanese felt they could not take this risk. The resulting conflict was the largest geographical conflict in history, spanning tens of thousands of miles of ocean. It was the most bitter war ever waged by Americans, frequently without quarter, and involved the most massive naval and industrial construction and logistical efforts in history. It scarred its participants and shaped an entirely new world in the process. Hopefully we will never see its like again.

RIGHT: Dead and wounded sailors lie scattered about the deck of an Imperial Navy Type D escort caught by Far East Air Force B-25 bombers off the Indo-China coast on April 13, 1945.

The enemy of our games was always Japan, and the courses were so thorough that after the start of World War II, nothing that happened in the Pacific was strange or unexpected. Each student was required to plan logistic support for an advance across the Pacific, and we were well prepared for the fantastic logistic efforts required to support the operations of the war.

—Fleet Admiral Chester W. Nimitz

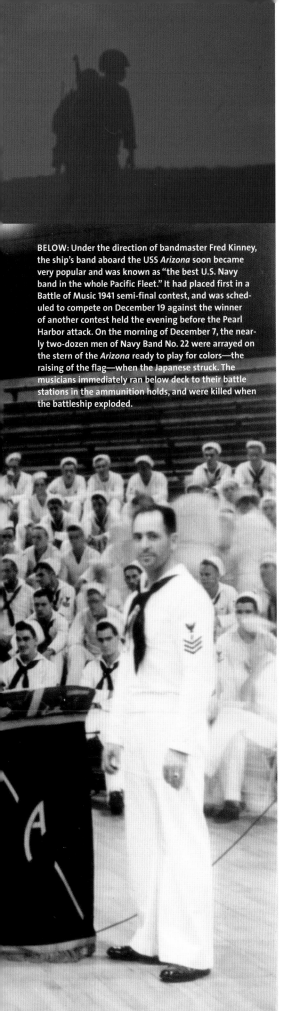

BELOW: Under the direction of bandmaster Fred Kinney, the ship's band aboard the USS *Arizona* soon became very popular and was known as "the best U.S. Navy band in the whole Pacific Fleet." It had placed first in a Battle of Music 1941 semi-final contest, and was scheduled to compete on December 19 against the winner of another contest held the evening before the Pearl Harbor attack. On the morning of December 7, the nearly two-dozen men of Navy Band No. 22 were arrayed on the stern of the *Arizona* ready to play for colors—the raising of the flag—when the Japanese struck. The musicians immediately ran below deck to their battle stations in the ammunition holds, and were killed when the battleship exploded.

Chapter One

THE ROAD TO WAR

ecember 6, 1941 was a tense day throughout the Pacific. For the United States, relations with the Japanese Empire had been *so* strained for *so* long that the nerves of many in FDR's administration had become dulled to the dangerous possibilities that each new day brought. The situation had been building for a very long time. Shortly after the end of World War I there was a scare over the issue of Japan's high-handed actions inside China that threatened America's "Open Door" trade policy. In the United States, racist immigration laws—especially those targeting the Japanese-American population in California—further worsened tensions. This crisis was defused in 1921 by the Washington Naval Conference, at which Japanese diplomats agreed to limit Japan's battleship fleet to three-fifths the size of the U.S. Navy in exchange for the United States maintaining the status quo of its naval bases and facilities in the western Pacific. The resulting naval and diplomatic treaties defused a very dangerous situation in the Pacific, but did not eliminate the basis for conflict—China itself—between the two nations.

There were elements in the Japanese military that were deeply offended by the Washington Naval Treaty and the "inferior" position it assigned the Imperial Japanese Navy (IJN). As the prosperous 1920s gave way to

ABOVE: General Claire Chennault, one of the first Americans in action against the Japanese. Chennault was a maverick in the Army Air Corps, who preached the merits of pursuit (fighter) aircraft in violation of the strategic bombing orthodoxy. He retired from the Army in the late 1930s at the rank of captain after a long, losing struggle to convince the Army Air Corps of the value of pursuit aviation. Soon afterwards he went to China as a civilian advisor to the brand new Chinese Air Force. He was later placed on the active Army list again and became famous worldwide with his group of volunteer American aviators who flew for the Chinese Air Force as the "Flying Tigers."

RIGHT: Japanese troops bound for the Sino-Japanese conflict leave Tokyo on a troop train. Most went to Nagasaki, and then across the Yellow Sea to the Japanese puppet state of Manchukuo (Manchuria) and on to northern China. For the Japanese, the war in the Pacific started in 1937 when they provoked an "incident" with the Nationalist Chinese government of Chiang Kai-shek at the Marco Polo bridge in northern China.

worldwide economic crisis, the militant elements inside Japan—spurred in their efforts by Japan's signing of the London Naval Treaty in 1930 that limited military shipbuilding—began to undermine the basis for peace in the Far East. The London Treaty imposed similar limits on other classes of warships—submarines, cruisers, and destroyers—that the Washington Treaty imposed on battleships. The Japanese senior naval leadership was now far more militant than at the time of the Washington Conference and wanted parity, not inferiority, to the American fleet in other classes of warships. Japan's signing of the London Naval Treaty sparked violent attacks on the treaty's advocates in Japan and resulted in the assassination of Prime Minister Osachi Hamaguchi.

Not long after, ambitious and insubordinate officers of the Kwangtung Army (KTA) stationed along the railway in southern Manchuria plotted a takeover of that vast Chinese province in order to provide Japan resources for further expansion in Asia. In 1931, these officers engineered an "incident" at Mukden along the railroad, a bomb exploding near a Japanese barracks, and then swiftly followed it up with a well-coordinated conquest of Manchuria—

all without the approval of the government in Tokyo. They then established a Japanese-puppet state, Manchukuo, under the last Manchu emperor, Pu Yi.

It was this act, more than any other, that soured Japanese-U.S. relations for the remainder of the 1930s. When Japan was castigated in the League of Nations in 1932 for its aggressions, the Japanese delegation responded by walking out of the organization. Japan, already stung by international condemnation, deepened its alienation from the community of nations when it announced in January 1935 that it would no longer consider itself bound by either the Washington or London Naval treaties. In fact, Japan had already violated the treaties and had plans for warships well in excess of treaty limits, especially the super battleships *Yamato* and *Musashi*. By 1936, the situation in Japan had become chaotic. Radical young army officers from the militant "Imperial Way" sect who were dissatisfied with civilian policies revolted against the government. Their revolt was suppressed, but the message to subsequent governments had the effect of allowing the army to set—or veto—national policy. The result was another army-

engineered "incident" in China in 1937 and the subsequent outbreak of war with Chiang Kai-shek's Nationalist government.

Japan's brutal behavior at Shanghai, Nanking (Nanjing), and elsewhere only strengthened the resolve of both the Chinese Nationalists and the Communists—now ostensibly in a united front against the Japanese—to continue the struggle from the farther regions of China. Additionally, Japanese aircraft had sunk the U.S. gunboat *Panay* in the Yangtze River. War was only narrowly averted with the United States, which now began to apply increasing economic pressure in addition to diplomatic measures to force Japan to abandon its Chinese conquests. The Americans also instituted a policy of material support for the Nationalist Chinese using the famous "Burma Road" linking Burma (now known as Myanmar) and China through the Himalayas, to provide military equipment to Chiang Kai-shek's Army against the Japanese. This included the "loan" of U.S. Army Major General Claire Lee Chennault who helped establish an effective Chinese Air Force.

During this period, President Franklin D. Roosevelt's policy was one of using "soft" economic and diplomatic power and proxies to

apply pressure on the Japanese. First, he built the Navy up as much as he could. In 1940, Congress approved his administration's proposal for a "Two-Ocean Navy," ostensibly for defense but really as a deterrent to Japan should it think of going to war with the United States. This act, at a stroke, established the basis for the largest and most modern fleet the world had ever seen. FDR's second set of actions revolved around the idea of the United States serving as the "Arsenal of Democracy." Instead of becoming directly involved in the war in Europe or in Asia, Roosevelt would provide supplies to those fighting the Axis powers of Germany, Italy, and Japan. China would fight the Japanese directly while Britain—and later the Soviet Union—were supplied to deal with Germany.

The final set of FDR's actions consisted of a series of economic sanctions and restrictions. They were the most critical in bringing on the war, although he probably did not realize it. In 1939, the United States terminated its decades-old commercial treaty with Japan in response to Japan's continued aggression in China. The following year, FDR ordered the Pacific Fleet to remain permanently "forward" at Pearl Harbor, instead of California. This resulted in the removal of its commander, Admiral James O. Richardson, who had protested this move as too provocative. The United States followed these actions in the summer of 1940 with an embargo on the sale of aviation gasoline and high-grade scrap iron to the Japanese. The Japanese responded by moving into northern Indochina at the "invitation" of the new Vichy-French government, formed after Germany's victory over France. The United States then expanded its embargo to include all scrap metal. It was at this point that Japan formally joined the Axis Powers of Europe in the Tripartite Pact, an action strenuously opposed by Admiral Isoroku Yamamoto of the Combined Fleet.

The strained atmosphere in Japan and lack of diplomatic accomplishment by the civilian-led cabinet resulted in the eventual fall of Prince Konoye's "unity" government and its replacement by the militarist government of prime minister and general, Hideki Tojo. By the summer of 1941, Japan's economic situation was becoming critical. Japanese forces had already moved into northern Indochina in September 1940, and further bullied the Vichy-French into accepting 50,000 Japanese troops into the remainder of the country. In response to this latest aggression, the United States—which supplied the majority of Japan's fuel oil needs—cut off Japan's ability to negotiate the oil leases necessary to buy fuel from American suppliers. This last act gave Japan only one-and-a-half years of fuel reserves, since the British and Dutch had followed suit by denying the Japanese access to their oil resources as well. It was this effective fuel embargo that steeled the militaristic Japanese government's determination to go to war to capture the fuel and resources of the Dutch East Indies. It also convinced the Japanese that they must attack the United States, whose Philippine possessions lay across Japan's strategic sea lines of communication with its prospective conquests to the south.

December Sixth— The Japanese

HIROHITO, THE SHOWA EMPEROR—The day before the Japanese attack on Pearl Harbor found Emperor Hirohito still engaged in meetings—begun on December 2 (December 1 in the United States)—with his war advisors. Previously in late November after receiving U.S. Secretary of State Cordell Hull's proposal that Japan withdraw from China in order to provide a "basis for peace," Hirohito had decided for war. This proposal was in part misrepresented to him by his advisors as being much less conciliatory than he had hoped, but in any case there was very little else he felt he could do because of the implicit threat of his removal

OPPOSITE: The launching of the USS *Missouri* in 1944. The most famous of the *Iowa*-class battleships, the keel of the "Mighty MO" was laid in January 1941, eleven months before the war started. At 57,000 tons maximum displacement, she was built to tangle with the massive *Yamato*-class battlewagons, but this "clash of the Titans" never occurred.

BELOW: Marines wade ashore at Culebra, Puerto Rico, from an experimental armored landing barge as part of fleet maneuvers held during the winter months of 1923–1924. The amphibious techniques developed by the Marines between the world wars prepared them for the grueling combat they would face in the Pacific.

RIGHT: Admiral Isoroku Yamamoto had conceived and planned the strike on Pearl Harbor, yet warned that Japan would likely lose the war if it could not be wrapped up quickly. As a young man, he had studied at Harvard and later served as Japan's Naval Attaché in Washington. Yamamoto's nearly six years in the United States gave him insights into an America that was incomprehensible to his warrior colleagues raised in a homogeneous, and in many ways still-closed, society. What they beheld when looking across the Pacific was a chaotic, mongrel nation suffering under the weight of a weak, inefficient democratic process; what Yamamoto saw was vitality and inner strength.

ABOVE, LEFT: Admiral Chuichi Nagumo. ABOVE, RIGHT: General Tomoyuki Yamashita. RIGHT: General Hideki Tojo was appointed in the summer of 1941 as the Prime Minister of the Japanese government after the fall of the "national unity" government of Prince Konoye and the imposition of a comprehensive oil embargo by the Americans. A militant fire-eater, Tojo was still subject to the will of Japan's consensus-style political process and the Emperor. According to some accounts, he had hoped that he would not become the Prime Minister because he regarded himself as too pro-war. His image and name would become synonymous with Japanese treachery to most Americans.

as emperor if he was seen to give away Japanese gains in China to appease the Americans. Hirohito's fears were well-founded as there were elements in the army that were ready to replace him on the throne with one of his presumably more compliant princely brothers. By December 1, he had issued an Imperial rescript—a unique instrument of Imperial authority used to elicit action or demand obedience—that directed the Japanese armed forces to attack the United States, as well as to seize the remainder of what it called the Southern Resource Area. Typically, the rescript claimed that Japan's actions were taken in self-defense against the western powers.

THE JAPANESE AMBASSADOR—Ambassador Kichisaburo Nomura, also an admiral in the IJN, had arrived in the United States in February 1941 for what was seen by contemporaries as a last round of diplomatic activity in order to avoid a wider war in the Pacific. On November 20, Nomura delivered his government's final proposal for peace. It was basically an ultimatum for American non-interference in the western Pacific and East Asia. On November 26, Nomura relayed the American response—a counterproposal meant to serve as the basis for further discussions—to his government. It seemed clear that war was imminent and the U.S. Chief of Naval Operations in Washington, Admiral Harold R. "Betty" Stark, took the extraordinary measure of issuing a "war warning" to U.S. forces in the Pacific. On December 6, Secretary of State Hull transmitted—via his diplomatic channels—a personal letter from FDR to Hirohito that "begged" the Japanese to reconsider and return to the table for further talks. On the last day before war, Nomura and his staff (one of whom was the head of Japanese covert intelligence collection in the United States), spent the remaining hours decrypting and transcribing a lengthy fifteen-section message being sent by the Foreign Ministry in Tokyo. Part Fifteen was Japan's declaration of war and was intended to be delivered prior to the Pearl Harbor attack.

ADMIRAL CHUICHI NAGUMO—Admiral Nagumo was arguably the most powerful man afloat on December 6, 1941. Underneath him was the largest and most deadly aircraft carrier task force of all time—*Dai Ichi Kido Butai,* or the First Mobile Striking Force. This fleet consisted of Japan's six largest aircraft carriers—*Akagi* (Nagumo's flagship), *Kaga, Soryu, Hiryu,* and the newer *Shokaku* and *Zuikaku*—plus numerous destroyer, submarine, and cruiser escorts. Embarked on these impressive ships was the First Air Fleet, Japan's carrier air force, consisting of over 420 modern fighter, bomber, and torpedo aircraft.

The weight of command bore heavily on Nagumo. His chief, Admiral Isoroku Yamamoto, commander of the Combined Fleet, was opposed to the course of events that had led Japan to join the Axis alliance and was rumored to be on a target list for assassination by reactionary pro-war fanatics within the Imperial Army. He regarded the Pearl Harbor operation as a serious gamble that might result in disaster and had managed to convey and imbue his subordinates with a similar attitude of dread and angst.

Nagumo realized, much as did British Admiral John Jellicoe in World War I, that he could "lose the war in an afternoon": in Nagumo's case, if defeated by the powerful and dangerous U.S. Navy. Nevertheless, duty to his emperor overcame all of his doubts and on December 6, he swung his naval-air armada south toward the Hawaiian Islands. Ten minutes later, he raised the same flag that his illustrious predecessor Admiral Heihachiro Togo had hoisted prior to Japan's pivotal 1905 victory over the Russians in the Tsushima Strait. He added to the drama of the occasion by sending a signal similar to that sent by Admiral Horatio Nelson at Trafalgar—"Every man will do his duty."

GENERAL TOMOYUKI YAMASHITA—Meanwhile, more than 5,000 miles to the southwest, the Japanese invasion convoys had already left their ports of call—mostly from French Indochina—to descend on Malaysia. The commander of the ground forces, General Yamashita, was embarked on the light aircraft carrier *Ryujo.* Yamashita suffered several tense days and nights after the invasion convoy departed Cam Ranh Bay in Indochina [Vietnam]. First the alarm came when an unidentified submarine had been reported in the area to be transited by the convoy. Then, before it turned north into the Gulf of Siam [Thailand], a British Hudson reconnaissance aircraft detected the convoy. However, bad weather soon made the force invisible and it turned north and remained undetected thereafter. At 9:05 A.M. on December 7 (around 9:00 P.M. along the West Coast of the United States on December 6), the Japanese invasion convoy broke into four groups for the invasion of Siam and Malaysia.

BELOW: The genial and always-smiling Japanese Ambassador Kichisaburo Nomura (left) and special envoy Saburo Kurusu yuck it up with the Washington press corps several days before the Japanese attack on Pearl Harbor.

December Sixth— The Americans

ABOVE: Members of the War Plans Division meet with Brigadier General Leonard T. Gerow of the U.S. Army General Staff in his War Department office on November 26, 1941, less than two weeks before Pearl Harbor. The group, responsible for strategic planning for the coming war, are (left to right) Colonel Lee S. Gerow, Colonel Charles W. Bundy, Lieutenant Colonel Matthew B. Ridgway, Brigadier General H.F. Loomis, General Gerow (who served as the War Plans Division's chief), Colonel Robert W. Crawford, Lieutenant Colonel Stephen H. Sherrill, Colonel Thomas T. Handy, and Lieutenant Colonel Carl A. Russell.

From mid-November to December 5, 1941, Op-20-G, the Navy communications office tasked with the decryption of vital MAGIC and PURPLE signal intelligence from Japan, had worked overtime. Their performance had been magnificent. The intelligence they provided was, above all, timely. That is, the system intercepted and decrypted signals smoothly and got them to the strategic intelligence "consumers" at the highest levels of the American government rapidly. On December 6, this admirable performance suffered its first real setback during the worst of all possible signal intercepts, the lengthy Japanese diplomatic cable to Ambassador Nomura in Washington that would constitute Japan's declaration of war against the United States— a declaration that was supposed to be delivered just prior to the Pearl Harbor attack. Most of the key strategic decision makers in Washington, D.C., went to bed that night without having been informed that the Japanese were sending their diplomatic entourage instructions to destroy codes and ciphers, and that a critical final section of the message had yet to be decrypted. A number of

factors explain this apparent intelligence failure—the long working hours and stress of the previous months, the extreme length of the Japanese dispatch, and the fact that what seems so clear now to historians in hindsight was, in fact, just another curious message that may or may not have contained a declaration of war.

Commander Alvin D. Kramer of the Office of Naval Intelligence (ONI) waited patiently in his office on the night of December 6 for the completion of six copies of the recently decrypted Japanese diplomatic MAGIC intercept. He had decided that he would hand-deliver all six copies to their recipients instead of waiting for the next morning. The copies were going to FDR; Secretary of the Navy Frank Knox; ONI Captains T.S. Wilkinson and Royal E. Ingersoll; Admiral Richmond K. Turner, the head of the War Plans Division of the office of the Chief of Naval Operations; and the Chief of Naval Operations (CNO) Admiral "Betty" Stark. Kramer got his wife to drive him around Washington since the duty driver was not on site. Shortly before 9:30 P.M., Kramer arrived at the White House and gave the president's copy of the decrypt to acting naval liaison officer Lieutenant Robert L. Schultz.

PRESIDENT FRANKLIN D. ROOSEVELT— December 6 dawned quietly for FDR. He was aware that the situation was tense, but had decided to leave the initiative for peace or war with Japan. The ongoing negotiations between Secretary of State Hull and Ambassador Nomura had shown little progress, but it seemed unlikely that Japan would attack in the midst of diplomatic negotiations. At the end of a midday budget meeting, the president remarked that, "We might be at war with Japan although no one knew." Later that night, Lieutenant Schultz was shown into the Oval Office with the packet that Commander Kramer had hand-delivered earlier. It included a number of dispatches, but the key diplomatic MAGIC intercept was at the bottom of the pile. FDR rapidly read the entire fifteen-page document. When he was finished he said, "This means war." However, he had little idea of where or when the first attack would occur.

THE PHILIPPINES—On December 4, the defense of the Philippines had been placed in a condition of "three-day readiness," which indicated that war could occur in as little as three days. Total blackout had been ordered for all military and naval facilities, antiaircraft batteries were cleared to fire on unknown

aircraft, and Admiral Thomas C. Hart—commander of the Asiatic Fleet—expected war to break out at any moment. If the Japanese decided to strike, Admiral Hart was convinced that his base would be at the top of the list. His naval facilities in Manila Bay represented the only deepwater, protected port from which the Navy could operate in the western Pacific. Like Port Arthur, Manchuria, in the Russo-Japanese War, the Japanese would almost certainly move to neutralize the Cavite Naval Base and the airfields (especially Clark Field) scattered across northern Luzon [Philippines] at the first opportunity. By December 6, Hart was executing instructions previously provided by CNO Admiral Stark to pull back most of his naval forces, except his PT boats and submarines, from their exposed position in Manila Bay. The defense of America's "Port Arthur" would rely mostly on land and air power.

Meanwhile, Hart's nominal commander, General (or Field Marshal, to use his Philippine title) Douglas MacArthur had thought he was taking the proper precautions in dispersing as much as possible his air forces. He had been

BELOW: Pearl Harbor—looking west on October 13, 1941. The body of water curving from upper to lower left and center is the Southeast Loch. It is from the area at upper left and the main channel along the upper right that Japanese bombers launched their torpedoes at "battleship row," along Ford Island (upper right). The supply depot is at upper center, part of the Submarine Base is at lower left, and the Navy Yard is in the upper left. Alongside the submarine tender USS *Holland* at left is the *Sturgeon* (SS-187), *Spearfish* (SS-190), *Saury* (SS-189), *Seal* (SS-183), and *Sargo* (SS-188). The gunboat USS *Niagara* (PG-52) is alongside the wharf, ahead of *Holland*. Ships docked at the supply depot, upper center, are minelayer USS *Oglala* (CM-4) and the SS *Maui*, operated by the U.S. Army. The two battleships moored by Ford Island are USS *Oklahoma* (BB-37) at left and USS *Arizona* (BB-39), both of which were judged to be unsalvageable after the Pearl Harbor attack.

ABOVE: Major General Jonathan M. Wainwright (right), the commanding general of the Philippine Division, and his aide, Captain John R. Pugh, observe a July 1941 river crossing exercise near Fort William McKinley during a steady rain. Located south of Manila, Fort McKinley was the division's main base and headquarters of the U.S. Armed Forces-Far East (USAFFE). Wainwright had been given his Philippine command in September 1940, but hoped to be available for combat in Europe where the war was already raging. He feared that if war broke out with Japan, he would be "stuck in the Philippines missing everything." Captured at the conclusion of a lengthy, well-executed defense of the Bataan Peninsula in April 1942, he was finally freed after Japan's surrender in September 1945.

given specific orders not to fire the first shot. Nevertheless, he felt he had taken as many precautions as he could with the forces he had. These forces, he felt, were grossly inadequate to the task of defending the Philippines, and so one can understand his somewhat paradoxical attitude in wanting both to defend the islands and buy time for more forces to arrive in order to increase the chances for their successful defense. On the night of December 6, he wrote, "Every disposition had been made, every man, gun, and plane was on the alert."

On November 27, Admiral Husband E. Kimmel, the intelligent and aggressive Commander in Chief of the U.S. Pacific Fleet (CINCPACFLT), received Admiral Stark's "war warning." He immediately convened a meeting at Pearl Harbor of the major commanders about preparations for war. Pacific Fleet commander of aircraft carriers, Vice Admiral William "Bull" Halsey, Jr., and Army Lieutenant General Walter Campbell Short attended this meeting. The main topic of discussion was the very risky, and potentially provocative, move to reinforce the air components of both Wake and Midway islands with additional aircraft in anticipation of the blow that all felt must soon

fall. Both Japanese behavior and the warnings coming out of Washington dictated action. Because of the limitations placed on Army fighters for over-water flights—they were not authorized to fly beyond 15 nautical miles from shore—it was decided to reinforce both the Wake and Midway garrisons with Navy and Marine aircraft. Accordingly, twelve F4F Wildcat fighters of Major Paul Putnam's Marine Fighter Squadron 211 (VMF-211) were on-loaded aboard Halsey's flagship, the aircraft carrier USS Enterprise out of Pearl Harbor. When Kimmel asked Halsey if he wanted battleships for escort, Halsey turned them down due to their much slower speed compared to his carriers, cruisers, and destroyers; he wanted to be able to outrun any Japanese forces he might encounter and strike at them with his aircraft from a distance.

Several battleships did accompany Halsey until his force was beyond sight from shore, after which the battleships separated for target practice and a return to Pearl Harbor. This step was taken to deceive any spies as to the real nature of Halsey's mission. The other Pacific fleet carrier at Pearl Harbor, the USS Lexington, was to perform a similar delivery mission to Midway, except the planes were scout bombers and not fighters. This decision to send both carriers and their escorting cruisers and destroyers out at the same time, while unbeknownst to U.S. military leaders the main striking power of the Japanese Navy was approaching stealthily from the north, was to have momentous consequences on the course of the Pacific War. It was Admiral Kimmel's decision, and one for which he has gotten almost no credit. The third Pacific fleet carrier, Lexington's sister ship USS Saratoga, was already en route to the West Coast of the United States for routine maintenance in a naval yard.

Halsey departed Pearl Harbor at first light on November 28 and delivered the fighters to Wake without incident, unaware of the huge Japanese carrier force to the north. On December 5, Lexington and her escorts—also blissfully unaware of the Japanese—pulled out of Pearl Harbor bound for Midway. Halsey had intended to be back in port by Saturday or

LEFT: A reconnaissance of the Lingayen Gulf area on Luzon Island—where Japanese forces would invade in December 1941 and the United States would follow in 1945—is conducted by the 57th Infantry Regiment. Third from the right is Captain Harold K. Johnson, who would survive his imprisonment by the Japanese to become the Army Chief of Staff during the Vietnam War. At far left is Lieutenant J.E. McColm, who would be killed in action. His brother George, a naval officer, would later become one of the principal planners for the invasion and occupation of Japan.

BELOW: "Philippine Scouts" of the 57th Infantry take part in an October 1941 field exercise. Members of this unit were regular U.S. Army soldiers and not the country's own national army, which was also under American command.

early Sunday morning, but heavy weather east of Wake on the return trip damaged one of his destroyers, slowing the force on December 6 and delaying his arrival until the morning of the December 7, 1941. Halsey spent most of December 6 on stormy seas, worrying over the damaged destroyer and the delayed return to his homeport.

Ensign Archie Mills, Naval Aviation Pilot-in-Training at the Naval Air Station in Corpus Christi, Texas—where the initial training for the PBY Catalina flying boat took place—discusses what he was doing the night before Pearl Harbor. (The PBY-5 Catalina was the Navy's standard long-range patrol aircraft at that time.)

I finally got my wings at Corpus Christi, Texas, and was about the three-hundredth naval cadet that went into that station. Let me tell you how I was selected for PBYs. They would read the roster and would draw a line—one group would be fighter pilots; they would draw another line—you're dive-bombers; draw a line, you're scouts; draw a line, you're patrol boats. And there was a lot of tears shed. Oh, we cried. I wanted to be a fighter pilot so bad. I probably wouldn't have been very good. I was probably a much better PBY pilot. We could switch around if we could get someone to, but no one wanted to fly boats! Only the last stage of the training was in PBYs—the first flights were in SNJs [monoplane trainer aircraft]. I got through Corpus in November 1941 and was waiting for an assignment. We had to wait until there was a place to put us.

The First Shot

On the other side of the 180th meridian—the International Date Line—it was already December 7. In Malaysia, the British military commanders were fighting a losing battle trying to prepare for the storm they knew would soon break upon them. Up until December 5, the British ground commander Lieutenant General Arthur

E. Percival had been trying to get the colonial government to agree to a redeployment of troops to pre-empt any Japanese invasion by occupying the excellent harbor of Singora (which, in fact, the Japanese did indeed plan to seize). However, greedy plantation owners complained about any pre-emptive troop movements and preparation on their land, and by December 6, Percival had settled into waiting for the Japanese to strike.

Also that day, a PBY Catalina flying boat of American manufacture took off from Kota Bahru in British Malaya to search for reported Japanese convoys that had last been sighted steaming west from Thailand toward the Kra Peninsula, which connected Thailand with Malaysia to the south. This aircraft was shot down at 1:30 that afternoon by Japanese aircraft providing cover to the invasion convoys. The British mistakenly assumed that this plane had been lost due to bad weather or engine failure and remained ignorant of the immense blow about to fall on His Majesty's possessions in Malaysia, Singapore, and Burma.

Before sunrise on December 8, Tokyo time, the IJN and IJA launched their coordinated attacks at Singora and Kota Bharu. About an hour later, the first wave of *Dai Ichi Kido Butai*'s striking air groups arrived over Pearl Harbor, Hawaii. Several hours later, Japanese aircraft from Formosa [Taiwan]—Mitsubishi "Betty" medium bombers—struck at Clark Field and Cavite Naval Base in the Philippines. Never before in the history of warfare had any nation launched such finely synchronized attacks on the land, air, and sea over such a broad geographic area and in so short a period of time. The geographic scale of this attack even exceeded that of the Nazis' Operation Barbarossa (the invasion of the Soviet Union) less than six months before. The Pacific War had begun.

BELOW: Aichi D3A Type 99 bombers start their engine warm-up for the raid on Pearl Harbor as the carrier *Soryu* follows close behind, December 7, 1941. The D3A was code-named "Val" by the Allies. The main punch of the *Kido Butai* (Striking Force) also consisted of Nakajima B5N Type 97 "Kate" torpedo bombers and the deadly Mitsubishi A6M Type 0 fighter, code-named "Zeke" but better known as the Zero.

If we are ordered to do it [go to war with the United States] then I can guarantee to put up a tough fight for the first six months, but I have absolutely no confidence as to what would happen if it went on for two or three years.

—Admiral Isoroku Yamamoto to Prime Minister Prince Konoye
prior to the attack on Pearl Harbor

BELOW: Mitsubishi A6M Zero fighters aboard the carrier *Akagi* prepare for takeoff during operations in the Indian Ocean. After striking the U.S. Pacific Fleet at Pearl Harbor, Japanese carriers supported the invasions of Wake Island and the Dutch East Indies, then chased a three-carrier British force from its Indian Ocean base at Colombo, Ceylon, in April 1942. The quilted appearance of the *Akagi* was a result of the common practice among Japanese carrier crews—when they had ample foreknowledge of approaching combat—of using tightly rolled mattresses to provide extra protection from bomb splinters. In addition to being secured on the "island" structure rising from the flight deck, mattresses and rope screens were used along the gun galleries just below deck's edge. A similar effort—though far less systematically and comprehensively applied—was carried out on the USS *Yorktown* and possibly other American ships. The circular composite antenna atop the *Akagi*'s bridge is not radar, but likely a radio direction finder [RDF] or perhaps an early navigation beacon based on an RDF design.

Chapter Two
RUNNING WILD

The famous statement on the opposite page is often misquoted. Most versions have Admiral Yamamoto, the commander of Japan's Combined Fleet, stating that he will "run wild for six months" in the Pacific before the weight of the United States' industrial power could come to bear and influence events. The misquote is more descriptive. Japan's navy and army literally did "run wild," winning battle after battle and engagement after engagement. By the end of the first five months of the Pacific War, Japan had attained all of its strategic and operational objectives— except the most vital, an offer to negotiate peace with the United States.

Ironically, Japan was undefeated but not victorious after these conquests. The United States, surprisingly, had remained on the defensive and relied on delaying actions, raids, and last stands to buy time that was desperately needed while the Americans attempted to bring their cumbersome war machine into full gear. Besides, the United States was committed to a policy of "Europe First," since Germany was seen as the greatest threat to the Allied coalition. Japan, on the other hand, could choose to switch to a defense of its gains or it could remain on the offensive and hope that after a few more well-placed blows, the United States would see reason and negotiate a peace settlement favorable to the Empire.

Hickam Field

USS *New Orleans*

USS *San Francisco*

USS *St. Louis*

Fuel Storage

USS *Helena*

USS *Oglala*

USS *Cassin*
USS *Downes*
USS *Pennsylvania*

USS *Oklahoma*

USS *West Virginia*

USS *Vestal*

USS *Tennessee*

USS *Arizona*

USS *Nevada*

At extreme left, above the cruiser *San Francisco*, one of Lieutenant Commander Kakuichi Takahashi's nine D3A1 "Val" dive-bombers exits the area after striking targets on Ford Island along Battleship Row. Japanese aircraft, however, did not attack the vitally important fuel tank farm between Hickam Field and the harbor, which remained untouched throughout the raid. This photo taken by Petty Officer Takeo Shiro, navigator aboard the of Kate attack-bomber of Lieutenant Heita Matsumura from the *Hiryu*, was used in a wide range of Japanese propaganda such as a postage stamp [inset] that carried an extra surcharge to raise money for the war effort.

USS *Shaw*

USS *California*

USS *Neosho*

USS *Maryland*

FORD ISLAND

海軍省許可濟第七八三號

Japan chose the latter course of action, a choice that not only doomed it to decisive defeat, but one that ultimately shortened the war.

Pearl Harbor—How Important?

The United States has been criticized for not being ready for the war that came; yet in most details, strategic planners got it right. They expected attacks on the Philippines, Guam, Wake, as well as the resource-rich British and Dutch colonial possessions. All of these occurred on December 7–8 or shortly thereafter; but not foreseen was Admiral Yamamoto's attack on Hawaii, far across the Pacific from Japan. Militarily, the Pearl Harbor attack was nothing more than a spectacular and highly successful raid. However, had it never occurred, the United States would still have gone to war because of all the other assaults against America's possessions in the Pacific.

Admiral Nagumo's hundreds of naval aircraft caught the Pacific Fleet completely unaware on December 7, 1941. In addition to sinking or damaging all eight of the battle-ships present, the Japanese crippled the U.S. Army Air Forces. More than 3,200 military and civilian casualties were incurred. However, once sober minds evaluated the damage, it was realized that the critical repair facilities and fuel depots surrounding Pearl Harbor were virtually untouched. The results of Pearl Harbor were materially insignificant as far as the Japanese conquest of the Southern Resource Area was concerned because the U.S. fleet had little chance of reaching American possessions in the western Pacific in time to prevent the loss of Wake, Guam, and even the Philippines once hostilities broke out.

LEFT: On "Battleship Row," concussion waves from the torpedoed *West Virginia* and *Oklahoma* spread out across Pearl Harbor as smoke rises from Hickam Field, attacked minutes earlier at 7:55 A.M. The attack in the harbor started at 7:57. In this photo, taken at approximately 8:03, fuel oil pouring from the ships' ruptured sides flows across the surface of the water. Both are listing heavily to port, and the *Oklahoma* would later capsize. Directly across the channel, smoke from the cruiser *Helena* and the minelayer *Oglala* obscures most of the battleship *Pennsylvania*.

The wakes of multiple torpedo tracks and splash points where they entered the water are visible, as well as the geyser of a yet another hit on the *West Virginia* that has begun to rise amid-ships, just beyond its rear mast and superstructure. Within seconds, it will tower hundreds of feet over the ship. The running motor of a torpedo launched by an aircraft from the carrier *Hiryu* created the large area of froth on the surface, directly above the *Tennessee*. The torpedo was intended for the battleship *California*, but was dropped too high and became lodged in the mud. It was later recovered.

Flying as low as 10 meters, Lieutenant Asao Negishi reported that he and wingman Petty Officer Gunji Kaido almost struck a small boat—a church launch from Merry's Point near the submarine base—while on their way to launch against the *California*. This same area, at center left, became the focus of attention more than five decades later when a photo and marine analysis pointed to the possibility that concussion waves in the shallow harbor might have caused one of the Japanese midget submarines to be temporarily pushed to the surface in this same area where many aircraft-borne torpedoes passed or were dropped.

USS *Oklahoma*

USS *West Virginia*

USS *Maryland*

USS *Vestal*

USS *Nevada*

USS *Tennessee*

USS *Arizona*

ABOVE: Battleship Row at 8:06 A.M., as seen by the high-level Kates from the *Kaga* targeting the inner row *Arizona*, *Tennessee*, and *Maryland*. An OS2U-3 Kingfisher floatplane (arrow) topples into the *West Virginia*'s gushing fuel oil as the ship begins to settle stern-first into the bottom mud. Ahead, the *Oklahoma*, with much of its port-side deck already awash, is nearing the point where it will capsize. The *Nevada* (center left), partially obscured by smoke, loses fuel from a single torpedo hit. The *Arizona* is still relatively undamaged.

RIGHT: A schematic of the Japanese attack prepared by Commander Mitsuo Fuchida, who, as Commander, First Air Fleet, led the air strike and also commanded the *Akagi*'s air group. Long red arrows represent torpedoes launched and their targets. The amount of damage believed to have been inflicted is marked on each ship: "\" = minor, "\\" = moderate, "\\\" = serious, and "X" indicates destroyed. A small "x" represents a bomb strike or damaging near miss, and Fuchida also indicated oil slicks and catastrophic fires. English-language text and key in light red were added by American intelligence analysts after the war.

BELOW: Fires on the destroyer USS *Shaw* reached its forward magazine at 9:30 A.M., and the bow disintegrated in a spectacular explosion inside floating dry dock YFD-2. This photo was taken from the southern end of Ford Island across the channel near where the sinking *Nevada* (center right) was beached to avoid blocking the harbor entrance. Amazingly, the *Shaw* was repaired and back in action for the Guadalcanal campaign in 1942. YFD-2 also sank but, like most of the battleships, was raised and repaired. Miraculously, YFD-2 was one of the few repair facilities damaged in the attack.

Richard Fiske, Marine Corps bugler, was assigned to the USS West Virginia *anchored on "Battleship Row" along Pearl Harbor's Ford Island.*

I was the Marine bugler—there were two of us. The ship carried ninety-five Marines and two Marine buglers, two clerks, two cooks, and two radiomen were part of the crew—you know Marines have been stationed aboard Navy ships since 1775. I had just come back from "Cinderella liberty" where you have to be back aboard ship at least by midnight. If you don't, they turn you into what they call a brig rat and you go down there and then go up before the old man [ship's captain] and, normally, if you were absent a little bit you'd get restricted to the ship about fifteen days or ten days, depending on how the old man feels. The master at arms woke me up at four o'clock and I got my act together, reported to the officer of the deck [OOD], and said, "Sir, I have the watch."

I sounded reveille at five thirty and then, at six o'clock, sounded chow call. After we finished eating, I went back on the quarterdeck to sound the morning colors. At about twenty minutes to eight, we saw a whole bunch of airplanes coming in and naturally we thought this was going to be a drill because from a distance you can't tell whether they were...at that time, our airplanes had a blue field and white star and a red circle. So I went up there and sounded first call for colors like I normally would do and all these airplanes were coming in. Stanley Bukowski, one of the orderlies says, "God dang it, we got a drill this morning"—there was quite a few of them. The planes were from the mountains, coming in this way, about 1,500 to maybe 2,000 feet. They had the torpedoes and we said, "Well God darn, are they gonna practice a torpedo run on us?" Stanley said, "Well, I guess they are." I said, "Let's go watch them drop the torpedoes, then I'll run back and sound general quarters." So we went over to the port side. There was five coming in and three headed toward the *West Virginia*. We watched them drop the torpedoes and watched the wake coming out. The next thing I remember, there was this hellacious explosion, right by frame eighty-

LEFT: A crewman is rescued from the oil coating the harbor as sailors on the *West Virginia*'s bridge peer down at the wreckage of their ship. Beyond the *West Virginia*, the *Tennessee* has settled to the harbor bottom. Nine torpedoes slammed into the *West Virginia*, but her rapid settling by the stern had prevented her capsizing as the *Oklahoma* did. Although there was considerable doubt that the *West Virginia* could be made seaworthy due to the massive damage below the waterline, extensive patching by Navy salvage experts enabled the ship to be refloated in May 1942, and it returned to duty in July 1944.

The lightly damaged *Tennessee* had originally been pinned tight against the forward mooring quay by her sister ship, the *West Virginia*. The concrete structure was carefully chipped away so as to not further damage the *Tennessee*, and the battleship was eventually towed with great care through the space between Ford Island and the *Arizona* after the narrow passage was deepened by dredging. In company with the *Maryland* and *Pennsylvania*, the *Tennessee* moved out to sea on March 20, 1942, and sailed to Puget Sound, Washington, where she received additional repairs and, eventually, upgrades in radar and antiaircraft protection so that she could return to war.

seven about almost the center of the ship. It blew us to the starboard side of the ship—and the ship is 118-feet wide. God, we were covered with oil and soaking wet and Stan, he looked at me and he said, "What in the world?"

Our first sergeant came up. It blew him out of his office. He almost got killed, and was soaking wet with seawater and oil and he said get your butts to your battle stations. So I grabbed the bugle and took off and went up to the bridge. Then there were some more explosions—I didn't even get to sound morning colors. I was up on the bridge with Lieutenant White and there were some more explosions in the forward part of the ship. The ship was rocking and then there was another explosion toward the stern, which we didn't know it at the time, but it blew our rudder completely off of the ship. We were looking at one another and Lieutenant White says, "By God, this is hell of a way to start a damn war."

Robert Kinzler of the U.S. Army's 27th Infantry Regiment, Headquarters Company, was stationed at Schofield Army Barracks near Wheeler Field, Oahu, when the Japanese planes arrived.

I was in the army, stationed at Schofield Barracks. I got back to the barracks at about 2:00 A.M., so was very much asleep at five minutes to eight when there was a terrific explosion. We thought that there had been an explosion in one of the mess halls. We dressed as quickly as we could, and ran outside. When we got to the second level of our barracks building, a plane flew over, no more than 50 feet from us and just a little higher than we were. Not having any aircraft identification instruction, we thought it was either a Navy plane or perhaps even a Marine plane. It wasn't an Army plane.

We went down to breakfast. But no sooner had we sat down than we got the alert calls. From that point on, we had to get our equip-

ment together and move out to our assigned battle station, which in our case was the Roosevelt High School football stadium at the base of the Punchbowl [a nickname the soldiers gave to the extinct volcano now known as Diamond Head at the end of Waikiki Beach]. The plane we had seen was a Japanese dive-bomber, later nicknamed Val. Fixed landing gear; two men in the cockpit; greenish color, huge; red circle on the fuselage. Still, we had no idea at that time what it was nor who it was.

Nathan Heilman was a staff sergeant in the Army Air Corps stationed at Hickam Field on December 7, 1941.

The day the war started, a fellow by the name of Charles Bartlett was wounded and I heard him hollering for help and I went over a wall and before I got over the wall there was a Zero [Japanese fighter plane] that came down and sprayed bullets, and two-by-fours and dirt and everything hit me on the head and shoulders and I thought this was it. Well, he went by and I heard this guy screaming because he had hit the guy on the other side of the wall. So he was all wounded in the legs and I said to the guy, a corporal, "Hey Mack, come on and help me get this guy into the truck. They used to come with pickup trucks from the hospital. About that time, another Zero came by overhead spraying and this other guy dropped the wounded soldier and left me alone with him. I thought, "What am I going to do?" So, it wouldn't have done any good, but I laid on top of him trying to protect him. Then when the truck finally got there, another fellow helped me pick him up and we threw him like a sack of potatoes and we got out of there. You know, to safety.

I saw our barracks get hit with a bomb and when they get hit with a bomb they squat. They go down and all of sudden collapse. The fire station was hit, but they had managed to get all the prisoners out—the fire station had the brig attached to it— before it was bombed. Our hangar got hit once. It was the same thing, it just squatted down and then it exploded, blew the doors

off and everything. The very next day we had airplanes that came in from the States, which landed on golf courses, parking lots, and wherever they could because Hickam Field and all our planes were blown up. The engines and everything were blown up out of the planes.

Colonel B.E. Allen managed to take off in a B-17 from Hickam Field during the Japanese attack on the base.

At the time of the attack, I had a squadron with only three B-17s because we had given up most of our B-17s and sent them on out to the Philippines. I was concerned, primarily, with saving at least one of these B-17s and attempted first to take off empty, since it was empty, and save it. I flooded one engine in the attempt—and the hustle and bustle, trying to get four engines started—and abandoned the idea of trying to takeoff since I had to takeoff across the coral, not on the runway. I then did manage to get it loaded with bombs, and was sent out with the information that there were two Japanese carriers to the south. Very shortly after takeoff, I found an American carrier to the south. Then with this personal

BELOW: A Mitsubishi A6M2 Zero-Sen fighter, code-named "Zeke," lifts from the deck of the *Akagi* in early 1942. The pilot's seat is raised and the canopy left open for the take-off. With its 330-liter (87 gallon) drop tanks, this early, lightweight Zero model could range 1,930 statute miles from its home base while fully loaded. Although armed with two 7.7mm machine guns in the upper fuselage and a 20mm cannon in each wing, its ability to out-fight nearly every enemy aircraft it came up against at the beginning of the war was principally due to its magnificent maneuverability. This superiority would be short-lived.

DONALD GAY STRATTON

ABOVE: Seaman First Class Donald G. Stratton, one of the few survivors of the *Arizona*.

BELOW: A newly arrived B-17 sits destroyed on the tarmac at Hickam Field. Miraculously only one of the crew was killed, strafed by a Zero fighter as he ran down the runway. These aircraft were being ferried out to General Douglas MacArthur in the Philippines in a last-minute attempt to make this U.S. possession defensible against the expected Japanese invasion.

feeling that the Japs, if they attack, and obviously they had, would come from the north, I made a maximum range search to the north. The weather was bad. For that part, we had some clear areas, some rainy areas, and I'd have to get down on the deck [low altitude near sea level] and up to altitude at times to take maximum advantage of visibility.

How close I ever came to that carrier task force, I don't know. But with one airplane it would have been an unusually fortunate situation if I had stumbled across a task force. But, at least, I was headed where they turned out to be, despite the fact that everyone expected that they had come from the southwest.

Seaman First Class Donald Gay Stratton was among the few to survive when the battleship Arizona exploded, killing more than a thousand crewmen.

We finished breakfast and I picked some loose oranges on the tables to take down later to my buddy in the sick bay. I came out on the forecastle deck via the number two casement and heard some sailors up on the bow of the ship yelling and pointing toward Ford Island [off Pearl Harbor]. They were jumping up and down

and pointing, and I looked over toward Ford Island, and I seen the planes bombing and all the smoke and the bombs, and I swear I saw the water tower topple over. So, I headed for my battle station, which was in the port antiaircraft director on the foremast's sky-control platform, one deck above the bridge.

All of our antiaircraft guns were firing. There was a ready box of ammunition behind each gun, and they were locked up. Of course we broke the locks and we were firing at the planes as they came in and I had a very good vantage point. I could back a hatch on the overhead of the director and stick my head out. And I seen the *West Virginia* get hit, and I seen the *Oklahoma* capsized, and I seen the torpedo planes coming in over the ferry landing and the wakes of the torpedoes heading right for us. And of course you know the *Vestal* [repair ship, AR-4] was tied up outside of us but they claim we didn't get any torpedoes, but I still say two of them had our name on it.

We were firing at the high-altitude bombers because we figured they were doing us more damage than anything else. Every shell has a fuse on it that's cranked on to try to explode at the right height, but we were very short; we weren't reaching the planes at all. And, of course,

the dive-bombers were also coming in. You could, on my position there, practically reach out and touch them as they went by.

All at once we'd get a big thump. That ship weighed 33,600 tons, and it just shook like an earthquake had hit it. The big bomb had hit near the number two turret on the starboard side, and went down into the fuel and the ammunition and the aviation gas, and exploded. There was a fireball and smoke that went, what?…about 400 or 500 feet in the air, I guess, and just engulfed the whole foremast. Very few escaped from the bow of the ship back to aft of the foremast, while from the stack on aft, there was quite a few that weren't hurt. Oh, some were blown over the side; some of them abandoned ship and got over to Ford Island.

We were kind of stymied up there on the foremast; we couldn't go up or down, inside this gun director, and a little sailor next to me opened the hatch and jumped out, and I never did see him again. And Vincent Lomax had gone to get some more ammunition and I never did see him again. But I reached out to close the hatch and that's where I got most of

my burns on my left side. Anyhow, we were kind of squatting down behind some of the bulkheads there, and trying to keep out of the fire, and doing the best we could, and we were just getting burned something terrible. Our hair is burnt and the skin on our arms just came off like big socks. We just pulled it off and threw it down. It was in the way.

The captain and the admiral and the chaplain were all killed on the bridge just below our station there. And of course this…the sailors were…you could see them down there, just trying to get aft, trying to get over the side, trying to get…pull their clothes off that were afire. I recognized some of them. I could look from my station up there and look down at the deck and see them, the sailors, scrambling around some of the guns there. It was terrible.

And of course we were trying to figure out a way we could get down the ladder, get on deck, and get off the sky-control platform. And, you know, there's a starboard side director up there also that had probably as many men as we did. There must be forty, fifty men or so that manned that station, port and starboard both, but there

ABOVE: A plume of black smoke is ejected from the stack of the USS *Arizona* as its forward magazine erupts in flame. Several minutes earlier, at 8:00 A.M., the lead group of high-altitude Kates from the *Kaga* dropped a bomb that hit the side of the No. 4 turret and glanced off into the deck below where it started a small fire. The conveyer belt of high-altitude Kates continued over the battleships berthed closed to Ford Island, and at 8:06, one dropped its 1,760-pound, armor-piercing bomb to starboard of turrets No. 1 and 2, causing the magazine to explode. It was long assumed that the Imperial Fleet's top bombardier, Petty Officer Noboru Kanai, aboard one of *Soryu*'s aircraft made the devastating hit. More likely, it was accomplished by a Kate from the *Hiryu* under the direction of Lieutenant Commander Tadashi Kusumi.

ABOVE: Admiral Husband E. Kimmel, Commander of the U.S. Pacific Fleet and Army General Walter Short were made the scapegoats for the Pearl Harbor disaster. They had received a "war warning" from Admiral "Betty" Stark ten days before, and acting on this order, Kimmel had sent his aircraft carriers and escorts—including some of its few oilers—out of Pearl Harbor to reinforce the Wake and Midway Island defenders. These actions, never recognized at the time, allowed the most critically important part of the Pacific Fleet, its oilers and the aircraft carriers, to survive.

BELOW: Long after the Japanese strike, the charred remains of the *Arizona* still smoldered as Navy crews began the task of finding what they could salvage from the wreck.

were only six of us who went across to the *Vestal*, which was tied up alongside. We gave a holler to a seaman [Joseph George] on board, and he throwed us a heaving line. So we catch this, and, then he ties on the heavier line and we pull that across, and we tie it onto the *Arizona* on the wing there where the director was. And we crawled hand over hand across that line to the vessel, which was probably 60, 70 feet across at amidships, and about 45 feet in the air.

We were pretty burned. Our hands were... our hands were just raw, and, in the meantime, my fingernails had all come off. But, anyway, I get down to the middle of the line, going down-way, it was fairly easy. But, then, the pain comes up. I just about give up a couple times, but they kept urging me on, and, oh, you can make it, you can do that. Anyway, I'm here. And had a lot of help from up above, I'm sure.

Seaman Stratton spent nearly a year in Navy hospitals recovering from the burns over 60 percent of his body before being honorably discharged. Although his 1C classification exempted him from further military duty, he re-enlisted and served aboard the destroyer USS Stack in time for invasions of Leyte, Luzon, and Okinawa.

Once the reality of war set in, the Navy did what it had planned to do: methodically island-hop across the Pacific. Pearl Harbor served not as a morale-destroying defeat but rather as a rallying cry that motivated Americans to greater efforts as it hardened their hearts. This hardness, when combined with the Japanese code of warrior *Bushido*—a concept of honor that demanded suicide if one was perceived to have "dishonored" the sacred emperor—would be a critical factor that made the Pacific War one of the most merciless, brutal, and intense conflicts in history. It would be a "War Without Mercy."

Catastrophe in the Philippines, Guam, and Wake

BOTTOM: USS *Sealion* in 1939, one of the twenty-nine U.S. submarines based at the Cavite Naval Base in Manila Bay when war broke out. Admiral Thomas Hart, the commander of the Asiatic Fleet, intended to use his submarines to interdict Japanese invasion convoys and isolate any Japanese force that succeeded in landing.

Japan's lightning bolts against U.S. forces in the Far East had to wait for the sun to rise because they would literally come from the clear sky. Air power was still mostly a daytime weapon at this stage of World War II, and the Japanese aircraft waiting to strike the Philippine naval and airbases had to wait for morning. When they arrived, they found the Americans totally unprepared, despite the fact that notification of the attack on Pearl Harbor occurred at 2:20

A.M. on December 8 in Manila and that General Douglas MacArthur was personally warned soon after.

The early days of war in the Philippines are not among the brighter moments of General MacArthur's military career. Through a series of miscues and miscommunications, as well as a classic underestimation of the enemy, Japanese bombers and fighters found Lieutenant General Lewis H. Brereton's B-17 bombers on the ground. At one stroke, the Japanese eliminated half of MacArthur's air force and the majority of his bombers. There were more than 250 casualties, including eighty killed—many of them valuable pilots. The actions taken by MacArthur and his staff in the Philippines that fateful day were never investigated in contrast to numerous official investigations of Pearl Harbor.

With air superiority essentially achieved by their initial strike, the Japanese returned on December 10 to pound Cavite Naval Base. The U.S. Asiatic Fleet suffered few losses, but that was simply because Admiral Hart had already moved most of his major units to the south. This attack caused extensive damage to the shore facilities, destroying the Asiatic Fleet's reserve of torpedoes, and sank a submarine and a minesweeper. The defense of the northern Philippines was now the responsibility of the combined U.S. Army and indigenous Filipino forces that would be virtually without naval or air support in their quixotic mission.

Navy Pharmacist's Mate Wheeler B. Lipes recalls his decision to go into the U.S. submarine service, and the bombing of his submarine at the Cavite Naval Base in the Philippines.

ABOVE: *Sealion* amidst the wreckage at Cavite after the Japanese attacks on December 10, 1941.

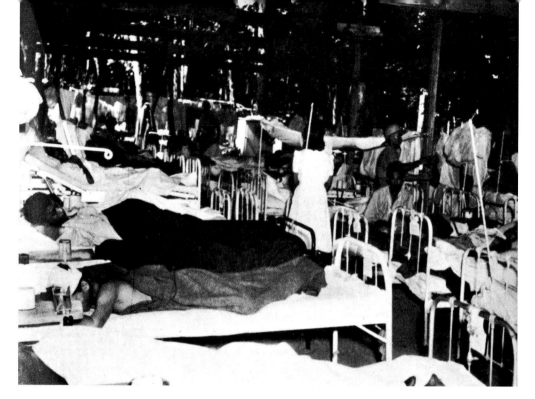

ANN BERNATITUS

One day I just decided I wanted submarines. The personnel officer thought that I had a hole in my head. There weren't any subs available then, but I went looking for one and eventually got aboard the [USS] *Sealion* [SS-195]. The *Sealion* was almost finished with its overhaul and was tied alongside her sister ship, the *Seadragon* [SS-194], at the Cavite Navy Yard.

When the bombers came at noon on the tenth of December [1941], they just leisurely wiped out the yard. One bomb went right down the after engine room hatch. The shrapnel from that one killed some people on the *Seadragon*'s conning tower and punched holes in her pressure hull. I was in the water for a while and was picked up on the perimeter of the navy yard late that night with the yard burning and exploding. The *Seadragon*'s pharmacist's mate was slightly wounded in the arm by shrapnel and he transferred himself off the sub, which left a vacancy. I was the logical choice to replace him. My escape from the Philippines was made possible by that event. [Admiral Thomas C. Hart moved most of the remaining submarines south after this devastating attack.]

As part of a squadron of submarines that was feeding Bataan, we would leave our torpedoes, except those in the tubes, in Cebu, take on forty to sixty tons of food, and run it into Corregidor [another Philippine island]. As Bataan was being overrun, we were taking people off Corregidor.

 Ensign Ann Bernatitus, Nurse Corps, U.S. Navy, stationed in the Philippines remembers the day the war started.

Bertha [Evans St. Pierre, another nurse] said that her boyfriend at Cavite on Sangley Point phoned her around six o'clock [in] the morning, and she came running up the steps and into my room. "Ann, war's been declared." When we heard about Pearl Harbor, they started sandbagging around the hospital because it wasn't on a solid foundation, just on these corner posts that held it up. And it was a three-story building. They assigned us so many hours duty and then somebody would come and relieve us.

I remember I was coming off duty some time in the early morning hours when the siren went off that the planes were coming to bomb Nichols Field. When the war was declared, all the patients who could go back were sent back to duty. They sent the Filipinos home. Anybody who couldn't be moved ended up under the hospital. The [commanding officer] then decided to evacuate the patients to Sternberg

ABOVE: The naval yard on Cavite burns after the Japanese air attack. Because of the destruction of the bulk of MacArthur's air forces on December 8, 1941, this facility was essentially defenseless and the U.S. Asiatic Fleet was ordered to evacuate south.

Hospital in Manila, and decided that two nurses and two corpsmen had to accompany them. That afternoon, they took us to the nurses' quarters at Sternberg. You wouldn't believe it. When those nurses came off duty, they always served tea and those nurses were having tea. War had been declared and they were having tea.

On December 10, the Japanese bombed the Navy yard at Cavite again. They were bombed by approximately 125 planes flying at 20,000 feet, and we were out in the courtyard of the nurses' quarters watching all this. There were foxholes dug there. The patients who were brought in were given first aid at the Navy hospital and transferred to Sternberg immediately. About this time, General MacArthur declared Manila an open city. And why did I

get picked to go to Bataan? Only for one reason. When he declared Manila an open city, they were sending surgeons out to Bataan. They weren't picking general medical men. The fact that I had been Dr. [Carey] Smith's ward nurse and I had a background in operating rooms, he picked me. Anyway, the convoy took off for Bataan. There were twenty-four Army nurses, twenty-five Filipino nurses, and me—the one Navy nurse.

As we passed through the villages, the natives came out and cheered us giving us the "V" for victory sign. Many times during the trip, the bus would have to stop and we would dive into gutters along the roadside because the Japanese planes were overhead. Late that afternoon, we arrived at Camp Limay, Hospital

PHILIPPINE DIVISION

Made up of both American soldiers and well-trained Philippine Scouts, the Philippine Division was part of U.S. Forces Far East headquartered in Manila. After the Japanese invasion, it successfully covered the withdrawal of Philippine and American forces into the Bataan Peninsula of Luzon in December 1941. Japanese attacks in mid-January were repulsed, but the division's counterattacks were not able to prevent it from being flanked and forced to withdraw. Made cautious by heavy losses, the Japanese did not attack again until late March. Weakened by malnutrition, sickness, and prolonged exposure to combat, the Philippine Division's counterattacks failed and its combat units were destroyed one by one. On April 8, 1942, the 57th and the 31st Infantry Regiments were lost near the Alangan River, and the 45th Infantry surrendered two days later. Approximately 40 percent of the division's soldiers would die while prisoners of the Japanese.

Number One. There were twenty-five wooden, one-story buildings—fifteen of them wards. A water pipe outside each ward provided water. The utility room for the bedpans and what have you was the back porch. The buildings were in a rectangle with the operating room building at the upper end with a generator and water towers alongside. At the further end was the building housing the nurses' quarters and the officers' mess hall. The remaining buildings were along each side. Behind the buildings on the left side of the beach was a warehouse in which were stored the equipment and supplies for the hospital. In the center of this area was grass and trees and foxholes dug everywhere. We were assigned two to a room.

Meanwhile, the Japanese strikes continued relentlessly at other disparate locations throughout Southeast Asia and Micronesia. Poorly defended Guam in the Marianas, the so-called "Gibraltar of the Pacific," fell easily on December 10. Only at the tiny Wake Island atoll in the middle of the ocean did the Navy and Marine Corps defenders give the Japanese juggernaut its first temporary setback. Here it was the Japanese who were guilty of underestimating the enemy and overestimating their own capability. Despite being softened up by bombers flying out of the Marshall Islands, a Japanese amphibious assault on December 11 was bloodily repulsed by Wake's defenders with the loss of several Japanese warships.

The news of the successful repulse was a ray of sunshine in an otherwise very stormy sky. It served to bolster morale and had the impact of hastening an attempt to reinforce the island with additional resources and defenders. Unfortunately, the relief force under Rear Admiral Frank Jack Fletcher was fatefully delayed in its departure from Pearl Harbor and was over 425 miles away from Wake when the gallant defenders surrendered. More than 1,600 Americans became prisoners.

BELOW: Japanese Mitsubishi Ki-21 "Sally" bombers from Formosa [Taiwan] over Corregidor Island in Manila Bay. Due to a series of miscues, the bulk of General MacArthur's air forces, especially his precious bombers, were caught on the ground and destroyed. Even if the Pearl Harbor raid had never occurred, the United States would have entered World War II due to Japanese invasion of U.S. possessions such as Guam, Wake, and the Philippine islands.

The Heroic Defense of Wake Island

Wake Island is a postage stamp-sized spit of sand in the middle of the Pacific Ocean. It is thousands of miles from land in all directions and this is what made it so important to both Japan and the United States. In American's pre-war contingency plan to fight the Japanese (Plan Orange), Wake was critical as an air and seaplane base from which the U.S. Navy and Marine Corps could provide either warning of Japanese moves or scouting in advance of the fleet as it methodically fought its way through the various island chains to the south of the outpost to retake the Philippines (which were expected to fall to the Japanese).

Despite the expiration of the Washington Naval Treaty in 1937, which allowed the United States to partially fortify the island, the Americans were very slow to build up Wake's defenses. This was because President Roosevelt and Congress wanted to avoid needlessly antagonizing the Japanese government and provoking an early war that the country was not ready for. Initially, the only funds allocated were earmarked for a seaplane base. During peacetime, it became an essential outpost to keep an eye on suspected Imperial forces in the Marshall Island archipelago some 500 to 700 miles south.

As for the Japanese, Wake was a critical part of their plan to conquer the so-called East-Asia Co-Prosperity Sphere. However, its function after capture was for a defensive, not an offensive, strategy against the United States by serving as a pillar in the Imperial Navy's first chain of island fortresses that the Americans had to pass if they tried to contest Japan's conquests. Essentially, Wake would be an unsinkable aircraft carrier, provide key intelligence, and serve as a logistics support base to far-ranging Japanese reconnaissance submarines.

Fortification of Wake became more and more a priority as relations with Japan deteriorated. Just prior to the war, the island also became critical to the U.S. Army, which intended to use it as a transit station for heavy bombers being sent to reinforce the Philippines. Overall command of the island's defense force was in the hands of Navy Commander Winfield Scott Cunningham. He had more than 1,200 civilian construction personnel, a few sailors, Marine Fighter Squadron VMF-211 flying the relatively new Wildcat fighter, and the 450-man First Marine Defense Battalion commanded by Major James Devereux. This was all that was to defend the three small islands comprising the Wake Atoll. The fighters had only recently arrived as a part of measures that Admiral Husband Kimmel took upon receiving the "war warning" from Washington, D.C. The twelve fighter planes and Devereux's coastal defense artillery batteries formed the heart of the

were trained for amphibious assault. These men were effectively outnumbered by the Marines, sailors, and armed civilians ashore, and paid dearly for violating their enemy's—the U.S. Marine Corps'—commonsense amphibious doctrine that mandated having an "unquestionably superior" force when storming a defended island.

Early on the morning of December 8, 1941, Japanese land-based bombers in the Marshall Islands took off—before even the first bombs fell on Pearl Harbor—to begin softening up Wake for an amphibious assault on December 11. The bombing caused extensive damage to the atoll's infrastructure and reduced its Marine fighter squadron to a mere four aircraft with little aviation gasoline left for flight operations. Nevertheless, despite widespread destruction, the critical Marine-manned 5-inch batteries remained largely untouched.

Major Devereux wisely held his fire as the Japanese invasion ships approached to give the impression that his batteries had been knocked out. The Japanese blithely accommodated him, sailing to within 5,000 yards before the Marines unleashed a hail of accurate and deadly fire upon them. The light cruiser *Yubari* with Kajioka embarked, was hit multiple times and immediately turned away, but the

defense, and here were only .50- and .30-caliber machine guns for ground-based antiaircraft defense. Devereux's main punch was his 5-inch guns, organized into three batteries (two each), and three batteries of 3-inch guns (four each).

On the Japanese side, in addition to numerous land-based bombers in the Marshalls, the invasion force—under the command of Rear Admiral Sadamichi Kajioka—consisted of three light cruisers and six destroyers escorting assault and garrison troops embarked on two old destroyers and two transports. A pair of submarines was also in support as scouts. Only 450 of Kajioka's troops

Japanese destroyer *Hyate* was sunk. As the Japanese withdrew, they were attacked by the Marines' four remaining Wildcat fighters, and another destroyer, the *Kisaragi*, was sent to the bottom. Kajioka cancelled the assault and withdrew to the Marshall Islands, licking his wounds.

The news of the successful repulse of the Japanese at Wake was a bright spot on an otherwise dark canvas. It served to bolster morale and had the impact of hastening an attempt to reinforce the island with additional resources and defenders. Events, however, conspired against the relief expedition from the very beginning. It was not until late on December 15–16 before a task force built around the carrier *Saratoga*, under Rear Admiral F. Jack Fletcher, was able to set out from Pearl Harbor.

Fletcher's biggest problem was the slow oiler *Neches*, which could barely make a 13-knot speed. As a result, four destroyers, the *Neches*, and the seaplane tender *Tangier* (loaded with Marine reinforcements) departed ahead of Fletcher for Wake on December 15. The

Saratoga followed with three cruisers and nine destroyers. Fletcher joined forces with his "slowpokes" during the afternoon of December 17 and sent the four destroyers escorting *Neches* and the *Tangier* back to Pearl, as they would only slow the force down once it was time for the destroyers to refuel.

Now weather, time, and distance, combined with decisions in Pearl and Washington to delay, fatally, Fletcher's mission. The task force was 425 miles away from Wake when dire messages from Commander Cunningham indicated that the islands would soon fall, and Washington's relief of Kimmel as its Pacific commander had a direct impact on the outcome. Vice Admiral William S. Pye, Kimmel's interim replacement, decided to recall Fletcher after receiving a message from Cunningham, now under attack by a second Japanese invasion force, stating that the "issue was in doubt." Fletcher's task force turned back to the east at the same time as the Japanese concluded their conquest.

The Japanese had indeed returned with superior forces. After their initial repulse, they continued to pummel the islands with land-based bombers. By December 22, a second invasion flotilla was in position, this time supported by the Pearl Harbor veteran carriers *Soryu* and *Hiryu* to the north and a heavy cruiser force in direct support of Kajioka's beefed-up invasion force, which now consisted of at least 2,000 troops.

By this time, all of the Wildcats had been destroyed and the Japanese stayed out of range of the Marines' batteries when they launched their amphibious assault waves. With the heavy cruisers and Japanese naval aviation providing fire support, these troops landed and by dawn of December 23 were firmly established ashore. Cunningham knew by this time that no help could be expected and after consulting with Devereux, he ran up the white flag and surrendered the gallant garrison at around 8:00 A.M., although some of the defenders, who had not gotten the word, fought on into the afternoon. More than 1,600 Americans became prisoners. Most of them were sent to prison camps around Shanghai, although 100 civilian workers were kept to repair the damage to the island's facilities. All were later executed.

The heroic defense was over, but Wake became the first in a number of morale-boosting operations that kept America's flagging spirits up in that first fateful year of the Pacific War.

"I Shall Return"

At the same time, events in the Far East had gone from bad to worse. Without the ability to interdict Japanese invasion forces, by either land or sea, it was only a matter of time before the Japanese successfully established themselves on the main Philippine island of Luzon in late December. With his air force destroyed, and most of the pitifully small naval forces being evacuated to the south, General MacArthur was holding a very poor hand of cards. His plan for the defense of the Philippines now bore a disturbing similarity to the Texans' plan at the Alamo. Instead of trying to prevent the Japanese from landing, MacArthur decided to pull back into a fortified

line of defense on the peninsula of Bataan, located between Subic and Manila Bays. Here he would defend until relieved by the Navy's Pacific Fleet. Yet any hope of executing this course of action had gone up in the pall of smoke rising over Pearl Harbor on December 7. Nevertheless, MacArthur had little choice other than to try and hold out, or at the very least tie up Japanese forces and prevent their use elsewhere.

In the largest of their amphibious operations to date, the Japanese landed over 50,000 troops of General Masaharu Homma's Fourteenth Army at the pristine beaches on Lingayen Gulf on the northwestern side of Luzon on December 22, 1941. Fortunately for MacArthur's field commander, Major General Jonathan Wainwright, Homma was more inter-

ABOVE: The famous tunnel complex on Corregidor, also known as "The Rock." MacArthur, his staff, and the defenders sheltered here, deep under Malinta Hill, during the Japanese siege of Bataan. After MacArthur's escape via PT boat, this outpost held out until just before the Battle of the Coral Sea in May 1942, and signals intelligence from the personnel in the radio intercept tunnel at Monkey Point played a key role in both the Coral Sea and Midway battles.

RIGHT: Filipino and American soldiers retreating after the Japanese invasion of the Philippines at Lingayen Gulf in December 1941. In many respects, the Philippine campaign was the U.S. Army's last battle of World War I. Fought with antiquated weapons like the Springfield rifle, Stokes mortar, 2.95-inch mountain gun, French-made 75mm and 155mm artillery, light tanks, and no close air support, it saw the Army's last mounted charge when G troop, 26th Cavalry attacked a Japanese force of tanks and infantry on January 16, 1942. The regiment's horses were subsequently eaten by the starving American and Filipino troops. The bulk of the U.S. ground forces during the Philippine Campaign were, in fact, Filipino. Poorly trained and wretchedly supplied, they fought well until the bitter end under both Philippine and American officers. After the surrender at Bataan, they made up the core of the guerrilla bands that formed around leaders of both nationalities, and coalesced into an increasingly effective national underground force that operated, according to circumstances, independently and in conjunction with MacArthur's headquarters.

ested in capturing Manila than destroying his opponent and Wainwright's withdrawal into the Bataan Peninsula was accomplished relatively smoothly. Bataan was simply not prepared for the 80,000 troops (including 20,000 Americans) who retreated into it. Large stockpiles of food did exist, but they were scattered across Luzon and in the confusion of the retreat, most of these supplies fell into the hands of the Japanese. After only one week in their new defenses, the "battling bastards of Bataan" were already on half rations.

The retreat to Bataan involved much hurry and confusion. Here Colonel Harry A. Skerry of the 11th Philippine Infantry remembers how a bridge was blown before his troops could get across.

The engineer lieutenant responsible for the bridge had left the destruction of the bridge to his platoon sergeant and departed for the rear. The platoon sergeant detailed a private and departed with the rest of his men. The private, not to be outdone, had found a civilian, instructed him how to light the dynamite, paid him one peso, and then left to join his platoon. The civilian, after hearing the shooting, became excited and blew the bridge.

Not all of the retreat was this confused or tragically comical. In another case, Lieutenant Colonel William A. Wappenstein describes the heroism of an American-led Filipino artillery outfit that covered his unit's withdrawal toward Bataan.

Every man of the 21st Infantry [regiment] who came out of Tarlac alive should get down on his knees and thank God for that redheaded son of bitch [First Lieutenant] Savoie [who advised the Filipino 3d Battalion Field Artillery Battalion]. He was everywhere he was needed at the right time. He kept the guns in almost three hours after he could have withdrawn to give us a chance to break off. We were all out and the enemy back into Tarlac before he pulled up a gun.

Ensign Bernatitus recalls the difficult working conditions as a nurse at Bataan and Corregidor.

The first few days I was assigned ward duty, but this was changed and I was reassigned to the operating room. You know, they really left me alone. I only worked when Dr. Smith worked. He was the one who took care of me. The Army nurses didn't bother me. Everyone was involved in setting up the hospital. All

Death March on Bataan

In early 1942, American and Philippine forces on the Bataan Peninsula had held out against Japanese attacks for more than three months. By April however, the ravages of disease and malnutrition had taken a heavy toll on the 100,000 defenders, and the Imperial Army was finally able to break through the weakening defenses. Although I Corps still held in the west, the collapse of II Corps' line in the east forced the surrender of Bataan on April 9, 1944.

Prisoners were collected on the southern tip of the peninsula and, within days, 72,000 of them were sent on a forced march to the San Fernando train station some 65 miles to the north. Huge numbers died along the way as the sick and starving stumbled from the ragged lines only to be shot, bayoneted, or in some cases, beheaded by the guards escorting the wretched procession. Estimates vary on the number of dead, but the U.S. Department of Veteran's Affairs places it at 650 Americans and 16,500 Filipinos.

Upon reaching the train station, the POWs were given a bowl of rice before being crammed aboard freight cars that would take them most of the way to Camp O'Donnell. There was little relief for the men once they reached the half-finished training center for Philippine army recruits that would serve as the principal POW camp on Luzon for the rest of the war. But the ordeal was far from over. U.S. Army medical doctors, who set up a makeshift hospital at the camp, estimated that between April 15 and June 10, approximately 1,500 more American and 22,000 more Filipino soldiers died, including 546 POWs on May 27, 1942.

BELOW: Surrendered U.S. troops just prior to the infamous "Death March." The faces of these GIs reflect the scale of the Bataan debacle. The Japanese expected to find large caches of food after the surrender and had made no arrangements to feed their captives.

RIGHT: One of Corregidor's eight 12-inch "disappearing guns" fires on distant Japanese targets during the defense of the Bataan Peninsula. These weapons retracted back into their gun pits for reloading when fired, and had a range of more than 16 miles. The massive and plentiful coastal defenses situated on islands in Manila Bay denied the Imperial Navy access to the excellent harbor for months after the rest of Southeast Asia had fallen to the Japanese, and guarded the back door to the American and Filipino troops on the peninsula. Their ability to directly support forces on Bataan was, however, hampered by a shortage of high-explosive ammunition more suited for use against land targets than the armor-piercing shells used against ships, nor did they have star shells to provide illumination for night fire.

Corregidor fell to the Japanese on May 6, 1942, five months after the strike against Pearl Harbor because, unlike on Wake Island and Bataan, the tactical defense of the island against a vastly inferior invading force was very poorly organized, in spite of the fact that the garrison had long known that an invasion was coming.

the supplies and equipment were crated and stored in the warehouse on the beach. The crates were neither marked nor stored as units, so the Navy crates had to be opened before you found the items for your particular unit. I recall a crate being opened and in it were surgical gowns wrapped in newspapers dated 1917.

The operating room was a long, narrow building with approximately seven or eight tables set up in the center. Along the window openings were the cabinets with supplies. There were shutters with a stick to keep them open. We were washing the dirty dressings

that they used during an operation. We would wash them out and refold and sterilized them and use them again. I'm a bit vague on how we sterilized the gauze and linen but it seems to me it was done in a pressure cooker operated by kerosene. The instruments were sterilized by placing them in a foot tub filled with Lysol, then rinsed in alcohol. The period of sterilization depended on how fast they were needed. As the patients were brought in, they were assigned to a table by Dr. [Alfred A.] Weinstein of the Army Medical Corps. The team assigned to that table took care of the patient regardless of what type of surgery was indicated. Casualties were heavy and the operating room was an extremely busy place.

Every operating table would be filled. They would come in from the field all dirty. You did what you could. There were lice; I kept my hair covered all the time. He [Smith] did a lot of leg amputations because we had a lot of gas gangrene out there. I remember one patient we were operating on. Dr. Smith didn't want to sew him back up. He had died. I remember telling him that I didn't want him to do that if anything happened to me. He said, "I'll sew him up just to shut you up."

We got there on December 24 and on January 23, 1942, Camp Limay moved to Little Baguio farther down the [Bataan] peninsula. We had two meals a day: 9:00 A.M. and 4:00 P.M. The wards were just concrete slabs with corrugated roofs. They were open on the sides. The operating room was on a little knoll. On March 3, the hospital was bombed, even though the warehouse on the beach had a big red cross. Outside the operating room was a bench. I almost killed myself trying to get under that bench. The alarm would sound and then you could hear the bombs coming down—a whistling sound. On [March 30] the Japanese apologized. It had been a mistake. That hospital was right next door to the ammunition dump.

On April 7, the following week, they bombed us again. It was terrible. The second time we were bombed, they hit one of the wards. There were patients who were tied in traction. The nurses had to cut the ropes so they could fall to the deck. There were pajamas in the treetops. By that time, [the Japanese] had stopped advancing for a while. Things were kind of quiet at the front lines. But we were getting a lot of patients with malaria, dysentery, all that. We ran out of beds. You'd go to bed at night and when you awoke the next morning you'd get out there and there would be all these two- or three-decker bunks made of wood and patients in them. There wasn't much surgery going on, but the nurses taking care of the sick were very busy. When Dr. Smith was operating, Dr. [Claude] Fraley got the job of being an assistant to the colonel in charge of the whole outfit, Colonel [James W.] Duckworth. He would go to the Navy facility down at Mariveles

BELOW: Soldiers of the two Japanese battalions that stormed Corregidor push their way through defensive works. Although small in number, the invading force was amply supported by artillery and air power, as well as a demoralized U.S. command structure that rightly felt abandoned on the remote outpost.

There was a heightened feeling that life was to be lived from day to day, without illusions of an ultimate victory. Many sought forgetfulness in gambling. There was no other way to spend the accumulated pay that bulged in their pockets and they rattled the dice or played endless bridge, rummy, and poker.

—Maude R. Williams

[at the southern tip of the peninsula] and scrounge instruments and whatever. The [submarine tender, USS] *Canopus* (AS-9) was there and the men aboard would make things we needed in the shops on the ship. I remember Dr. Fraley would go down to Mariveles scrounging for food. One time he came back with lemon powder. After that, everything was lemon. After I got home I didn't want any lemon.

On April 8, we were transferred to Corregidor. That's when the front lines collapsed. About eight o'clock they told us to take what we had—and we didn't have much—and put us on buses. I left Dr. Smith and Dr. Fraley there. Later on, Dr. Smith showed up on Corregidor; Dr. Fraley didn't.

I think I had all I owned in a pillowcase. To get to Mariveles, they had a road they called the Zig Zag Trail, with a drop-off on both sides. We met the fellows coming up, going to the front lines. Anyway, we got down to the dock at Mariveles and we had to stay there for a while waiting for a boat. Some of the men that were there asked us where we were from. They were shocked to find us nurses. Finally when the boat arrived, I remember sitting in the passageway on a wicker chair. I was carrying my camera; I never gave that up and brought it home with me. They were shooting back and forth over us.

When we got to Corregidor I don't think the people there knew we were coming because that night we had to sleep two in a bunk. I remember the following morning, the Army chief nurse came to me. She took me out to what we called the hospital exit to show me what Bataan looked like with the ammunition dumps going up. I felt real bad because I knew one of the officers that was left there to do the job. You wouldn't believe. They had bombs and everything. The Army nurses still over there were further up the peninsula and they were being evacuated too, but they didn't get to Corregidor until the next day. I was less scared on Bataan than I was on Corregidor. When the Japanese bombed, the whole place just shook.

We were in the tunnel which ran...straight through [Malinta Hill] and the laterals went off it. At the end of [the hospital lateral] would be another lateral. The main tunnel was where MacArthur and Wainwright had their headquarters. I didn't do much work when I got to Corregidor because I had

WESTERN UNION

CLASS OF SERVICE

This is a full-rate Telegram or Cable-gram unless its de-ferred character is in-dicated by a suitable symbol above or pre-ceding the address.

1220

A. N. WILLIAMS
PRESIDENT

NEWCOMB CARLTON
CHAIRMAN OF THE BOARD

J. C. WILLEVER
FIRST VICE-PRESIDENT

SYMBOLS

DL = Day Letter

NT = Overnight Telegram

LC = Deferred Cable

NLT = Cable Night Letter

Ship Radiogram

Time of receipt is STANDARD TIME at point of destination

The filing time shown in the date line on telegrams and day letters is STANDARD TIME at point of origin.

1944 MAR 8 PM 5 26

WA144 NL=WASHINGTON DC 8

E T STONE

=MANAGING EDITOR SEATTLE POST INTELLIGENCER SEATTLE

WASH=

TO THE MEMBERS OF THE BATAAN WIVES AND MOTHERS CLUB AT THEIR
MEETING TOMORROW I SEND WARD GREETINGS AND INEXPRESSABLE BUT
HEARTFELT SYMPATHY NOT ONLY TO THOSE WHO SORROW FOR THEIR
HEROIC DEAD BUT TO THOSE WHO LIVE IN HOPE FOR THE OTHERS
THAT REMAIN I BELIEVE THEIR HOPE IS JUSTIFIED BELIEVE THAT
THE SITUATION IN THE JAPANESE PRISON CAMP IN THE
PHILLIPINES AND IN JAPAN AND ELSEWHERE WILL BECOME BETTER NOT
WORSE AND THAT THE JAPANESE LEADERS WILL TAKE STEPS TO
IMPROVE THEIR RECORD MEANWHILE LET US ALL CONCENTRATE ON

VICTORY=

JOSEPH C GREW.

dysentery. Of course, the Army was in charge, so Dr. Smith wasn't working either. I remember only doing one amputation with him. It was not a clean tunnel. It was just rock. We went on April 8 and left on May 3.

Despite all these misfortunes, MacArthur's troops did accomplish their "new" mission of wrecking the Japanese timetable. The fight now settled into a siege, with disease and hunger afflicting both the Japanese and the Filipino-American forces. Meanwhile, FDR and General George C. Marshall, the Army Chief of Staff, realized that it might be catastrophic for American morale if MacArthur was captured and perhaps executed by the Japanese. MacArthur was given orders to escape through the loose Japanese blockade and go to Australia to stand up a new command charged with organizing a counter-offensive against the Japanese. He delayed his departure until March 11, when he finally boarded a PT boat with his family and staff for a 600-mile run to an airfield on the southern Philippine island of Mindanao. Upon

MacArthur's arrival in Australia he announced, "I shall return." In the meantime, the horrors in Bataan continued to their inevitable conclusion. In April, General Edward P. King ordered his famished and disease-ridden troops— some 78,000 Americans and Filipinos—to surrender with Major General concurrence. Wainwright and a forlorn hope of 14,000 troops held on into May on the island of Corregidor at the mouth of Manila Bay.

Maude R. Williams served on both Bataan and Corregidor as a hospital assistant. Here are her almost poetic memories of the harrowing life on "The Rock".

Under the deepening shadow of death, life on Corregidor took on a faster, more intense tempo. The smallest and most simple pleasures became sought after and treasured as they became increasingly rare and dangerous—an uninterrupted cigarette, a cold shower, a stolen biscuit, a good night's sleep in the open air.

There was a heightened feeling that life was to be lived from day to day, without illusions of

an ultimate victory. Many sought forgetfulness in gambling. There was no other way to spend the accumulated pay that bulged in their pockets and they rattled the dice or played endless bridge, rummy, and poker.

Jam sessions attracted great crowds, which gathered in the dark and hummed softly or tapped feet to the nostalgic swing of the organ, a haunting guitar, or a low-moaning trombone. Sometimes a nurse and her boyfriend of the evening would melt into a dance...The eyes of the onlookers would grow soft and thoughtful, while other couples would steal out into the perilous night.

Still others sought the consolations of religion and the symbols of another world, a better world of sweet and eternal peace. The Catholics gathered at dawn in the officers' mess of Malinta Tunnel where one of the tables was converted into a simple altar, and kneeling on the bare cement under the high white-washed vault they listened devoutly and a little desperately to the same hushed phrases that had been whispered in the Catacombs.

Your name was called and you stepped out of the crowd because everybody was gathered around to see this. Wainwright shook [my] hand and wished [me] Godspeed and he said, "Tell them how it is out here." And then I got in a car and they took us out of the tunnel down to the dock. Everything was pitch-black.

—Ann Bernatitus

Nurse Bernatitus describes her evacuation from Corregidor aboard the USS Spearfish *(SS-190) and the subsequent nerve-racking transit down to Freemantle, Australia.*

On May 3, we were evacuated from Corregidor. I don't know how I was picked. I remember the planes came in first to evacuate people. Two Navy PBYs [seaplanes] took several Army nurses and fifteen other passengers on April 29. We were called to the mess hall and told we were going to be leaving that night. They stressed that weight didn't matter as much as size. All I had was a duffel bag. I always said that I didn't want to go off there on an airplane. I would rather go by submarine. We were dreaming that that's exactly what was going to happen.

They told us we would meet after dark in front of [Major General] Wainwright's head-quarters. But then the Japanese started shelling us, so they canceled us [leaving on the PBYs]. We were told to meet, I think, two or three hours later. Your name was called and you stepped out of the crowd, because everybody was gathered around to see this. Wainwright shook [my] hand and wished [me] Godspeed and he said, "Tell them how it is out here." And then I got in a car and they took us out of the tunnel down to the dock. Everything was pitch-black.

When we got down there, we got on a boat that was even smaller than the one that took us to Corregidor. Then we shoved off. We had to go through our own minefields to get to the submarine. We learned later that it was taking us so long to get out there that the submarine wasn't sure Corregidor hadn't already fallen. Finally we saw this dark shape and we came alongside of it. You could hear the slapping of the water between the two objects. Then someone said, "Get your foot over the rail." And then someone just pulled me, and then the first thing I knew I was going down the hatch. I got down there awfully fast. There were six Army officers, six Navy officers, eleven Army nurses, and one Navy nurse. There was also one civilian woman, and two stowaways—one navy electrician's mate and one who was with the Army transport.

When they first said seventeen days [at sea], I thought I couldn't make it. But I did. When we first got aboard, I was in the control room. Everything was lighted up and there were all these valves and what have you. They took us into the officers' mess. That's where we sat and they gave us tea and chocolate cake. We hadn't seen chocolate cake and tea in a long time. The chefs [mess cooks] gave up their quarters for us. It was just a cabin with a sink in it. Four of us would go to sleep in a hot bunk. [Hot bunking or hot-racking is the practice of several people taking turns sharing one bed to sleep in shifts].

BELOW: General MacArthur and his chief of staff Lieutenant General Richard K. Sutherland. Sutherland had a notorious reputation as an arrogant and over-bearing taskmaster. He was evacuated along with his more "Olympian" boss prior to the fall of Corregidor.

Our luggage we brought with us was on the deck in that same room. I was one of the four picked to go to bed right away.

The next morning when my eight hours were up, four others went to sleep. You just had to kill time any way you could. Most of our time was spent in the crew's mess. Someone had a Victrola [record player] that was playing all the time. The crew would come with magazines they had stashed away someplace. We would sit and talk. And, of course, the boys loved it. The crew was fed first. Anything they served was wonderful for us. We hadn't seen food like that. They gave us one bucket [of water] for four of us when we went to bed. And that was for bathing and washing. Of course, if you went to the john you had to have an escort. Down in that submarine, the only thing you heard was the sound of the screws turning. You know, after awhile, the gals were cooking for the boys.

They initiated us when we went under the equator. I had just gotten up and I had to stand in a pan of water or something. [Known as the "crossing the line ceremony," it's still observed on all U.S. Navy warships today.] You know, while we were on that submarine we remained submerged during the day and at dusk we would surface to charge our batteries. When we came up, we came up at an angle. And then someone opened a hatch and we felt this gush of nice fresh air come through. We had hardly done this when whish, down we went again. Well, that was an experience. They thought they sighted something. Everything was turned off and everybody was sitting around doing nothing. You could watch the men. Those who had shirts on, you could just see those shirts gradually turning from tan to brown with perspiration. We must have been submerged for several hours, just barely crawling. But everything turned out okay.

As the American and Filipino forces battled bravely against the Japanese, the Allies agreed to establish an American, British, Dutch, and Australian Command under the British field

BELOW: The conquering invader—Lieutenant General Masaharu Homma and his staff come ashore at Lingayen Gulf. The Japanese had the most extensive amphibious forces of any nation at the start of World War II.

marshall, Sir Archibald Wavell. The goal was to halt the Japanese advance to the south. Wavell's naval commander was Admiral Hart, which caused considerable resentment by the Dutch. The principal weapons in Hart's inventory were his twenty-nine submarines, some of the latest design. But the weapons, and training, for these vessels were woefully inadequate to the task at hand. However, Hart's force did include a number of surface forces from all four nations, including several heavy and light cruisers, as well as several squadrons of destroyers. They received their baptism by fire when the Japanese invaded the island of Borneo in late January. During the first major surface action of the war, U.S. destroyers slipped in among Japanese transports at Balikpapan at night, sinking four of them—and they would have sunk even more if not for their defective torpedoes.

The event that really doomed the Dutch East Indies (today Malaysia and Indonesia) was the fall of Singapore, Britain's "Gibraltar of the Far East." Hong Kong—the other pillar of Imperial defense—had fallen in December and in a brilliant campaign that had begun on the first day of the war, General Tomoyuki Yamashita conducted a blitzkrieg against the British in Malaya under Sir Arthur Percival. In perhaps the greatest defeat for the Allies in the Pacific War, Percival was pushed out of the Malay Peninsula into Singapore. Worse, he was unable to repel an assault against the vulnerable rear of the island bastion by the Japanese coming across the Strait of Johore. Percival surrendered over 130,000 soldiers and other personnel on February 15, 1942. Many of these men—along with thousands of other slave laborers from the captured colonies— would die of disease, famine, and neglect while

RIGHT: The heavy cruiser USS *Houston* at Tjilajap, Java in February 1942. Some forty-six of its crew were killed almost instantly when a Japanese aerial bomb penetrates the cruiser's No. 3 turret at center. A harbor crane later re-trained the now destroyed turret to face aft, and the war at sea continued as Admiral Hart's meager naval forces of a few destroyers and cruisers of the ABDA command attempted to defend the Dutch East Indies.

BELOW: *Houston*, on the right, readies to depart Darwin, Australia as Admiral Hart's flagship. Surviving defeat at the hands of the Japanese naval forces in the Java Sea, *Houston* was sunk along with the Australian cruiser *Perth* attacking Japanese invasion forces in the Sunda Strait on the last day of February 1942.

building the infamous Thailand-Burma railroad for the Japanese.

Shortly after the fall of Singapore, Wavell advised the Combined Chiefs of Staff (CCS) that protecting the remaining Indies was hopeless and turned over their defense to the Dutch who were adamant in fighting to the bitter end. The naval forces that remained were put under the command of the Dutch and, in late February during a day/night battle in the Java Sea, the Japanese smashed what little Allied sea power remained. The two major survivors, the cruisers USS *Houston* and HMAS *Perth* both perished in the Sunda Strait as they withdrew to the south. On March 9, the Dutch East Indies surrendered.

The Japanese now had nothing to impede their advance to the very shores of Australia. Earlier in February, Nagumo's *Kido Butai* (Mobile Strike Force) had conducted a punishing attack on Darwin in northern Australia. Moving south from their bases in the Marianas and Truk in the Carolines, the Japanese had captured the excellent harbor at Rabaul in the Bismarck Archipelago and turned it into an impregnable fortress. Elsewhere they occupied the British Gilbert Islands (including Tarawa), parts of the northern Solomons, and established themselves along the northern shores of New Guinea.

Back at Pearl Harbor, a new commander had arrived. He was a mild-mannered Texan who had experience in both surface ships and submarines—Admiral Chester W. Nimitz.

Nimitz was a "team player." His first action was to retain the staff of Admiral Kimmel and leave existing command structures in place. This had a calming influence. Additionally, Nimitz decided to conduct an active defense. His biggest limitation was in the numbers of escorts and oilers that he had available for his remaining ships. Because the carriers were 10 knots faster than the battleships, he decided to make them the center of his strategy for defense and devoted most of his destroyer and cruiser escorts to them. He formed these into carrier task forces built around a single carrier instead of the multi-carrier formations favored by the Japanese. It was Nimitz, a non-aviator, who adopted the carrier-centric strategy that would defeat the Japanese Navy.

At the end of Admiral Yamamoto's "wild run," the Japanese had indeed achieved incredible results. But these results were not what they anticipated. Their geographic objectives had been accomplished but their strategic objectives—the destruction of the U.S. Fleet and initiation of diplomatic negotiations to end the war—had not been attained.

ABOVE: A new sheriff in town. Admiral Chester Nimitz arrives to take command of the Pacific Fleet. Nimitz immediately set to the Herculean task of improving morale and getting his fleet back into fighting trim. His first action was to "let bygones be bygones" by retaining Kimmel's excellent staff. Nimitz left the witch-hunting to Congress.

As far as I am concerned, war with America starts now. We'll get our revenge by God.

—Admiral Kanji Kato,
at the 1922 Washington Naval Conference

Chapter Three

CORAL SEA AND MIDWAY

Not long after the fall of the Dutch East Indies, the American Joint Chiefs of Staff (JCS) under the leadership of General George C. Marshall oversaw the implementation of a new, and divided, command structure for the Pacific. This decision was driven principally by service rivalries. MacArthur was put in charge of the Southwest Pacific Theater and Nimitz of the Pacific (often called Central Pacific) Theater. The dividing line between the two theaters ran right along the line of the next axis for Japanese offensive operations: through New Guinea and down the Solomons.

The Doolittle Raid and After

Nimitz soon began to conduct limited strikes against the Japanese. These raids had little real physical impact and their principal value lay in boosting both the morale and confidence of the Pacific Fleet, as well as giving Nimitz's inexperienced carrier aviators much-needed flying time in a relatively benign combat environment. In April, the Americans launched their

JAMES H. DOOLITTLE

PREVIOUS PAGES: Smoke streams from the *Mikuma* as Douglas SBD Dauntless dive-bombers from USS *Hornet* prepare to attack the burning Japanese heavy cruiser on June 6, 1942, during her desperate retreat west after the Battle of Midway. Earlier strikes by *Yorktown* and *Enterprise* SBDs have left her dead in the water, and the *Hornet*'s aircraft have brought 500-pound bombs to finish the job.

ABOVE: Army Air Force flight crew preparing .50-caliber machine gun ammunition on the flight deck of USS *Hornet* as it nears the launch point for their raid on the Japanese mainland, April 18, 1945. The ammunition box in center is marked "A.P. M2, Incndy. M1, Trcr. M1," indicating the ammunition types inside: armor-piercing, incendiary, and tracer. Note the wooden flight deck, with metal aircraft tie-down strips in place of every eighth plank.

most audacious effort to date—the Doolittle Raid on Tokyo. The idea was to place B-25 medium bombers aboard the carrier *Hornet*, escorted by the *Enterprise* and under Admiral Halsey, and then stealthily steam across the Pacific to a launch point about 500 miles from Tokyo. Lieutenant Colonel James H. "Jimmy" Doolittle was selected to command the bombers.

Even though the carriers were detected well short of the launch point by Japanese picket ships, Halsey launched Doolittle's force as planned early on the morning of April 18 when about 650 miles from Tokyo. Doolittle's bombers achieved complete surprise and completed their attack runs with no casualties, but most planes ended up crash-landing short of their Chinese airfield destinations due to lack of fuel. Although the raid caused little physical damage and death in Tokyo, it provided a huge boost to U.S. morale—both civilian and military. For the Japanese military leadership, the dishonor associated with the bombing led to the assignment of hundreds of veteran Japanese aviators back to Japan for defense of the homeland. These pilots and aircraft would be sorely missed in the year to come.

Lieutenant General Jimmy Doolittle tells how he was chosen to lead the Tokyo Raid.

The thing was to select an airplane that would go 2,000 miles carrying 2,000 pounds of bombs and take off short. So I was briefed on the Tokyo plans, and given the job of selecting and modifying the aircraft and selecting and training the crews. During the middle of that operation, I went in to General Arnold [head of Army Air Corps], and said "I know more about this mission; I know more about the B-25s; I know more about the crews than anyone else; I would like to lead it." And he said, "Well, I need you badly here, Jimmy, and I'd rather you stayed on my staff." He apparently saw the disappointment on my face, and said, "Well, I'll tell you what, if it's all right with Miff—General "Miff" Harmon was then his chief of staff—then it's all right with me." I saluted briskly and ran as fast as I could around to Miff's office....

The Japanese now found themselves at odds about what to do next. The Imperial Japanese Navy (IJN) General Staff proposed

LEFT: Lieutenant Colonel James H. Doolittle (left front), leader of the attacking force, and the *Hornet*'s commanding officer, Captain Marc A. Mitscher, pose with a 500-pound bomb and B-25 crewmen during ceremonies on the carrier's flight deck.

BELOW: Army Air Force B-25B bombers lashed securely to the deck below the *Hornet*'s bridge and forward of the midships aircraft elevator. The plane in the upper right is tail number 40-2242, mission plane No. 8, piloted by Captain Edward J. York.

that the next step should be to sever Australia's lines of communication. Some officers proposed that Australia itself be invaded, but the Imperial Japanese Army (IJA) vetoed this plan, claiming that they simply did not have enough troops to secure an area so large. As for Admiral Yamamoto, he was convinced that the only way to bring the Americans to the bargaining table was to finish the job of destroying their navy. Yamamoto first advocated an invasion of Hawaii, but both the Army and the Navy General Staffs opposed this plan. He then proposed the seizure of the American base at Midway, at the far western end of the Hawaiian Islands.

When Doolittle's aircraft dropped bombs near sacred Edo Castle in Tokyo, the Japanese Army—and especially the Navy—felt they had let the emperor down and were humiliated. All resistance to Yamamoto's Operation MI to seize Midway evaporated. Unfortunately for Yamamoto, approval of his plan to defeat the U.S. Navy did not cancel existing plans to continue the advance in the southwest. Naval planners also saddled his Combined Fleet with the mission of seizing the westernmost islands in the Aleutian chain [between Alaska and Siberia] because it was thought that Doolittle's raid may have originated from there. All this led to a fatal watering down of the striking forces Yamamoto would have available for Midway.

INSETS: Lieutenant Colonel Jimmy Doolittle spearheaded Doolittle's Raid, the first American strike on Japan's homeland, on April 18, 1942. Sixteen bombers took off for the mission and all were lost, with eleven crewmen captured or killed. Pictured here are four of the crews that were handpicked for this critical attack.

Crew No. 1 (above), plane #40-2344, was tasked with bombing Tokyo. Members of the 34th Bombardment Squadron included, Lieutenant Colonel James H. Doolittle, pilot; Lieutenant Richard E. Cole, copilot; Lieutenant Henry A. Potter, navigator; Staff Sergeant Fred A. Braemer, bombardier; and Staff Sergeant Paul J. Leonard, flight engineer/gunner.

Crew No. 3 (above, center) of the 95th Bombardment Squadron, plane #40-2270, also targeted Tokyo. Pictured here are Lieutenant Robert M. Gray, pilot; Lieutenant Jacob E. Manch, copilot; Lieutenant Charles J. Ozuk Jr., navigator; Sergeant Aden E. Jones, bombardier; and Corporal Leland D. Faktor, flight engineer/gunner. Corporal Faktor was killed during his bailout attempt over China.

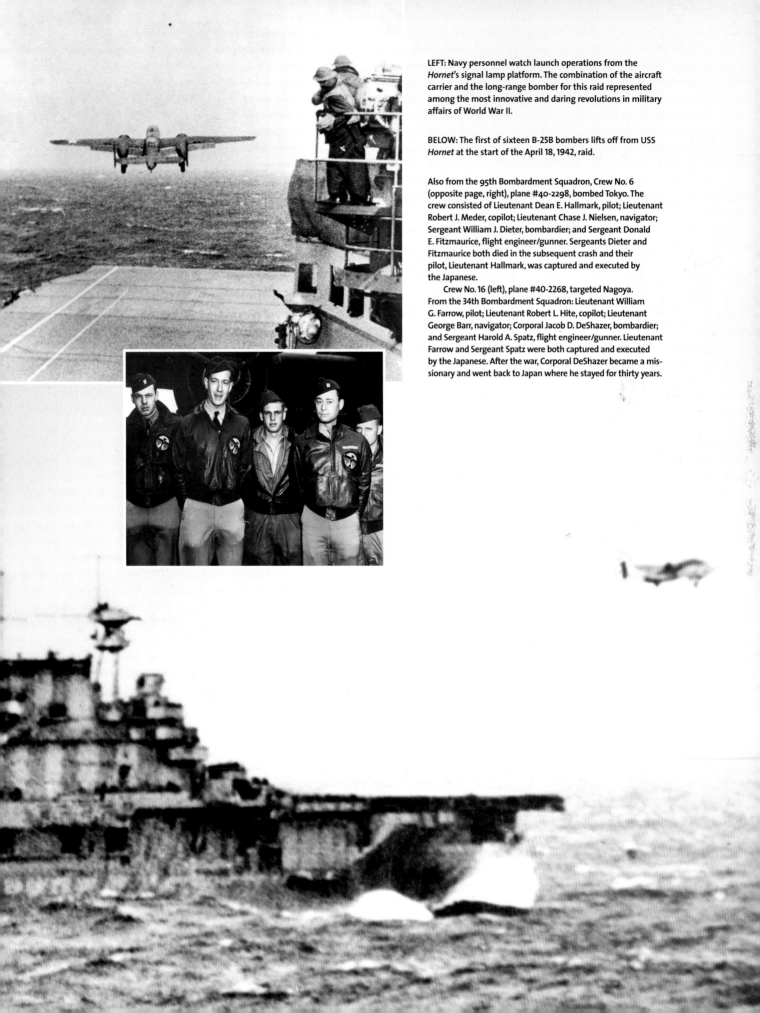

LEFT: Navy personnel watch launch operations from the *Hornet*'s signal lamp platform. The combination of the aircraft carrier and the long-range bomber for this raid represented among the most innovative and daring revolutions in military affairs of World War II.

BELOW: The first of sixteen B-25B bombers lifts off from USS *Hornet* at the start of the April 18, 1942, raid.

Also from the 95th Bombardment Squadron, Crew No. 6 (opposite page, right), plane #40-2298, bombed Tokyo. The crew consisted of Lieutenant Dean E. Hallmark, pilot; Lieutenant Robert J. Meder, copilot; Lieutenant Chase J. Nielsen, navigator; Sergeant William J. Dieter, bombardier; and Sergeant Donald E. Fitzmaurice, flight engineer/gunner. Sergeants Dieter and Fitzmaurice both died in the subsequent crash and their pilot, Lieutenant Hallmark, was captured and executed by the Japanese.

Crew No. 16 (left), plane #40-2268, targeted Nagoya. From the 34th Bombardment Squadron: Lieutenant William G. Farrow, pilot; Lieutenant Robert L. Hite, copilot; Lieutenant George Barr, navigator; Corporal Jacob D. DeShazer, bombardier; and Sergeant Harold A. Spatz, flight engineer/gunner. Lieutenant Farrow and Sergeant Spatz were both captured and executed by the Japanese. After the war, Corporal DeShazer became a missionary and went back to Japan where he stayed for thirty years.

Coral Sea

ABOVE: Destroyers lend assistance as crewmen abandon the USS *Lexington*, mortally damaged by fires and explosions during the afternoon of May 8, 1942. Note the shredded wingtip on the SOC-3 Seagull scout plane on the cruiser *Minneapolis* in the foreground.

RIGHT: U.S. Navy torpedo and dive-bombing planes attack the carrier *Shokaku* on the morning of May 8, 1942. The ship was heavily fire-damaged during the Battle of the Coral Sea, and was unable to take part in the subsequent Japanese attempt to invade Midway Island.

The operations in the southwest Pacific occurred first. The opening phase involved a two-pronged assault code-named Operation MO. It had two objectives: the seizure of the island of Tulagi in the southern Solomons and the capture of Port Moresby on the southeastern tip of New Guinea on the Coral Sea. With New Guinea and the southern Solomons in their possession, the Japanese would then be poised to push into the Coral Sea and sever Australia's lifeline to the United States across the South Pacific. Unfortunately for the Japanese, Nimitz had a dedicated team of code breakers who, by April 1942, were able to inform him of the outline and objectives of MO. Nimitz recognized the opportunity to strike a blow that might seriously damage the Japanese. He

already had Admiral Fletcher's *Yorktown* task force operating in the area and immediately dispatched *Lexington* to join him. Additionally, MacArthur dispatched a combined force of Australian and American cruisers and destroyers under the Australian Admiral John G. Crace to operate under Fletcher's tactical command.

In a confused series of engagements during the first week of May, 1942, the American and Japanese navies clashed in the Coral Sea. It was the first naval battle in which neither side's ships saw the other. The Americans lost the large carrier *Lexington*, an oiler, and a destroyer as well as suffering damage to the *Yorktown*. The Japanese lost the light carrier *Shoho* and suffered damage to the veteran Pearl Harbor carrier *Shokaku*. Admiral Shigeyoshi Inoue, the Japanese commander in Rabaul, made the critical decision to turn the Port Moresby invasion force around and try another day. That day would never come. It was the first operational defeat of the war for the Japanese.

The Japanese did not see it this way, however. They believed they had sunk two, if not three, of the American carriers. In reality, the Americans—due to the incredible efforts of the sailors aboard *Yorktown* and the dockworkers at Pearl Harbor—had three big aircraft carriers available to oppose Yamamoto's fleet when it came to attack Midway. To Nimitz's credit, and with the help of his code breakers, he decided to risk them all

on another battle to whittle down the Japanese fleet. The Coral Sea fight had also reduced the forces available for Yamamoto's great battle. Both of the large carriers used at Coral Sea were unavailable for the Midway operation: one suffered structural damage and the other sustained critically reduced air groups. Yamamoto had also dangerously diluted his available naval air striking power by agreeing to the Aleutian operation that subtracted the air groups of two medium carriers. Thus, the results of the Coral Sea were two-fold: It stopped the Japanese advance in the south and compromised the chances for success for the operation at Midway—fatally as it turned out.

🎙 *Lieutenant Commander Paul D. Stroop was the flag secretary and tactical action officer for Admiral Aubrey Fitch, Commander of Carrier Division One, aboard the aircraft carrier* Lexington *at the Battle of the Coral Sea when the Japanese naval strike from the carriers* Zuikaku *and* Shokaku *found Admiral Fletcher's forces. Here he describes the attack that eventually resulted in the loss of the "Fighting Lady Lex".*

At eleven o'clock we began getting radar indications that enemy aircraft were approaching, and I remember making an entry in the war diary at that time because I thought maybe later on

I wouldn't be able to make entries in the log— I was keeping the war diary in longhand, in a ledger on the bridge—I made the entry at 1120 "under attack by enemy aircraft," and that turned out to be exactly right. At 1120 we began seeing enemy aircraft overhead, and they came down in a very well coordinated attack. They attacked with torpedo planes and dive-bombers. Well, you're a little curious and you're quite scared and you wonder what the outcome is going to be. I can remember standing on the bridge and watching the enemy dive-bombers come down. These were fixed-landing-gear dive-bombers…and you were convinced that the pilot in the plane had the bridge of your ship right in his sight, you knew it, and this didn't look good. Fortunately, they were not strafing, because if they'd been strafing I'm sure that they would have made the topside untenable, but they didn't strafe in their dives.

The minute he released his bomb, you could see the bomb taking a different trajectory from the aircraft itself, generally falling short because their dive wasn't quite as steep as it should have been for good dive-bombing, and you knew that that particular bomb wasn't going to hurt you. It might hit the side of the ship. I watched this a number of times. I was fascinated to watch the bomb leave the air-

plane and realize then that it was probably going to fall short. The torpedo planes came in about the same time—a fine, nicely coordinated attack—and launched their torpedoes at about, I'd say, a thousand yards. They were down to flight deck level when they dropped the torpedoes. And, of course, they were successful in having excellent dive-bombers.

I believe, they got three hits on the *Lexington*. We got, I believe, four torpedo hits. I might add that in the account that was finally sent out later, only two torpedo hits were recorded officially. I personally think this is wrong, and that the *Lexington* probably took four.

All the torpedo hits were on the port side and pretty well distributed along the length of the ship, because immediately after the attack we took a port list and I watched some of the torpedo planes passing from port to starboard. It was pretty discouraging to see these Japanese at it. They'd launch their torpedoes and then some of them would fly very close to the ship, you know, to get a look at us; they were curious and sort of thumbed their noses at us, and we were shooting at them with our new 20mms [antiaircraft guns] and not hitting them at all. The tracers of the 20mms were falling astern of the torpedo planes. It was very discouraging to see enemy planes pass within range of your guns and not be able to knock them down. You were completely helpless, you were depending on the training that had been given to the fighter pilots in the air, and you were dependent on the training and practice the gunners had had. The commanding officer of the ship, Captain [Forrest] Sherman, was very busy twisting his ship, trying to avoid torpedoes, and I think he was successful in some cases, but he wasn't successful completely.

We had fighters overhead and they were credited with knocking down some Japanese planes. As a mater of fact, we saw one or two come tumbling down. We'd also taken some of the dive-bombers and put them on close in patterns as defense against the torpedo planes, figuring that they could overtake them possibly and disrupt the torpedo plane attack. They were not successful and the torpedo planes pretty much got through. The *Lexington* took, I think, three bomb hits. One of the most spectacular ones was on the port gun gallery.

A bomb exploded and immediately killed, burned, gun crews in that area. I remember walking down there when the attack was over and here were the Marine gunners and they were burned right at their stations on the guns. That particular bomb started a fire down in the officers' country the next deck below the admi-

ral's—flag officer's living quarters were set on fire and killed a couple of stewards who were down in the pantry in that area. I remember that particular situation because I considered going down later and getting into the stateroom and taking some gear out of the safe and it couldn't be done.

We had another bomb hit in the after part of the island, or stack, and another one pretty well aft in—I think in the boat pocket where the captain's gig [a large auxiliary boat for going ashore or ship-to-ship] was stored. All these bombs, of course, started fires, which we figured that we could control and put out. We learned a lot, of course, from this action that ships of that kind were tinder; they had too much flammable stuff aboard. The furniture in the admiral's cabin, for example, was wood and fabric and that burned. Paint all over the ship had an oil base and wherever we got a fire, why, the paint on the bulkhead burned. That was something that had to be corrected. We learned that our fire-fighting equipment was not adequate, that we needed to redesign our hoses and hose nozzles so as to have fog instead of solid water. These were lessons, of course, that come out of the war and which were quickly used to improve situations on other ships.

BELOW: A Nakajima B5N Kate torpedo bomber is shot down during the Coral Sea battle. This was the first time Japanese carrier aviators faced real resistance from other carrier aviators. Their losses to the rookie Americans decimated two air groups and prevented Japan's two biggest and newest aircraft carriers from participating in the Midway operation.

BELOW: Midway—the prize that became the fatal bait—as seen looking west across the southern side of the atoll, November 24, 1941. Eastern Island and its air station are in the foreground while Sand Island, location of most other base facilities, is across the entrance channel. Additional channels were blasted through the reef around Eastern Island to dock areas at the southern end of the north-south runway and the hangar area opposite Sand Island.

Midway

Yamamoto and Admiral Nagano of the Imperial Naval General Staff both believed that the weight of the Combined Fleet, especially its battleships, must prevail. On the other side of the Pacific, Nimitz's code breakers led by Lieutenant Commander Joseph Rochefort were reading Japanese naval signals and through subterfuge already knew that Midway was the target. Nimitz reacted decisively to this intelligence. He deployed all of his carriers to a position northeast of Midway to ambush his attackers. The American task forces were geographically separated into two groups—the *Yorktown* TF under Admiral Fletcher, and a second carrier force composed of the *Enterprise* and the *Hornet* (of Doolittle raid fame) under Rear Admiral Raymond A. Spruance. (Spruance replaced Halsey who had been hospitalized due to a severe attack of dermatitis.) Fletcher,

the victor of Coral Sea, was the overall commander but gave Spruance considerable latitude in conducting his own operations. Fletcher would also have the "unsinkable aircraft carrier" of Midway, with its Marine, Navy, and Army Air Corps aircraft available to attack the Japanese. It would be an even fight as far as aircraft numbers went, even though the Japanese aviators were still superior at this point in the war to their improving American counterparts.

On the morning of June 3, 1942, a PBY-5 Catalina flying boat sighted the main Japanese armada (but not Nagumo's carrier force) 700 miles west of Midway. Despite this, Yamamoto pressed on with not a single change to his plans. "USS Midway" struck at the Japanese first on the afternoon of June 3 by launching B-17 bombers to attack a group of enemy transports and, later that night, radar-equipped PBY Catalinas attacked the IJN's Midway Occupation Force of troop transports.

Lieutenant Commander Archie Mills, USN, gives an account of the first Naval Aviation attack on the Japanese Fleet by PBY amphibious patrol planes fitted with aerial radar.

After the attack on Pearl Harbor, we were given two weeks leave before being sent to Hawaii. I was assigned to VP-21 but at Pearl Harbor was told VP-21 had been wiped out in Australia, so was sent instead to VP-24. One day, the word came down that three volunteer crews were needed for "special training" [a euphemism for a dangerous combat mission]. I was so anxious to fly, I signed up. Our crew's PBY used the Mark 13 torpedo, an unreliable weapon, mounted under the wing. There were four Catalinas for the mission—three from VP-24, one from VP-51. We were ordered to Midway and arrived at five in the afternoon on June 3, 1942. We went into the underground bunkers for briefings where we were handed a sealed envelope containing our orders, not to be opened until we were in our aircraft. We were to proceed 460 miles on a given heading in a four-plane formation seeking the Midway invasion fleet. Once airborne, we were to be in absolute radio silence. I was the copilot in the lead aircraft piloted by Lieutenant [junior grade] Hibbert. As the lead aircraft, we had a Lieutenant Richards of VP-44, one of their senior PBY pilots, with us and he functioned as the mission commander.

It was a long, quiet ride, but after midnight we made contact and then we saw the Japanese Fleet. We were down moon so didn't present a silhouette to the Japanese ships. It was real tight, like making a critical putt on the green or the key at bat in a baseball game. We just hoped we had not flown all that way without being able to do the job...and then we saw all these ships. We were a bit surprised at how easy it had been to find the fleet—your breath is a little short and throat is a little dry.

We attacked in a very loose formation, sequentially, to avoid collisions. We selected one of the bigger ships to attack, descended to 3,000 feet and released the torpedo from a glide profile. After long seconds, there was a tremendous orange explosion indicating a

direct hit, and later we learned we had struck the *Akebono Maru*, an oiler. We flew over the remainder of the fleet because it was nighttime and we didn't want to go through the AA [anti-aircraft] fire already in progress behind us, since we also would have been silhouetted against the moon. One PBY probably missed a ship with its torpedo—although we heard an explosion—and the third Catalina dropped and missed, possibly due to a malfunctioning torpedo. In the end, our aircraft experienced no enemy fire from the ships or from aircraft. Some airplanes were sighted, but they were most likely scout planes from one or more of the Japanese cruisers.

We could not loiter due to fuel concerns and headed back to Midway. We flew solo on the return trip. The confusion of the attack dispersed our three aircraft and each proceeded independently in radio silence. When we were within radio range of Midway, we copied a blind radio broadcast that Midway was under attack and so we had to continue to either Lisianski or Laysan Island, east of Midway. We selected Lisianski. One of the PBYs ran out of fuel and ditched, but the crew was later rescued by a Navy ship.

Yamamoto and Nagumo still had no idea that the American carriers were present and decided to pummel Midway with the air power

ARCHIE MILLS

BELOW: The crew of Patrol Squadron 23 (VP-23), PBY-5A Catalina patrol bomber, that found the approaching Japanese fleet's Midway Occupation Force on the morning of June 3, 1942. (Kneeling) Aviation Machinist's Mate 1st Class John F. Gammell; Aviation Machinist's Mate 3d Class George Goovers; and Aviation Machinist's Mate 3d Class Patrick A. Fitzpatrick. (Back row) Aviation Machinist's Mate 2d Class Raymond J. Derouin; Chief Aviation Radioman Francis Musser; Ensign Gerald Hardeman, copilot; Ensign Jack H. Reid, pilot (on wheel); and Ensign Robert A. Swan, navigator.

ABOVE: Japanese aircraft carrier *Hiryu* maneuvers to avoid three "sticks" of bombs dropped during a high-level attack by Army Air Force B-17 bombers, shortly after 8 A.M. on June 4, 1942.

of *Kido Butai*—four large aircraft carriers—at first light of June 4. Not long after daybreak, a PBY located Nagumo's force and alerted the island of the incoming danger. Nagumo's strike found the Americans prepared for them, but easily sloughed off the Marine fighters. Despite heavy damage to some of the facilities, the Japanese lost over thirty-eight aircraft to Midway's defenses and probably another thirty were too damaged to be used again soon. The Japanese strike commander radioed to Nagumo that a second air strike would be necessary. In the meantime, Nagumo experienced his first air strike of the day—attacks that would tax his own air defenses for the next four hours.

 Colonel B.E. Allen remembers the Army Air Corps role his bomber played at Midway in June 1942.

We had sent two squadrons out to Midway based on some advance intelligence of a possible Japanese attack. My squadron was not one of them, but on the day that the Japs attacked the Aleutians—which was the day before their planned attack on Midway—my squadron was on a fifteen-minute alert, so we were sent out there...without a toothbrush or anything else. I was the second-ranking squadron commander there. Colonel [Walter Campbell] Cam Sweeney was commanding the other squadron. We worked together. The first day we went on two sorties attacking the Japanese carrier task force. Sweeney's squadron was pretty well worn out. They had been out there for about ten days, flying day and night on search missions. His squadron was withdrawn that night and I had command of the remaining B-17s the following day. We never could relocate the Japanese task force, but we did locate a battleship and a couple of cruisers that we attacked on the second day, and on the third day there was nothing to be found within range of the B-17.

Now the American carriers got in on the act and all three launched strike packages at what they believed to be Nagumo's location. Most of *Hornet's* air group never found the target. Meanwhile, in an incredible stroke of luck, dive-bombers from both the *Yorktown* and *Enterprise* groups arrived almost simultaneously overhead of the Japanese force.

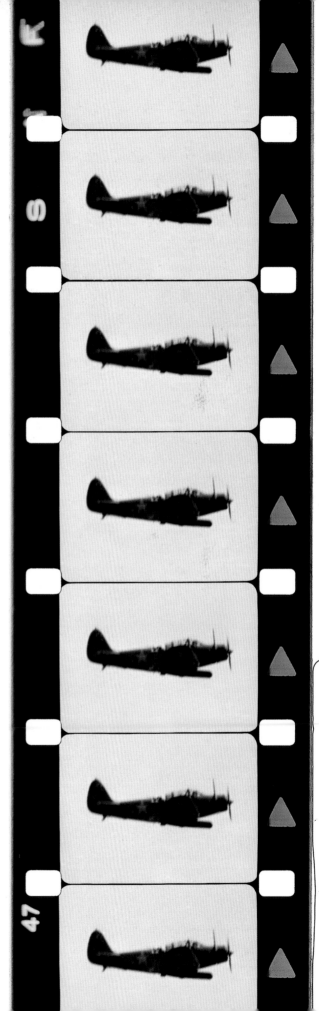

Ensign George Gay, the sole survivor of VT-8 at Midway remembers the battle.

RIGHT: A Douglas TBD-1 Devastator torpedo plane—an obsolescent death trap—carrying a Mk. XIII torpedo, en route to attack the Japanese carrier force during the morning of June 4, 1942. This plane is thought to be from Torpedo Squadron 3 (VT-3), launched from USS *Yorktown* at approximately 8:40 A.M.

Torpedo 8 had a difficult problem. We had old planes and we were new in the organization. We had a dual job of not only training a squadron of boot [inexperienced] ensigns, of which I was one of course, we also had to fight the war at the same time. When we finally got up to the Battle of Midway, it was the first time I had ever carried a torpedo on an aircraft and it was the first time I had ever taken a torpedo off of a ship…had never even seen it done. None of the other ensigns in the squadron had either. Quite a few of us were a little bit skeptical and leery, but we'd seen Doolittle and his boys when they hadn't even seen a carrier before and they took the B-25s off. We figured, by golly, if they could do it, well we could, too.

It turned out the TBD [Douglas Devastator torpedo bomber] could pick up along the way. We learned everything that we knew about Japanese tactics and our own tactics from Lieutenant Commander [John C.] Waldron, Lieutenant [Raymond A.] Moore, and [Lieutenant James C.] Owens, as they gave it to us on the blackboards and in talks and lectures. We had no previous combat flying and we'd never been against the enemy; our only scrap with them had been in taking Doolittle to as close to Tokyo as we [could]. When we finally got into the air on the morning of June the fourth, we had our tactics down cold and we knew organization and what we should do. We could almost look at the back of Commander Waldron's head and know what he was thinking, because he had told us so many times, over and over, just what we should do under all conditions.

I didn't get much sleep the night of June the third, the stories of the battle were coming in, midnight torpedo attack by the PBYs and all kinds of things, and we were a bit nervous, kind of like before a football game. We knew that the Japs were trying to come in and take something away from us, and we also knew that we were at a disadvantage…we had old aircraft and could not climb the altitude with the dive-bombers or fighters and we expected to be on our own. We

BELOW: Torpedo Squadron Six (VT-6) Devastators prepared for launch on USS *Enterprise* at about 7:30–7:40 A.M. on June 4, 1942. Eleven of the fourteen TBDs launched from *Enterprise* that morning are visible, with the rest and ten Grumman F4F Wildcat fighters still to be pushed into position before launching. The TBD at the left front is No. 2 , flown by Ensign Severin L. Rombach and Aviation Radioman 2d Class W.F. Glenn. In little more than two hours, this plane and its crew—along with eight other VT-6 aircraft—were lost attacking Japanese aircraft carriers. The cruiser USS *Pensacola* is in the distance (right) and a destroyer is in "plane guard" position at left to retrieve the crewmen of any aircraft that might have to ditch after takeoff.

didn't expect to run into the trouble, but we knew that if we had any trouble we'd probably have to fight our way out of it ourselves.

Before we left the ship, Lieutenant Commander Waldron told us not to worry about our navigation but to follow him as he knew where he was going. He went just as straight to the Jap Fleet as if he'd had a string tied to them. I thought that there was a battle in progress and we were late. I was a little bit impatient that we didn't get right on in there then and when it finally turned out that we got close enough in that we could make a contact report and describe what we could see, the Zeros jumped on us and it was too late. They turned out against us in full strength and I figured that there was about thirty-five of them...I found out later that they operated fighter squadrons in numbers of about thirty-two and I guess it was one of those thirty-two-plane squadrons that got us.

It's been a very general opinion that the antiaircraft fire shot our boys down and that's not true. I don't think that any of our planes were damaged, even touched by antiaircraft fire—the Zeros shot down everyone. By the time we got in to where the antiaircraft fire began to get hot, the fighters all left us and I was the only one close enough to get any real hot antiaircraft fire, and I don't

think it even touched me and I went right through it, right over the ship.

I think we made a couple of grave mistakes. In the first place, if we'd only had one fighter with us I think our troubles would have been very much less. We picked up on the way in a cruiser plane, a Japanese scout from one of their cruisers, and it fell in behind us and tracked us and I know gave away our position and course and speed. If we'd had one fighter to go back and knock that guy down, catch him before he could have gotten that report off, I believe the Japs might have been fooled [about] the fact that our fleet was there.

We were still trying to find them and didn't, and the skipper [commanding officer] put us in a long scouting line, which I thought was a mistake at the time. I didn't ever question Commander Waldron...he wanted to be sure that we [found the Japanese] and that is the reason that we were well trained, and when he gave the join-up signal, we joined up immediately. I was only afraid that in the scouting line in those old planes we would be caught by Zeros [while] spread out and it would be much worse. As it turned out, it didn't make a whole lot of difference anyway.

I remember the first [Zero] that came down got one of the airplanes that was over

to the left. Commander Waldron on his air phone asked [Chief Radioman Horace F.] Dobbs and came out over the air if that was a Zero or if it was one of our planes and I didn't know whether Dobbs answered him or not, but I came out on the air and told him that it was a TBD. He also called Stanholpe Ring [the Carrier Air Group Commander or CAG] from "John E. One, answer" and we received no answer from the air groups. I don't know whether they even heard us or not, but I've always had a feeling that they did hear us and that was one of the things that caused them to turn north, as I think the squadron deserves quite a bit of credit for the work that they did. I've never understood why I was the only one that survived, but it turned out that way, and I want to be sure that the men that didn't come back get the credit for the work that they did. They followed Commander Waldron without batting an eye.

It was only a matter of time before the Japanese combat air patrols (CAP) were caught out of position, but by luck it was the worst possible moment. As the Japanese Zeros finished off the doomed torpedo bombers and dueled with the American fighters, the Navy dive-bombers screamed in from two different axes on the Japanese carriers. In a few minutes, *Yorktown*'s bombers had lit up the carrier *Soryu* and [Lieutenant Commander Clarence Wade] McClusky's *Enterprise* bombers had scored multiple hits on the carriers *Kaga* and *Akagi*. The Japanese were also caught with most of their strike aircraft in their below-deck hangars [which were completely enclosed by the walls of the ships]—armed and, in some cases, fueled. Japanese damage control systems, inferior to those on the U.S. ships, were quickly overwhelmed by the blazing infernos that the American bombs created in these hangar bays. Before long, all three carriers were burning from end to end as they were racked by secondary and tertiary explosions of bombs, torpedoes, and aviation gasoline. Eventually, all three carriers would sink or be torpedoed by their own escorts to prevent their capture by the Americans.

The battle wasn't over. The American dive-bombers had missed one Japanese carrier, the

Hiryu. She soon launched a strike that crippled the *Yorktown*. Spruance, however, located *Hiryu* and set her ablaze in the same manner as her three sisters. By early morning on June 5, Yamamoto made the decision—much as had happened at Coral Sea—to abandon the invasion and return to Japan, despite having a preponderance of naval surface power at his disposal. He was beaten and he knew it. As for the *Yorktown*, the Japanese submarine I-168 sank the veteran carrier and an escorting destroyer two days after she was first damaged. She was being towed back to Pearl Harbor for repair at the time.

GEORGE GAY

Lieutenant Joseph P. Pollard, USN, was a medical officer onboard the aircraft carrier Yorktown (CV-5). He remembers her role in the battle and how he was forced to abandon ship after devastating Japanese air attacks on June 4, 1942.

On May 30, USS *Yorktown* put to sea at 0800 and took a course said to be toward Midway at a speed of about 15 knots. There was gunnery practice most of the morning, using both towed sleeve and high-speed sled. The gun crews seemed good. Morale was excellent. I had the flight deck duty station when we took onboard our aircraft. One of our lieutenant commanders was killed at this time in a very unfortunate accident. A fighter drifted over the arresting cables, over the barriers, and sat down on the back of his plane. The propeller of the fighter split his headrest causing a compound skull fracture; the next blade pushed in the rim of the cockpit crushing his jaw, face, and neck, and severing the great vessels of his neck. Obviously, there was nothing I or anyone could do for him.

On June 2, our scouting aircraft were out morning and afternoon. Excitement was running high in the ship and morale was excellent. We were told that our submarines had reported a Jap invasion force [battleships, cruisers, destroyers, and transports] off Midway Island. We rendezvoused with the [carriers] *Hornet* and *Enterprise* and their escorts in late afternoon and remained with them overnight. [The following day] the scuttlebutt [speculation] was thick. We heard that land-based aircraft had

Japan's Midway Plan

For several months in 1942—due to their unexpectedly rapid successes virtually everywhere in the Pacific—the Japanese found themselves at odds about what to do next. The Imperial Navy General Staff under Admiral Osami Nagano proposed that the next step should be to cut off Australia's lines of communications. However, Admiral Yamamoto, the commander in chief of the Combined Fleet, had become convinced that the only way to bring the Americans to the bargaining table was to finish the job of destroying their fleet. This could be done, he maintained, by attacking Hawaii because the U.S. Navy must surely do everything in its power to keep Pearl Harbor from falling to Imperial forces.

Both the Army and the Navy General Staffs opposed this plan as logistically unrealistic. It was this opposition that gave birth to the Midway Operation, code-named MI. Yamamoto countered that a seizure of the American airbase at Midway, at the extreme western end of the 1,000-mile-long Hawaiian Island chain, would accomplish the destruction of the U.S. Pacific Fleet without forcing the Japanese Fleet to operate even farther from its bases. After Lieutenant Colonel Jimmy Doolittle's B-25 bomber raid, Yamamoto's operation MI to seize Midway was quickly approved and planning for the operation proceeded at a frenzied pace.

Unfortunately for Yamamoto, approval of his plan to defeat the U.S. Navy did not cancel the existing plans to continue the advance in the southwest Pacific against the Solomon Islands and New Guinea, while also seizing the American-held Aleutian chain in the northwest Pacific. The Japanese decided they could have their cake and eat it, too, by conducting—nearly simultaneously—all three operations: MO against Port Moresby, MI against Midway, and AL against the islands of Attu and Kiska in the Aleutian

LEFT: Admiral Isoroku Yamamoto, commander of the Combined Fleet. Yamamoto had been opposed to war with the United States and it is thought by some historians that he was assigned command of the Combined Fleet to get him aboard ship where he could be better protected from fanatical junior officer assassins in the Army and Navy.

BELOW: Lieutenant Commander Joseph Rochefort. Rochefort was Admiral Nimitz's chief cryptologist, or code breaker. It was Rochefort who broke the Japanese coded JN-25 signal that indicated that Midway was the objective for the Japanese Fleet. Rochefort's work was so secret that he wasn't recognized until well after the war for his significant, some say decisive, contribution to the victory at Midway. Rochefort's assignment to command one of the big Advanced Base Sectional Docks (ABSD) after Midway has been regarded as a slap in the face by some historians. However, the ABSDs were some of the most important units in the Pacific Fleet, without them the U.S. Navy could not maintain its battleships, cruisers, and carriers in the undeveloped anchorages of the Western Pacific. Command of one of them was actually a mark of esteem for Rochefort.

chain. Ironically, the admirals to whom these operational tasks had fallen—Shigeyoshi Inoue in the southwest and Yamamoto in the north—had both been opposed to Japan's signing of the Tripartite Pact with the Axis powers that had set their country on the final path to war. Now it fell to both of these men to

try to achieve victory in a war they essentially did not believe in.

After their "victory" in the Coral Sea (which was, in fact, a strategic defeat), the mood of the Japanese remained dangerously optimistic. They believed they had sunk both the *Yorktown* and the *Lexington*, two of the U.S. Navy's largest aircraft carriers leaving, at best, two and probably only one aircraft carrier to defend Midway. In fact, the Americans—due to the incredible efforts of the sailors aboard *Yorktown* and the dockworkers at Pearl Harbor—had three big aircraft carriers: *Yorktown*, *Enterprise*, and *Hornet*, potentially available to oppose Yamamoto's fleet. To Admiral Nimitz's credit, and with the help of his code breakers, he decided to risk them all on another punishing defensive battle to whittle down the Japanese fleet.

As for the Japanese, the aircraft carrier *Shokaku* was so badly damaged during the Coral Sea battle that she was no longer available for the Midway operation and her sister ship, *Zuikaku*'s air groups, had also been reduced to dangerously low levels during the fighting. It was decided instead to use the spare pilots from these two ships to beef up the air groups of the remaining four carriers of Admiral Nagumo's *Kido Butai* embarked on the Pearl Harbor-veteran carriers *Akagi*, *Kaga*, *Hiryu*, and *Soryu*. As it turned out, this would be a major error since the Japanese would find they had need of every one of their carriers at Midway. Worse, the Aleutian operation had subtracted the air groups of the medium carriers *Junyo* and *Ryujo* from the forces available for the main effort at Midway.

Admirals Yamamoto and Nagano acted as if Coral Sea had never occurred and believed that the weight of the Combined Fleet, especially its battleships, must prevail at Midway. Both failed to understand that the real center of power was now naval aviation and that with the losses from Coral Sea and the dilution due to the Aleutian operation, this power was greatly weakened where it was most needed. The fatal final plan for the Midway operation ultimately included six separate—and as it turned out, non-supporting—naval forces for both the invasion and the subse-

quent sea battle that Midway's seizure was anticipated to provoke.

Yamamoto's plan relied on surprise. He had to capture Midway before the Pacific Fleet could deploy. Then, with Midway in hand and its airbase neutralized as a factor—and possibly in use by Japanese planes—he would smash the Americans

BELOW: The USS *Yorktown*, which the Japanese believed they had sunk, receiving urgent repairs at the Pearl Harbor Navy Yard's Dry Dock No. 1 on May 29, 1942, for damage inflicted during the Coral Sea battle. She left Pearl Harbor the next day to participate in the Battle of Midway.

when they came to take it back. The plan, however, was complex and violated the principle of concentration by dividing his fleet into a half-dozen different forces—and these did not include those ships already assigned for Operation AL well to the north.

First there was the Mobile Carrier Striking force (*Kido Butai*) under Admiral Nagumo. His job was two-fold: provide air cover while supporting the invasion of Midway; then ambush any American naval forces coming out to meet the Imperial fleet. *Kido Butai* was composed of the finest and most veteran carriers and air groups in the Imperial Japanese Navy, as well as two escorting battleships. The second force consisted of a screen of Japanese submarines that would deploy in advance to report the movements of the Pacific Fleet from Pearl Harbor and any American warships in range of their torpedoes.

A separate Main Force of battleships was under Yamamoto's personal command from the new super battleship *Yamato* with her gigantic 18-inch naval guns, and also included the old, small

carrier *Hosho*. The Main Force's role would be to engage any U.S. naval forces remaining after Nagumo's *Kido Butai* had neutralized or destroyed the American aircraft from Midway and any carrier(s) that tried to intervene.

The fourth element was the Midway Invasion Force on transports carrying the special Ichiki Landing Detachment with their warship escorts. This group was to assault, seize, and occupy Midway while receiving the support of a fifth element, an independent cruiser covering force. Just to the north, but still some distance from Yamamoto and Nagumo, yet another group was Admiral Kondo's Second Fleet Main Body of cruisers: two fast battleships and the new light carrier *Zuiho*.

A brief review of these forces shows that Yamamoto's confidence had led him to scatter his battleships among three widely separated forces. His intent was to unite all of them at Midway for the final showdown. Finally, the principle of concentration, which was essential for the battleships, was employed only for the four big aircraft carriers. If they were to go down, the two remaining small carriers

could do little more than provide fighter cover for the battleships.

Yamamoto's key assumptions were that he would be able to strike at Midway undetected while at the same time receiving accurate and timely intelligence from his submarines about the size and location of the U.S. Fleet. In both cases, he was to be disastrously wrong. Nimitz's code breakers under Lieutenant Commander Joseph Rochefort were already reading Yamamoto's JN-25 radio transmission. In order to determine the target for the big attack that the Americans knew to be brewing, they had the garrison at Midway transmit "in the clear" (an uncoded message) that their water distillation unit was broken. The Japanese duly intercepted this transmission and soon the Americans were reading a Japanese message that the target for the upcoming naval operation had a problem with water distillation.

In summary, Yamamoto's plan had violated the emerging principle in naval warfare that widely scattered ships must be mutually supporting in their operations. He employed tactical concentration only for his most valuable assets—his carriers—yet left them relatively unsupported. At the operational level, it left two medium carriers (in the Aleutians) and two light carriers unavailable to respond if his plan ran into trouble. If these carriers were located, there was the potential for the Americans to knock most of them out with a single blow. Finally, in the critical area of aircraft—just as at Coral Sea—the Japanese would have about the same numbers of airplanes and pilots to employ as the Americans, but his plan relied on the Americans to act precisely as he assumed. It was with these dangerous flaws in his plan that Yamamoto set sail to Midway.

LEFT: Japanese prisoners of war, survivors of the aircraft carrier *Hiryu*, are prepared for transportation from Midway to Hawaii aboard the USS *Sirius* (AK-15), June 1942. They had been rescued by USS *Ballard* (AVD-10) a few days earlier. Note armed guards nearby, a crowd of onlookers, and widespread use of the old-style "tin hat" battle helmets.

picked up the Jap invasion force and bombed them and also that our submarines were active. A Jap task force was reported to have bombed Dutch Harbor [Aleutian Islands]. A Jap carrier force was reported northwest of Midway, consisting of three carriers [it actually had four] and their screen. We were said to be heading toward them.

On June 4, our scouting aircraft were dispatched. One returned about 0930 and dropped a message on our flight deck. The Jap task force of three carriers and their screen was reported to be 200 miles ahead, closing in on us at 25 knots. Everywhere there was an undercurrent of excitement. At any moment, the word might be passed to begin our attack. At any moment, we might be attacked.

Meanwhile, the *Hornet* had sent off her planes, then the *Enterprise* sent hers off. We could see them on the horizon like a swarm of bees—then they were gone. A report came in from Midway Island that the Japs were attacking. Apparently, the Japs had hit Midway with everything they had and had not expected to be attacked themselves. The...word came over the bullhorn, "Pilots,

BELOW: "Fighting Six," or VF-6, part of Air Group Six aboard the USS *Enterprise*, in January 1942. Lieutenant Commander Clarence Wade McClusky, Jr., seated fourth from the right, was also the air group commander and as such was flying in a Dauntless dive-bomber, not in a fighter, during air strikes. On a hunch, he followed a Japanese destroyer northwest of Midway, which led him directly to the four large carriers of *Kido Butai*. McClusky's dive-bombers arrived almost simultaneously with the air group from *Yorktown*, accidentally achieving the first multi-axis at-sea strike from geographically separated carrier forces. The result was a calamity for the Japanese.

FIGHTER SQUADRON VF-3

The "Fighting Three" was transferred to the USS *Lexington* in January 1942 after its carrier, the *Saratoga*, was torpedoed by a Japanese submarine. The following month, it struck Rabaul where Lieutenant Edward "Butch" O'Hare became the Navy's first fighter ace, shooting down five aircraft. VF-3 then played a key role in the Battle of the Coral Sea. The *Lexington* was sunk, however, and the squadron was moved to the *Yorktown* where it absorbed the surviving pilots of VF-42. Lieutenant Commander John Thach's combat maneuver, the "Thach Weave"—soon adopted by fighter pilots across the fleet—was successfully tested during the Battle of Midway, but the *Yorktown* was also lost, and VF-3 was recovered by the *Enterprise* and the *Hornet*. The severe attrition of U.S. carriers resulted in the squadron's prolonged assignment to Hawaii, where it was redesignated as the new VF-6 in July 1943. Retaining its "Felix the Cat" insignia, VF-6 returned to action aboard the *Independence*, and later, *Cowpens*, *Intrepid*, and *Hancock*.

man your planes." We put off our bombers, torpedo planes, and half-dozen fighters for their protection. Then we put up more fighters for our protection. We sat tight with no news for a while. There was a great deal of tension. There were small groups of people everywhere—talking in low tones. Everyone was wearing anti-flash clothing and steel helmets. All was quiet—too quiet.

Battle Dressing Station No.1, my duty station, was manned and ready. The morning wore itself away and the afternoon began. I became hungry and went down to the wardroom for a sandwich.

About 1400 [2:00 P.M.], our planes began returning. They had been out a long time and were low on gas. A couple of well-shot-up SBDs [Dauntless dive-bombers] made their crash landings. Then the fighters started coming aboard. Many were riddled with holes. We landed about five and then one came in too hot and too high. He began to float over the deck and it looked like trouble. The pilot recognized that he was in trouble and made a dive for the deck. He somersaulted and skidded away. I made a quick dive under the wreckage but the pilot was unhurt and

got out of the wreckage before I could get to him.

I began to run across the flight deck to my station but before I arrived there, general quarters sounded, Jap planes were upon us. I dived down the ladder for Battle Dressing Station No.1 and on my way saw one of our fighters fall on one wing and, like a shooting star, hit the drink. There was a puff of black smoke and that was all. Upon arriving at No.1, I lay flat on the deck and hoped that we would not get a bomb in the crowded dressing room, or anywhere for that matter. By this time, our AA [antiaircraft guns] was in full bloom—such a roar—first the 5-inch, then the 1.1s and 20mms, the 50 cal, and finally the hastily set up 30 cal machine guns along the rail. I knew then they were upon us.

Then all hell broke loose. I saw a burst of fire, heard a terrific explosion, and in less than ten seconds was overwhelmed by a mass of men descending from the gun mounts and flight deck into the Dressing Station. An instantaneous 500-pound bomb had struck just aft of the starboard side of the middle elevator and shrapnel had wiped out nearly all of the men from AA mounts No.3 and No.4

(1.1-inch) and also my corpsman who stood on the aft island ladder platform where I usually stood. Another corpsman was injured who was standing in the gear locker doorway.

I was overwhelmed with work. Wounded were everywhere. Some men had one foot or leg off, others had both off; some were dying—some dead. Everywhere there was need for morphine, tourniquets, blankets, and first aid. Station No.1 rapidly overflowed into the passageway, into the parachute loft, and into all other available spaces. I called for stretcher-bearers to get the more seriously wounded to the sick bay where they could receive plasma, etc., but the passageways had been blocked off due to the bomb hits. So we gave more morphine, covered the patients with blankets, and did the best we could. Many patients went rapidly into shock. All topside lights were out and I never realized that flashlights gave such miserably poor light.

There was no smoke in Battle Dressing Station No.1, which was fortunate. Water hoses were dragged into the passageway in an attempt to control a fire somewhere forward in the island—the hose had been perforated by shrapnel and sprayed water all over the deck and on some of my wounded who were lying in the passageway. Our water tank was very useful to us, as there

I saw a burst of fire, heard a terrific explosion, and in less than ten seconds was overwhelmed by a mass of men descending from the gun mounts and flight deck into the Dressing Station. An instantaneous 500-pound bomb had struck just aft of the starboard side of the middle elevator and shrapnel had wiped out nearly all of the men from AA mounts No.3 and No.4 and also my corpsman, who stood on the aft island ladder platform where I usually stood.

—Joseph P. Pollard

BELOW: Corpsmen treating casualties onboard *Yorktown*. The dead and wounded were the crew of 1.1-inch gun mount No. 4, in the center background, who were struck by fragments of a bomb that exploded on the flight deck just aft of the midships elevator. This view looks directly to starboard from the front of the same elevator as a bearded petty officer steps off it and over a fire hose. A fire extinguisher is at lower left.

was a great need for drinking water and none was otherwise obtainable.

I went up to the flight deck. The first thing that I noticed was Mount No.4 [gun]. A pair of legs attached to the hips sat in the trainer's seat. A stub of spinal column was hanging over backwards. There was nothing else remaining of the trainer. The steel splinter shield was full of men—or rather portions of men—many of whom were not identifiable. Blood was everywhere. I turned forward and saw great billows of smoke rising from our stack region. We were dead in the water and it suddenly dawned on me how helpless we were lying there. A repair party was rebuilding a portion of the flight deck. Then I was called aft where there were several casualties from shrapnel that came from a near-miss off the fantail. There were wounded also along the catwalk along the starboard side.

The fire by this time was discovered to be in the rag locker and was under control. This

stopped the billowing column of smoke that gave away our position and made us so susceptible to a second attack. Suddenly, there was a great burst of steam from our stack, then another, and amid cheers from all hands we got underway. Meanwhile, the Admiral [Fletcher] and his staff had gone over to the [cruiser] *Astoria* and it was said that we had orders to proceed to the States at the best speed we could make. We seemed to be doing all right and began getting the ship in shape. We were really beginning to have some hope that the Japs would not return, but alas and alack.

About 1600, our radar picked up enemy planes at 40 to 60 miles coming in fast. We had just begun to gas five F4F-4s [Wildcat fighters] that we had succeeded in landing just before the previous attack. Some had only 25 gallons aboard. Nevertheless, they took off posthaste. We were just hitting 22 knots but they took a long run and made it off. Just as the last one left the deck, I made

ABOVE: Looking forward on the flight deck of USS *Yorktown* (CV-5) shortly after she was hit by two Japanese aerial torpedoes, June 4, 1942. Men are preparing to abandon ship. The island's port side is at right, with the curved supporting structure for the Primary Flight Control booth at top. Knotted and unknotted lines in the foreground were apparently used to evacuate the island's upper platforms.

a dive for Battle Dressing Station No.1 and again the AAs began as before. By the time I could find an unoccupied place on the deck, there was a sickening thud and rumble throughout the ship and the deck rose under me, trembled and fell away. One torpedo hit had occurred. My thought was that we could take this one and get away with it perhaps, but not any more. Then another sickening thud and the good ship shuddered and rapidly listed hard to port.

We were completely helpless, but did not want to admit it. Just then, word came over the speaker, "Prepare to abandon ship." I was dumbfounded. It was uncomprehensible [sic]. A man lying beside me with one foot shot away and a severe chest wound turned his head toward me and asked, "What does this mean for us?" and turned his head away. He knew that he would have no chance in the water. But this man was later seen in the Naval Hospital in Pearl Harbor on the way to recovery. We listed more and more to port until it was almost impossible to stand on the slick deck. We searched frantically for life preservers for the wounded, taking some

from the dead. Our stretchers had gone below to the sick bay and we had difficulty finding enough for our wounded. All who could possibly walk did so.

I went up on the flight deck and walked along the starboard edge being very careful not to slip and skid the width of the ship and off the port side. The ship rolled slowly with the swells but the water was not rough and after each roll she returned to her former position. I thought a big wave might possibly capsize her. A bulkhead giving way below might also let her go over. Our list was about 30 degrees. The speakers were dead and when word was passed to abandon ship, it did not get to me. Several life rafts were in the water but the lines over the side were not long enough to reach the water. Lieutenant Wilson and I tied some lines together and lowered some wounded. Meanwhile the sick bay wounded were being lowered from the hangar deck.

Captain [Elliott] Buckmaster [*Yorktown's* commanding officer] came up to me as I was on the verge of going over the side at a place we had lowered some wounded on the starboard side aft of the island structure. There were several life rafts of wounded floating below me. He asked what I was waiting for. I told him I was waiting to get off all the wounded and that we had searched the topside structure and the catwalks and I was sure that we had every man that was alive from this area on the life rafts. He said something to the effect that "They said the captain should be the last to leave the ship. I'm ready to go now. Would you leave?" I chose a big line and went over the side. I stopped at the armor belt for a rest. It was at least 75 feet from the deck to the water and I still had some 20 feet to go. I worked along the armor belt to a spot that was immediately above a life raft. The line there was a small one and soon after I started down, a corner of my life jacket got inside my grip and I began slipping. The fingers of both my hands were rather badly burned before I realized it. Then I released the line and dropped the remainder of the way into the water and swam through the oil to the raft. We took on board several wounded who were close by until the

LEFT: A trio of furry Laysan Albatross ("Gooney Bird") chicks have a birds-eye view of burning fuel oil tanks on Midway's Sand Island following the Japanese raid on the morning of June 4, 1942.

BELOW: The *Yorktown*, adrift after her crew was ordered to abandon ship, rides with the North Pacific currents as the destroyer USS *Balch* stands by. The brighter-looking water surrounding the ship is caused by the reflection of the sky on an oil slick.

We were completely helpless, but did not want to admit it. Just then, word came over the speaker, "Prepare to abandon ship." I was dumbfounded. It was uncomprehensible [sic]. A man lying beside me with one foot shot away and a severe chest wound turned his head toward me and asked, "What does this mean for us?"

—Joseph P. Pollard

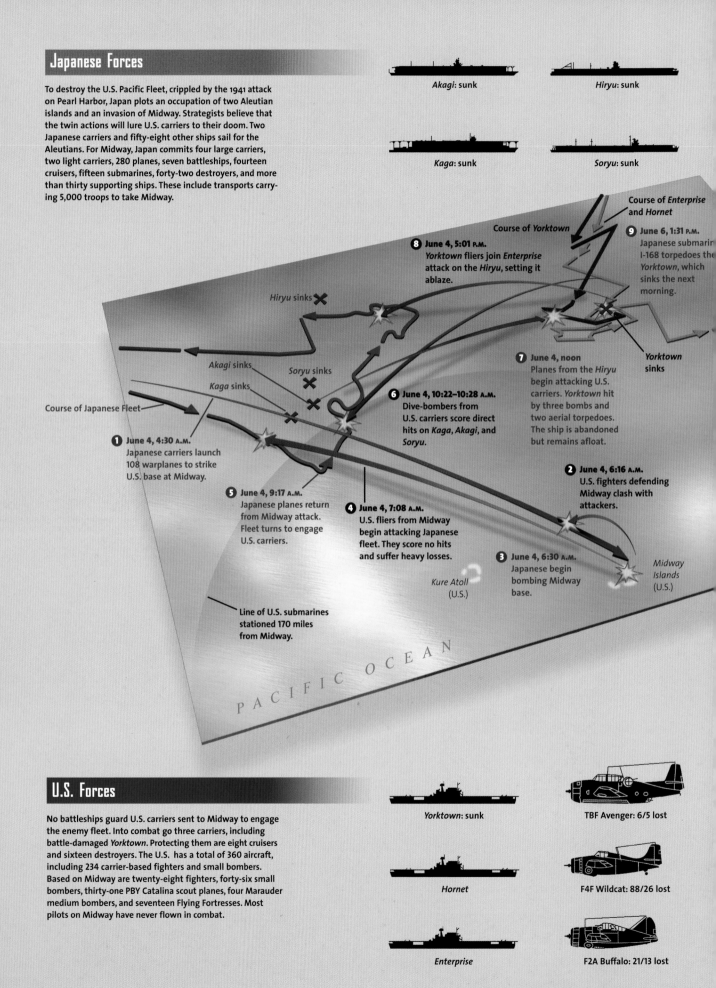

Japanese Forces

To destroy the U.S. Pacific Fleet, crippled by the 1941 attack on Pearl Harbor, Japan plots an occupation of two Aleutian islands and an invasion of Midway. Strategists believe that the twin actions will lure U.S. carriers to their doom. Two Japanese carriers and fifty-eight other ships sail for the Aleutians. For Midway, Japan commits four large carriers, two light carriers, 280 planes, seven battleships, fourteen cruisers, fifteen submarines, forty-two destroyers, and more than thirty supporting ships. These include transports carrying 5,000 troops to take Midway.

Akagi: sunk

Hiryu: sunk

Kaga: sunk

Soryu: sunk

Course of *Enterprise* and *Hornet*

Course of *Yorktown*

8 June 4, 5:01 P.M.
Yorktown fliers join *Enterprise* attack on the *Hiryu*, setting it ablaze.

9 June 6, 1:31 P.M.
Japanese submarine I-168 torpedoes the *Yorktown*, which sinks the next morning.

Hiryu sinks ✖

Akagi sinks

Kaga sinks ✖ ✖

Soryu sinks ✖

Course of Japanese Fleet

Yorktown sinks

7 June 4, noon
Planes from the *Hiryu* begin attacking U.S. carriers. *Yorktown* hit by three bombs and two aerial torpedoes. The ship is abandoned but remains afloat.

6 June 4, 10:22–10:28 A.M.
Dive-bombers from U.S. carriers score direct hits on *Kaga*, *Akagi*, and *Soryu*.

1 June 4, 4:30 A.M.
Japanese carriers launch 108 warplanes to strike U.S. base at Midway.

5 June 4, 9:17 A.M.
Japanese planes return from Midway attack. Fleet turns to engage U.S. carriers.

4 June 4, 7:08 A.M.
U.S. fliers from Midway begin attacking Japanese fleet. They score no hits and suffer heavy losses.

2 June 4, 6:16 A.M.
U.S. fighters defending Midway clash with attackers.

3 June 4, 6:30 A.M.
Japanese begin bombing Midway base.

Midway Islands (U.S.)

Kure Atoll (U.S.)

Line of U.S. submarines stationed 170 miles from Midway.

PACIFIC OCEAN

U.S. Forces

No battleships guard U.S. carriers sent to Midway to engage the enemy fleet. Into combat go three carriers, including battle-damaged *Yorktown*. Protecting them are eight cruisers and sixteen destroyers. The U.S. has a total of 360 aircraft, including 234 carrier-based fighters and small bombers. Based on Midway are twenty-eight fighters, forty-six small bombers, thirty-one PBY Catalina scout planes, four Marauder medium bombers, and seventeen Flying Fortresses. Most pilots on Midway have never flown in combat.

Yorktown: sunk

TBF Avenger: 6/5 lost

Hornet

F4F Wildcat: 88/26 lost

Enterprise

F2A Buffalo: 21/13 lost

A6M Zero: 106/94 lost

B5N Kate: 93/81 lost

D3A Val: 72/72 lost

U.S. Dauntless dive-bomber

SBD Dauntless: 128/48 lost

PBY Catalina: 31/1 lost

SB2U Vindicator: 21/6 lost

B-26 Marauder: 4/2 lost

TBD Devastator: 44/40 lost

B-17 Flying Fortress: 17/2 lost

raft was overflowing and the few of us with life preservers had to get out and swim or hold on with one hand. As each wave broke over our heads, the oil burned our eyes and noses like liquid fire. It was impossible to keep from swallowing some of it. Someone would swim alongside and say "Hold me up a minute please," and proceed to vomit the oil and then swim on.

We had nine stretcher cases and about twenty-five men on or hanging onto our raft.

We tried to flutter kick and paddle our raft away from the side of the ship, but each wave seemed to bring us back against her side. If she capsized, we would be carried down by suction and not have a chance. Finally, someone got the bright idea of paddling aft along the side of the ship and we began to make some headway. By doing this we finally got free of her stern.

Our destroyers were weaving back and forth about 300 yards away, picking up survivors. Captain Buckmaster swam alongside the raft that I was holding onto but would not come aboard as we were so overcrowded. Instead, he swam to a nearby raft and hung onto it. A passing motor whaleboat threw his raft a line and was towing it to the [destroyer] *Russell,* but with too much speed, and a mess attendant was pulled off. Instead of treading water, he began screaming and wearing himself out. Captain Buckmaster turned loose of his raft and swam to the mess attendant. They were both about gone when a man from our raft swam out and helped keep both of them afloat. We took the mess attendant aboard, but the captain preferred to swim.

About this time, the [destroyer] *Hughes* threw us a line—two or three of them. All were short and as enemy planes were reported coming in, our chances seemed to be at an all-time low; but the [destroyer] *Hammann* finally came alongside and got us. She was a wonderful ship. We had been in the water two-and-one-half hours [picked up at 1930]. Just as we hit the deck of the *Hammann,* there was another general quarters alarm [enemy planes] and she went to full speed, but the planes proved to be friendly. Fortunately, the Japs seemed unaware of our predicament.

RIGHT: Dead in the water, the crew of the heavy cruiser *Mikuma* attempts to jettison their oxygen-powered Type 93 Long Lance torpedoes, afraid they'll be set off by internal fires. The *Mikuma* and her sister ship, *Mogami*, had been reduced to roughly half speed from damage received during their collision while taking evasive maneuvers. Lagging farther and farther behind the retreating Imperial Fleet, they were discovered by a Midway-based PBY scout plane on June 6, 1942, and then pummeled mercilessly by wave after wave of aircraft from the *Hornet* and the *Enterprise*. Not all of the *Mikuma*'s torpedoes could be removed, and those that remained exploded, sinking the ship. The badly battered *Mogami* eventually made its way to the safety of Wake Island.

INSET: The burning *Mikuma* explodes during the third wave of attacks. The destroyer off its bow is either the *Arashio*, which managed to rescue many survivors, or the *Asashio*.

As Yamamoto sailed grimly back to Japan, he must have realized that his task had just become infinitely harder. His fleet—especially his carrier-based air power—was seriously wounded and the opportunity now existed for the United States to seize the initiative and launch a strategic counterstroke. This counterstroke, actually two, was not long in coming.

Upon their return to Japan, the IJN leaders, including Yamamoto, decided not to tell the Japanese people of the disasters at Midway and Coral Sea, and even withheld its extent from the Japanese Army. This deception ultimately exacerbated the defeat. Unaware that they had lost hundreds of experienced naval aviators—not to mention hundreds of veteran carrier personnel—the Japanese did not step up efforts to train and deploy their replacements. The conflict in the Pacific had now become a war of attrition. As for the northern forces attacking the Aleutians, they had accomplished their mission and captured the desolate islands of Attu and Kiska. Yet even this minor victory was pyrrhic since they soon found that these islands were virtually useless as air-bases. Even more critical was their loss of an intact Zero that crash-landed on the American-held island of Akutan. The Americans recovered this valuable prize and used it to help design an aircraft that would eventually give them qualitative superiority over the Japanese—the F6F Hellcat.

Lieutenant Commander Masatake Okumiya was assigned as the staff aviation officer aboard the light aircraft carrier Ryujo, *which was a part of the Japanese Navy's covering forces for the invasion of the Aleutians. Here he remembers the need to complete the invasion of Attu and Kiska so as to bolster General Yamamoto's propaganda that the various operations (which included Midway) had not been completely unsuccessful.*

We did not know of the American airfield at Umnak Island. At the time, our operations officers collected as many documents as possible. But at the time, I had only a map of Unalaska that had been made around 1920 and only some photographs taken by our merchant ships around that time. So, we had no correct [intelligence] about Dutch Harbor. If we aban-

OPPOSITE BOTTOM: Marines taking cover in a zig-zag trench stand by as 22,000 barrels of fuel burns out of control after the second day of Japanese air strikes against the Dutch Harbor Naval Operating Base, June 4, 1942. The Japanese carrier aircraft were launched from the light carriers *Ryjno* and *Junyo*. Code-named AL, the Aleutian attack—contrary to myth—was never a part of the Midway plan and was a completely separate operation intended to neutralize potential American bombing raids. Some senior Japanese officers on the Naval General Staff thought that General Jimmy Doolittle's famous raid on Tokyo had originated from these islands. The Aleutians invasion was most important for the role it played in further diluting the naval air striking power Admiral Yamamoto had available for the Midway gambit.

doned the intended occupation at Attu and Kiska, Admiral Yamamoto could not say we had no success. We lost the battle around Midway, but we occupied the Northern Islands [Attu and Kiska]. We needed the occupation to show some success to our people. [During air attacks on Dutch Harbor] I saw one B-26. The pilot was so brave. The plane, the B-26, made a very low altitude bombing; like torpedo bombing. The B-26 flew over our flight deck, and whoooom, flew just over our heads and dropped off the stern of our ship. Had he dropped a half second earlier, his bomb would have hit. Very brave!

Lieutenant Commander James F. Russell, U.S. Navy, talked with the B-26 pilot who made this attack after the flight and remembers the same incident a bit differently.

I spoke with [Captain Wayne] Thornborough when he came back to Cold Bay. He was the first one from whom we got authoritative information as to the [composition of the] Japanese formation—the ships there. He had been in the flight with [Lieutenant] Colonel [William] Eareckson. That flight was armed with Navy torpedoes, one torpedo for each B-26. We had told them the warhead of the torpedo is armed with a water impeller, little paddles that stick out to the side of the warhead, and as the water flows by, it turns the paddle and arms the warhead. We had warned them that if they flew very fast, we had no way of safetying the little impeller, and if they dove at high speed, they might very well arm the warhead. Thornborough told me that he made two approaches and each time the ships turned end-wise to him so he pulled up and climbed and dove his airplane as fast as it would go thinking he would arm the war head. Then he made the attack on the Ryujo. They saw the [torpedo] leave the airplane and go the length of the deck of the Ryujo and drop into the water astern.

After that, Thornborough came back to Cold Bay. We sat in the tent together, my communication tent. We sketched out the Japanese formation. He was very excited about the whole thing, and although he had

a good number of [bullet] holes in his airplane, it was flyable and he said, "I'm going to load up with 500-pound bombs and go back and get them." He did that, he flew, [and] didn't find them apparently. The last we heard from him, he was 10,000 feet on top [of the cloud cover] and trying to get down into Cold Bay [to land his aircraft]. We had rigged a field telephone from my little communication tent at Cold Bay out to the *Casco*, the seaplane tender, and I called the commanding officer, Commander Combes and said, "Please get on Captain Thornborough's plane frequency and try to coach him down through the overcast." Apparently he made a [descent] and hit the water because several days later we discovered wreckage on the beach—his nose wheel and the corpse of his radioman still strapped to his chair.

Lieutenant Commander Okumiya relates how the Japanese came to lose an intact Zero fighter to the Americans in the Aleutians and how the Americans used it to design the F6F Hellcat.

As the *Junyo* [a light aircraft carrier] group returned home, they were attacked by American fighters and received severe damage. At the time, we lost two Vals, dive-bombers, and our fighter pilots saw the two Vals shot down. The other two communicated to our flagship that they lost their way. So in total, four planes were lost at the time. Hours later, a pilot from Lieutenant [Michio] Kobayshi's fighter group, Flight Petty Officer Tadayoshi Koga, reported to his flight commander that he had been hit by antiaircraft fire and could not return to our carrier [Ryujo]. He made a forced landing on Akutan, the small island east of Dutch Harbor, which had been designated as an emergency landing site for crippled planes.

The sea was so cold...if we ditched on the sea, we could survive only a few minutes. On the island the pilot was [later] picked up by a submarine. We knew when we saw the F6F Hellcat that the Americans had exploited one of our Zeros captured at the Aleutian Islands. But, until that time, about one year later, we did not know of this.

LEFT: The Japanese Navy Zero, or "Zeke", fighter flown by Flight Petty Officer Tadayoshi Koga that crashed on Akutan Island just east of Dutch Harbor in the Aleutians provided a gold mine of information on the aircraft's characteristics and performance to U.S. avionics specialists. Koga died in the crash.

The greatest pity was that every Japanese commander was aware of all the factors [that contributed to their defeat], yet no one seemed to do anything about any of them. We stumbled along from one error to another while the enemy grew wise, profited by his wisdom, and advanced until our efforts at Guadalcanal reached their unquestionable and inevitable end—in failure.

—Rear Admiral Raizo Tanaka

Chapter Four

THE DEFENSIVE-OFFENSIVE

Prior to the climactic Battle of Midway, the strategic stage was already being set for the first American-Allied offensives of the Pacific War. The results of the Battle of the Coral Sea had unexpectedly presented new opportunities for the two commanders—General Douglas MacArthur and Admiral Ernest J. King—itching to go over to the offensive. As early as March 1942, King—alarmed by the Japanese seizure of Rabaul in the Bismarck Archipelago—had broached the idea of a counteroffensive through the Solomon Islands to capture this new Japanese base. Eventually, the Rabaul operation would be code-named WATCH-TOWER. After Midway, MacArthur—sensing the tide had turned—made an astonishing counterproposal to use his command to seize Rabaul in a three-week operation. He said he needed the majority of the available Army, Marine, and Navy forces then in the Pacific to accomplish this task.

The Navy agreed that Rabaul must be neutralized and wanted the operation performed by forces under Nimitz's command. Nimitz favored a more methodical advance up the Solomons, establishing command of the air and sea as they "climbed the ladder" of the nearly 500-mile-long chain of islands. The final result of the fight over who was to command

the operation to seize Rabaul was a compromise that established the entire offensive pattern for the war in the South Pacific for the rest of 1942 and early 1943.

Nimitz would execute the first phase by seizing the Japanese seaplane base and anchorage at Tulagi Island in the southern Solomons. MacArthur was to perform the second task, advancing along the northern coast of New Guinea at the same time as Navy and Marine forces advanced in the Solomons. The final phase, under MacArthur's overall command, would involve the capture of Rabaul. These three phases of WATCHTOWER became known as Task 1, Task 2, and Task 3. Admiral King nicknamed this period of the Pacific War the "defensive-offensive" because the United States would seize recently acquired Japanese territory and then defend it against the inevitable Japanese counterattacks.

Colonel General Frederick H. Smith, Jr., commanding the 8th Pursuit (fighter) group discusses the confusion, pessimism, and rigid command structure he found upon his arrival in Australia shortly after the fall of Bataan.

General [George H.] Brett moved his headquarters to Melbourne. He thought that anything else, anything much farther north, would be unsafe. He also was upset by

General MacArthur's arrival. He was the big "I am" before General MacArthur arrived, and he resented being superseded as Supreme Commander. However, he was made, by MacArthur, Commander of the Allied Air Forces, which was our American [forces] and the Royal Australians. General Brett did give me permission to make a reconnaissance to the Port Moresby area. Shortly thereafter, I got word to send a squadron to Port Moresby. I sent the 36th Squadron up there with Ed Hillery, squadron commander, and flew up there and spent several nights with them. Ed Hillery flunked it. He just found he was terrified at the thought of flying against the Japanese, so I had to relieve him and I appointed another officer as squadron commander. They lived in miserable conditions, unsanitary; the Aussies had had it before. They had a P-40 squadron there, which the 36th relieved and it was pretty miserable.

In typical fashion, the Japanese struck first. In a move of unprecedented audacity, the Japanese forces on the northern shores of eastern New Guinea advanced over the rugged Owen Stanley Mountains to attack MacArthur's Australian Allies in July 1942. They advanced along a mere path—the Kokoda Trail—that the Australians believed was unable to support any

meaningful operation. Their objective was again Port Moresby—this time by the land route—and MacArthur found himself on the defensive. The Japanese supported their advance with an amphibious assault at Milne Bay once more on July 25, but this was defeated in a hard fight by the Australians and a few U.S. Army combat engineers.

 Colonel Smith operated out of Port Moresby and witnessed the Battle of Milne Bay.

The first operation that involved aircraft from Whitey's [Brigadier General Ennis C. Whitehead] command was over in the Solomons. A search-and-destroy mission was ordered at just the start of Guadalcanal; I guess it was the south end of Bougainville Island, where intelligence reconnaissance had reported there was a convoy of Japanese ships assembled. I thought, with the weather being what it was, that it was a poor mission—from Seven-Mile Airdrome at Port Moresby clear over to the Solomons and back—because to be effective we had to have good visibility and there just wasn't. So I started my business of going on those missions, which I disagreed with, and I was on this mission and, as I had forecast, we didn't see a damned thing in the lousy weather. We dropped bombs—didn't even have H-2s or any radar sights, of course, nothing but regular Navy-developed sights.

When we got back to Seven-Mile, I found a message from General Whitehead that I was to report immediately to him. So I did. He informed me that the Japs had now put airplanes on Buna, an airdrome directly across the Owen Stanleys from Port Moresby. So I

ABOVE: Gunners of the 2/9th Light Anti-Aircraft Battery, Royal Australian Artillery stand watch with their 40mm Bofors at Milne Bay's Gili Gili Airfield, September 1942. A P-40 Kittyhawk fighter prepares to land on the main runway, which is steel planked in order to allow operations on the perpetually soggy ground. Four U.S. fighter squadrons were based here.

said, "Well, general, that means that Milne Bay is their next target." He said, "You really think so?" And I said, "Yes sir." I think we had two squadrons of the 8th Group at Milne Bay under the command of [William H.] Bill Wise: [Captain] Ben Green's squadron and the 80th under [Major] Greasley.

Sure enough, we ordered reconnaissance immediately and I believe it was early the next morning we saw a Japanese convoy heading into Milne Bay. General MacArthur had ordered in some two weeks prior to this time a brigade of Australian infantry into Milne Bay as a garrison, and we had two fighter squadrons there on steel-plank runways. We sent weather reconnaissance out after the Japanese had been seen to enter Milne Bay, and the weather reconnaissance observer reported the ceiling at 30,000 feet. So, at Whitey's direction, I ordered an attack by a squadron of B-17s on the convoy.

Well, what had happened was that the weather observer had reported the tops at 30,000 feet; actually there was practically no ceiling at all.

Two or three B-17s penetrated, individually, underneath, dodging hills and what not, and hit one transport. The rest of it aborted. It was a mission in which we got the wrong weather report. That was the 19th Bomb Group. To make a long story short, the Australians put up a very spirited resistance on the ground: The fighter aircraft strafed until their gun barrels were lopsided, and the Japanese were isolated, finally, and then decimated. In the meantime, of course, we were mounting missions against Rabaul as a principal target. We also bombed Lae and Salamaua to keep them under hack, and an airdrome at Gloucester Point on New Britain. These were generally our four targets in the late summer of 1942.

WATCHTOWER Task 1

With MacArthur's offensive moves on hold until the Japanese were defeated, the focus moved back to Task 1 and the American seizure of Tulagi. King, exercising his operational command prerogatives as Commander-in-Chief of the U.S. Fleet (COMINCH), had threatened to seize Tulagi with Navy and Marine forces only. The Joint Chiefs decided to sanction the operation with the Army to follow in support once the Marines were firmly established ashore in the southern Solomons.

On July 5, 1942, a B-17 bomber flying reconnaissance in preparation for the Solomons operation discovered that the Japanese were building an airfield on the neighboring island of Guadalcanal. There they would stage their medium bombers for a resumption of their drive to cut off Australia's lifeline through the South Pacific. King decided that this island, with its almost-complete airfield, must be seized in order to retain the strategic initiative against the Japanese. It was one of the most important strategic decisions of World War II. Guadalcanal proved to be a microcosm of the entire Pacific War—a war of amphibious

assaults; fierce naval, air, and jungle battles; increasing American strength; and, especially, attrition. This was the type of war the Japanese stood very little hope of winning.

The operation was under the command of Vice Admiral Robert L. Ghormley's South Pacific Command. On July 25, the invasion force that was to seize Guadalcanal arrived in the Fiji Islands. It was composed of seventy-six warships, including three of the Navy's four remaining aircraft carriers, and carrying the reinforced Second Marine Division under Major General Alexander A. Vandegrift. The Americans were already having internal squabbles among the various commanders of the force. Admiral Fletcher, victor at Midway and Coral Sea, argued with both the Marines and his amphibious force commander Admiral Richmond K. Turner over how long his carriers could remain in the restricted, submarine-infested waters off Guadalcanal to cover the invasion.

Time was running out. The Japanese—who had no idea of the scope of the U.S. invasion—were planning to activate their airbase on Guadalcanal sometime in August 1942, but on August 7 the Americans appeared off Guadalcanal and Tulagi and began landing. The Marines received a stiff fight from the

BELOW: Fires burn on Tulagi after bombing by U.S. carrier aircraft on August 7, 1942, the day U.S. Marines landed to recapture the island. Tulagi was initially the principal focus of the WATCHTOWER Task I operation and was only taken after bitter fighting with Japanese Marine defenders. The need to seize Tulagi's excellent anchorage and seaplane base were the reasons for the operation. Guadalcanal was only added as an afterthought because of the discovery of a Japanese airstrip on that island, which is to the south of Tulagi. This view faces north and shows the excellent anchorage between Tulagi and the larger, undeveloped Florida Island. The waters between Tulagi and Guadalcanal soon became known as "Iron Bottom Sound"—a veritable graveyard for everything from large battleships to diminutive PT boats. Just above the smoke in the foreground are the Tulagi Cricket Grounds, installed by the Australians before the war.

MERRITT A. EDSON

ABOVE: Merritt A. "Red Mike" Edson after the war as a Major General. The Marine Corps deployed both of its two elite Raider Battalions to the Southwest Pacific: Edson's 1st, and the 2d led by Lieutenant Colonel Evans F. Carlson. These units were developed before the war for special operations, and the Guadalcanal Campaign required them both—Edson's to seize Tulagi, and Carlson's to conduct raids behind Japanese lines in order to disrupt their logistics and troop flow.

RIGHT: Marines halt for a brief—and welcome— rest during a field march on Guadalcanal. Note the dense jungle foliage, lack of camouflage, and tightly packed march order. Although Japanese artillery would play an increasingly prominent role as the island fighting neared Japan, it was not a factor during the Guadalcanal Campaign.

Japanese defenders at Tulagi before securing their objectives. On Guadalcanal, 11,000 Marines simply waded ashore with no resistance as the Japanese construction workers abandoned their equipment and ran off into the jungle. Instead of landing on an idyllic island, they found a pestilential, monsoon-swept hellhole. The airfield (code-named CACTUS), strewn with Japanese bulldozers and earth rollers, was secured easily and without a fight. The Marines began to establish security perimeters, finished the airfield, and hunkered down for the Japanese onslaught that they felt must surely come.

Marine Lieutenant John B. Sweeney discusses his assignment to Lieutenant Colonel Merritt Edson's 1st Raider Battalion and the bitter fight for Tulagi Harbor that opened the Guadalcanal campaign.

I served under Edson. I began to hear about his background, and the few contacts I had directly with him, I got to admire him. And I think that was one of the things. I knew I was going to go to war and I wanted to be with someone that I had admiration for or who I felt was very competent in whatever he was doing. We were operating almost independently in the Tulagi campaign. There was a brigadier general [William Rupertus] in over-all command of that particular operation. He had two battalions. The 2nd Battalion, 5th Marines who came in behind us and did some mop-up work on the far end of the island which we had turned our backs on.

The unique part about that is that we were the spearhead, so to speak, of that attack. Tulagi was known to be the hardest nut to crack as far as coming in because the Japanese [at first] had only limited numbers over in Guadalcanal. They were building an airfield there, and not very much in the way of defensive forces. They were concentrated at Tulagi, which had an excellent harbor and a place for seaplanes to land and that sort of thing. They had several hundred, about 400 I believe, what they called special landing forces, people that we would call Japanese Marines. They were well-trained and very,

RIGHT: Gunner Angus R. Goss (left) teaching fellow Marines about demolitions. Goss was attached to Edson's Raiders and he jury-rigged TNT to poles for use against Japanese fighting from the numerous caves and bunkers on Tulagi.

BELOW: LVTs—landing vehicle tracked, or "amtracs" (amphibious tractors)—during a resupply operation at Guadalcanal. These are among the first LVTs, unarmored and newly fitted with machine guns for defense. The Marines foresaw the need for such vehicles during the interwar period, but stingy Navy budgets prevented their acquisition until just before the war. The Marines anticipated using them mostly for logistics, but they soon became the assault craft of choice for the coral-ringed Pacific islands. Amtracs were developed from a commercial vehicle used in Florida known as the "Swamp Gator," and there were very few of them available at this point in the war. The ship in the background is the Navy transport USS *President Hayes* (AP-39) shortly before she was reclassified as attack transport APA-20.

very bitter fighters to the end. In fact, we had no prisoners.

We were actually in two boats split up. The demolitions platoon with Bangalore torpedoes. These are about 6- or 8-foot-long iron pipes stuffed with TNT, a primer, and a fuse. If there were obstacles on the beach, barbed wire, any sort of concrete buttresses, that sort of thing, we were to go in and blow them up in order to make a way for the landing craft. It so happened that Red Beach, where we landed midway in the island, was not defended. Their entire defense was down on the lower part of the island, which was really the heart and brains of the command there. They had a few snipers,

and we lost one officer as a matter of fact. I moved my platoon and we left most of the Bangalore torpedoes back in the supply area at Red Beach and moved on down to what they call phase line A, which was a high piece of ground overlooking the main part of the island. During that time, I was really doing nothing but trying to keep abreast of what was going on and finding out if and when the demolitions platoon would be called into action.

As we moved in, B Company had moved across the island and there's where we received our first casualties. B Company was commanded by Captain [Herman] Nickerson and one of the platoon leaders was Eugene Key and he was

ABOVE: Marine officers on Tulagi, shortly after its capture in August 1942. Front row, left to right: Major Orin K. Pressley; Lieutenant Colonel Merritt A. "Red Mike" Edson; Lieutenant Colonel Harold E. Rosecrans; and Major Robert E. Hill. Brigadier General William H. Rupertus, who later commanded at Peleliu, is directly behind Edson.

> He [Sam Miles] was newly commissioned as a lieutenant JG [junior grade] in the Medical Corps. So he was a greenhorn and conscientious, dashed out to render some first aid to two people who he found were dead, and he was killed. So in the space of about thirty seconds, forty seconds, we lost the first three fatalities in the Guadalcanal operation.
>
> —John B. Sweeney

one of the six or eight officers at that time from my commissioning class. He and his platoon were moving out over some grassy area towards an objective that was on the far part of the island. His scout went into the area and was cut down with a machine gun blast.

Lieutenant Key, great officer that he was, maybe did the wrong thing at the time, but he dashed out to help the scout and he was cut down at the same time. We had one of those medical officers with us and this is another little tragic act. Sam Miles, who had joined us in San Diego just as we were getting ready to leave, he was a graduate of Princeton University and went to medical school. He was newly commissioned as a lieutenant JG [junior grade] in the Medical Corps. So he was a greenhorn and conscientious, dashed out to render some first aid to two people who he found were dead, and he was killed. So in the space of about thirty seconds, forty seconds, we lost the first three fatalities in the Guadalcanal operation.

The division across Sea Lark Channel [on Guadalcanal] didn't have a casualty until the second day. So, we started our casualties run there, unfortunately in a Hollywood type of scene. The next day I was detailed from a demolitions platoon to take over Key's platoon. I was trying to find out the names of everyone that was anyone in the platoon. The next day, we were patrolling in the area and did not get involved in any firefights at the time. We were cleaning up the so-called cricket ground area and another company had that particular job. The one task that we got was to try to blow up a cave that some Japanese had holed themselves up in and who were also holding up the advance on the beach side of the island. [Marine Gunner] Angus Goss, who was still with the demolitions platoon, came up to it and after looking it over tried to use his Rison gun to fire into the cave, threw a grenade in right afterwards, and the grenade popped out again and blew up right outside the cave. It blew Angus' shirt off and also wounded him, but not fatally, thank goodness, because he got angry, picked up his Rison again, and dashed up and into the cave and cleaned it out.

1ST MARINE DIVISION

Activated aboard the battleship USS *Texas* in February 1941, the 1st Marine Division launched the first American ground offensive operation of World War II with the invasion of Guadalcanal and seizure of the nearby Japanese seaplane base at Tulagi on August 7, 1942. The division blunted all efforts to retake Henderson Field and participated in operations at Cape Gloucester on New Britain from December 1943 through January 1944. Unexpectedly vicious fighting on Peleliu took a very heavy toll on the unit in September and October, and it entered yet another meat grinder during the Okinawa Campaign. The 1st Marine Division landed against little resistance on April 1, 1945, but the casualties quickly mounted as the Marines encountered the Shuri Line defenses. Progress was slow and tedious as the Japanese had to be blasted out—or sealed up—in every cave position. Okinawa was not secured until late in June 1945.

The same Colonel B.E. Allen who was at Midway commanded the 5th Bomb Group at Guadalcanal. Here he discusses the challenges of operating in the harsh environment of the South and Southwest Pacific.

I think the simple word Guadalcanal will conjure up many problems. We were initially without the service support; we were pretty much on our own fighting a jungle war. We had no jacks—we'd use coconut trees to jack up an airplane or pry up an airplane if we had a flat tire. The Japs were within three miles of the perimeter of the airfield and we had very much the same thing as they had. The problem was the distance of the supply line to us. We were concentrating our efforts at that time… in Europe as opposed to the Pacific. I did have, notwithstanding, some exceptionally well-trained crews and some exceptionally well-trained maintenance people. Otherwise, I don't think we would have ever hacked it.

BELOW: Soldiers from either the 25th or Americal Divisions prepare to move a soldier wounded during the January Offensive, the goal of which was to wrestle the Japanese out of the hills west of the original Marine perimeter on Guadalcanal. The strain of constant fighting is etched on the faces of these men. Note that one of the stretcher poles has broken and been replaced by an appropriately sized jungle tree.

RIGHT: As aircraft are recovered on the USS *Wasp* during the initial landings at Guadalcanal, key officers confer on the port bridge wing, or flag bridge. Wearing a helmet, the *Wasp*'s captain, Forrest P. Sherman, stands in front of Donald F. Smith, the carrier's air group commander. Facing the camera is Rear Admiral Leigh Noyes, in overall command of the task group, talking to the *Wasp*'s Air Group Commander, Lieutenant Commander Wallace M. Beakley. Note the wide variety of national identification symbols on the Dauntless SBD-3 scout bombers in the background. Sherman would command multi-carrier task forces later in the war.

It was not long in coming. For the Japanese air component, though, the campaign began poorly and remained that way for the remainder of the year. The 11th (naval) Air Fleet in Rabaul had just the range to get its Betty medium bombers to the southern Solomons. But once there, they had little time to deliver their attacks and would do so without land-based fighter coverage. What was worse, Japanese carrier aviation was so emasculated from the battles of Midway and Coral Sea that it could only provide temporary air coverage before it had to withdraw to refuel its few carriers in safer waters. The American carriers were under the same constraints and particularly vulnerable to Japanese submarines and land-based aircraft. Indeed, the first Betty attacks occurred on August 7, but were ambushed by Fletcher's Midway veterans. The following day, another strike from Rabaul made it to the landing areas, but lost many of their number while inflicting no significant damage.

By this point, Fletcher's escorting destroyers had run critically low on fuel and he withdrew to the relative safety in the south to refuel. Not long after, the Navy suffered the biggest American surface defeat of the war. A cruiser force under Japanese Admiral Gunichi Mikawa, hurrying south from Rabaul, annihilated one Australian and three American heavy cruisers in a night action off Savo Island with no ship losses to himself. Sailors and Marines alike nicknamed the strait between Tulagi and Guadalcanal "Iron Bottom Sound." However, in a stunning mistake, Mikawa turned north and left Turner's valuable transports and cargo ships unmolested, believing they would be easily mopped up after so great a naval victory. Turner left the next day, taking with him much of the Marines' heavy construction equipment and still-loaded supplies.

The Marines, at least for the next week or so, were without any naval support. Meanwhile, the Japanese continued to make critical errors. Underestimating both the size and fighting prowess of the Marines, they landed the Ichiki Detachment (one battalion) in an attempt to quickly recapture the airstrip, now named Henderson Field. On August 21, these troops were wiped out at the Battle of the Ilu River [Tenaru]. Additional Japanese reinforcements were turned back on August 24, thanks to the timely return of the U.S. Navy. By this time, Henderson Field was operating and included Marine, Navy, and Army aircraft.

Seabee Julian Gudmundson remembers the voyage to Guadalcanal and the harsh environment on the island.

The first mission was Guadalcanal and it took us 109 days get there—an LST is a flat, slow-moving boat. We were in the convoy and we'd run into a typhoon off New Caledonia and we lost one of our ships there. Then we got to Guadalcanal and landed and the word that [had] gotten out [was] that our ship was the one that had sunk. So they'd given all our machinery away and we had to beg, borrow, and steal before we could start any work. Our job was the water supply there and the electrical.

There were some Japanese still out in the woods. The natives loved our canned meat, so they would catch 'em—the Japanese troops—and bring 'em in, and trade 'em in for canned meat! Once we got there, we had to maintain the matting and help construct the regular asphalt runway for the Marines. It is pretty rough and dangerous for the aircraft to land on the Marston matting [the special matting used for expeditionary airfields]. We had bulldozers and other equipment to smooth out the runways 'til we got asphalt.

When we were on Guadalcanal, there was an ammunition ship that blew—about 200 yards offshore. I'll never forget that 'cause it was 11:30 at night this happened, and we woke up and our tent was being blown away.

The biggest threat was malaria. We didn't have enough quinine [anti-malarial tonic] to furnish there. Once we had to take a substance too, called Atabrine. It was a pill. A man was standing there and giving you your Atabrine every night and you had to take it before you could get a meal. And this made some people turn yellow.

Navy Seabee, Carpenter's Mate Valdemar Johansen remembers helping improve and repair Henderson Field during the Guadalcanal campaign.

It would have been more fun if they hadn't been shooting at us—we had some sniper problems and when you'd go down the strip

LEFT: The reason for all the fighting, Henderson Field looking northwest toward Lunga point, as photographed from a USS *Saratoga* aircraft in late August 1942. The airfield at Guadalcanal was named after Major Lofton R. Henderson (above), U.S. Marine Corps, killed in the Battle of Midway while leading an attack on the carrier *Hiryu*.

The dirt runway has yet to receive the Marston matting that will keep it operational in spite of the frequent tropical downpours, and the small taxiway within the circle is known as a "compass rose" which airman used to calibrate their planes' magnetic compasses. Aircraft, as well as tents and flimsy frame structures, are dispersed all across the center of this area in order to help minimize the damage from marauding Japanese warships and bomber aircraft from "up the Slot" that have already scarred it with shell holes. One nighttime raid on October 16, less than two months after this photo was taken, would destroy forty-one aircraft as the Japanese cruisers *Myoko* and *Maya* hammered the area with roughly 1,800 shells.

The well-groomed stand of palm trees at right is a small sliver of the giant Lever Brothers coconut farm that, before the recent Japanese invasion, had supplied the firm's copra used in soap products around the world. Although the trees provided little shade, the farm was a favorite campground for rear-area personnel (that is, if any place on Guadalcanal could be called a "rear area") because it was clear of jungle undergrowth like that along the Lunga River at left. Within a few weeks after this photo was taken, Marine artillery would fill much of the cleared area southwest of the runway. An auxiliary fighter strip a mile to the east, on the opposite side of the coconut trees, would become operational by the end of October.

THE SEABEES

After the attack on Pearl Harbor, use of civilian labor in war zones became impractical and the Bureau of Navigation moved to recruit men from the construction trades for assignment to newly formed Naval Construction Battalions (CBs or "Seabees") for operations overseas. During the war against Japan, the Seabees built 111 major airstrips at advance bases for both the Army and the Navy, 441 piers, 2,558 ammunition magazines, 700 square blocks of warehouses, hospitals to serve 70,000 patients, fuel tanks for the storage of one million gallons of gasoline, housing for one-and-a-half million men, and other critically needed infrastructure. This was all built and maintained on more than 300 islands spanning the Pacific and at sites ranging from tropical jungles to frozen Arctic islands. Through construction and fighting operations, the Pacific Seabees suffered more than 200 combat deaths and earned more than to 2,000 Purple Hearts.

Guadalcanal is a sink hole for the Japanese Air Force and their Navy.
—Vice Admiral John McCain

NATHAN F. TWINING

and [the bullets] start kicking up dust in front of you, you know what they are. You get underneath [the bulldozer] and lay there awhile and then go again.

General Nathan F. Twining was chief of staff to General Millard F. Harmon, who commanded the Army Air Corps units as Air Solomons, or AIRSOL, in the South Pacific. Twining later commanded the 15th Air Force in Italy. Here he discusses the Guadalcanal campaign.

Henderson Field, when our forces moved in there (the Navy actually built it for the Marines), was about one-third completed, I would say. And they went ahead and finished under wartime conditions, and did a terrific job. But it never was a real good operating field as we know 'em today. We couldn't get enough stuff in there, not enough equipment and supplies, and we were under attack all the time. The original Japanese Air Force—it was basically a Navy air force—was just as good as any.

They were well-trained, they had good equipment, and their Zero [fighter] was better than anything we had out there at the time, initially, in the first days. They did the job. They were never afraid to attack. But they didn't have enough aircraft, and not enough replacements coming in to take the place of the ones they lost. They didn't have a good training program, and there weren't enough people behind in the system, so it folded up and they couldn't support their forward units anymore.

At Guadalcanal, Admiral McCain [Rear Admiral, later Vice Admiral John McCain] the airman—"Clacker" McCain we called him—he was a wonderful air leader. He was the Navy's top airman in the South Pacific theater where I was operating. He said, "Guadalcanal is a sinkhole for the Japanese Air Force and their Navy." And that was the place the Japs felt must be knocked out. At that time, they practically quit fighting against MacArthur's forces in Australia. They were coming down the "slot" to knock Guadalcanal out, and they came pretty close to doing it a couple of times. We were in

OPPOSITE PAGE: Seabees from the 6th Battalion lay down Marston matting. The pierced steel planking provided a solid surface for aircraft to use in the rain-drenched tropics. The planks arrived in late September 1942, and were soon put into use for runways and, when available in sufficient quantities, walkways and aircraft aprons.

LEFT: An SBD Dauntless banks away from Henderson Field during a dive-bombing mission in early 1943. Considered obsolescent years before Japanese bombs fell on Pearl Harbor, the Dauntless was underpowered, short-legged, fatiguing to fly on long missions, and its wings could not be folded to ease flight deck operations. It was also a ship killer par excellence. A highly accurate dive-bomber, the aircraft was ruggedly constructed and capable of withstanding a considerable amount of punishment. The Dauntless remained the Navy's principal carrier dive-bomber through the Philippine Sea battle in late 1944, and continued to be effectively employed by Marine squadrons for close air support and antishipping missions until the surrender of Japan.

EVAN C. CARLSON

ABOVE: Lieutenant Colonel Evan C. Carlson, commanding officer of the 2d Marine Raider Battalion, made the term "gung ho" famous. He learned the Mandarin Chinese phrase during his time with the Marines in China and was an expert in jungle warfare, having earned a Navy Cross fighting the Sandinistas in Nicaragua. Carlson's son managed to join his father's outfit around the time of Guadalcanal Campaign, despite the elder Carlson's best efforts to try and keep him in another unit.

BELOW: The 2d Marine Raider Battalion comes ashore somewhere up "The Slot" via LCP(L) Eureka-type Higgins boats.

pretty bad shape up there—the Americans were—but we made it stick.

We got some new equipment and we got some new fighters for our little air force. Up to that time, we were flying the Air Cobras that could not get to sufficient altitude to fight against the Zero. But the Navy had some F6Fs [Hellcats] that could do the altitude work. We finally got the P-38 [Lightning]. It was our combat airplane—our combat fighter—and from then on our forces took over.

Nineteen-year-old Army First Lieutenant P.J. Dahl remembers flying the P-38.

All you had to do on this dude [the P-38] is be sure the guns worked, and the spark plugs were okay, and the harnesses were dry, and the engine worked. The system was relatively simple. They were rough airplanes you know, you could pull 10, 12, 15 Gs in the airplane. It was stressed for that. Ten percent of the time I am up there fighting [and] I am blacked out, and you scream, and do all you can to keep up, but that dark curtain comes down and you just keep going through that turn.

Lieutenant Evan C. Carlson, who served under his father, Lieutenant Colonel Evans F. Carlson, in the 2d Marine Raider Battalion, landed behind Japanese lines to conduct reconnaissance and disrupt Japanese communications.

The battalion was dispatched to Guadalcanal, where they were to patrol parts of the island that were important to the Japanese and that were not under the firm control of either side. This all started around the first of December and I was in E Company, the first platoon. These two companies were loaded up on World War I four-stack destroyers reconfigured especially to carry Raider companies. There were slightly over one hundred men in a typical company. We departed the New Hebrides and we proceeded to the coastal area of Guadalcanal about 40 miles down the coast from Henderson Field and its perimeter. This was an area that was devoid of [American] troops. In fact, there were a half-dozen army personnel, one officer, and—I think—five or six soldiers on the beach when we came off the destroyer and down the cargo nets at about two o'clock in the morning. Rubber boats carried us to the beach.

We started our patrol at daylight and this involved moving over the ground 25 or 30 miles a day with odd days spent for whatever purpose once in a while. We patrolled continuously; it seemed to me, for about thirty to thirty-one days. We covered all of the area of Guadalcanal, from the mountains to the sea, that was of immediate concern to the Marine commanders, General Vandegrift in particular. I should mention that there were just two of the six companies in the battalion for this mission at the outset. As the magnitude of the challenge became

clearer, the commanding officer [Carlson's father] ordered up more companies until the entire battalion was there. The battalion was reduced to five companies because one company had to be used for replacements.

We proceeded from our landing site, which was at Aola Bay, roughly paralleling the coastline, but moving inland. We covered the area in which the Japanese patrols might be operating. The U.S. commanders were intensely interested in learning how the Japanese moved their forces undetected into the vicinity of the U.S. perimeter and from there joined the attack against the Marines and later Army units in the perimeter. You can see what the importance of this would be, given that they had no hard evidence as to how the Japanese made it possible.

There were chance encounters in the main with [Japanese] patrols that generally were moving in our direction. We didn't know that around the next bend, in a jungle trail, we might encounter a Japanese patrol. When we did, it became rather interesting. Victory generally went to the patrol that started firing first. It was important to get something going at the instant that they had a look at the enemy patrol. I carried a Winchester 97 [shotgun] because it was easy to pull the trigger and the double-O buckshot that I was carrying was lethal charge and would hit at close range; it would cut a person in two.

We employed natives from the island under the direction of Sergeant Major Joseph Leuthen, who was chief of the constabulary on Guadalcanal and nearby islands. He recruited about fifty men who had fled their villages and were up in the hills somewhere to help us carry our equipment. We had especially heavy radios that we had selected because they were absolutely reliable. But they were a four-man carry and we appreciated the help. We fed them [the locals] canned corned beef.

On our part, we ate a sock full of rice, a half a sock full of raisins, and a handful of sugar. Also, a handful of expeditionary crackers called hardtack. I think they were World War I issue or shortly after. That was the ration for four days. No one gained weight on that. For a while, the lead guide would be right up front with the point until one got shot up six times without anything serious being damaged on him. He had a lot of holes in him, but we didn't put the natives at the front any more after that.

The campaign now turned into a fierce, back-and-forth struggle. At night, the Japanese Navy prowled the waters, bombarding the Marines and landing its troops (the "Tokyo Express") at remote beaches well away from the Americans. During the day, aircraft from Henderson Field flew against all comers in the

P.J. DAHL

ABOVE: P.J.Dahl standing in front of his Lockheed P-38 Lightning. This aircraft was another nail in the coffin of the Japanese air dominance and pilots like Dahl often used its incredible dive rate, firepower, and weave tactics to fly unscathed through much larger formations of the more agile, but fragile, Zero fighters. Note the Marston matting covering the airfield.

LEFT: On Guadalcanal, Admiral Chester W. Nimitz, decorates Lieutenant Colonel Evans C. Carlson, Commander, 2d Raider Battalion, during a September 30, 1942 ceremony. Major General Alexander A. Vandegrift, Commander, 1st Marine Division, is to Nimitz's left. Also receiving medals are (left to right) Brigadier General William H. Rupertus, Assistant Division Commander; Colonel Merritt A. Edson, Commander, 5th Marine Regiment; Lieutenant Colonel Edwin A. Pollock, Commander, 2d Battalion, 1st Marine Regiment; and Major John L. Smith, Commander, VMF-223.

P.A. DEL VALLE

ABOVE: Brigadier General Pedro A. del Valle commanded the Marine artillery on Guadalcanal.

air and at sea—but no one had dominance on land, sea, or air for more than a couple of hours at a time. The Japanese could not push the Marines off Henderson Field, but the U.S. Navy could not reestablish daytime control of the surrounding seas. Both navies had immense problems in getting supplies to their troops on the isolated island.

🎙 *An anonymous Marine officer visited the Army's 67th Fighter Squadron at Henderson Field and warned the pilots of the dire situation they were now operating in on Guadalcanal.*

We don't know whether we'll be able to hold the field or not. There's a Japanese task force of destroyers, cruisers, and troop transports headed our way. We have enough gasoline left for one mission against them. Load your airplanes with bombs and go out with the dive-bombers and hit them. After the gas is gone, we'll have to let the ground troops take over. Then our officers and men will attach yourselves to some infantry outfit. Good luck and good-bye.

🎙 *Brigadier General P.A. del Valle, commanding the 1st Marine Division's artillery on Guadalcanal, remembers the bombardment of his forces by the Japanese Navy—including battleships—prior to the landing of the Japanese 2nd Division.*

It was really wicked. The Japs had "bombardment ammunition," with reduced charges and instantaneous fuses for naval guns up to and including their 14-inch main batteries. Our division artillery CP [command post] received a direct hit by a 14-inch shell. The Japs started out by dropping flares at each end of the air-

RIGHT: A common sight in the South Pacific, an enemy plane hurtles toward the earth after being shot out of the sky by Cactus Air Force fighters.

field, and then proceeded to let us have it for three-and-one-half hours straight. He [the enemy] literally took out the airfield, destroying thirty-two airplanes. By the following morning, all we were able to get into the air was a single standard dive-bomber.

It was at this time that help from the air forces in the Southwest Pacific Area proved very valuable indeed. We were bombarded, from sea and air, sixty-four times in the first two months. It was a heavy emotional strain. The Jap bomber formation usually consisted of twenty-seven planes. Our fighters took a heavy toll on them, destroying upwards of 600 [over the course of two months]. The Jap was persistent, however, and kept coming back for more.

Lieutenant Colonel John A. Bemis, U.S. Marine Corps, discusses the arrival of heavy antiaircraft artillery and the attrition of the Japanese pilot corps.

When the 90mm AA guns arrived with mechanical-fuse ammunition, the Jap bombers moved upstairs [higher altitude] and stayed there, around 27,000 feet. Prior to this, they had been bombing from 12,000 to 14,000 [feet altitude]. On some occasions, the Jap bomber pilots would fly until they dropped, never breaking formation even though their planes were on fire and falling apart. Our 90mm AA guns got many of them. As of late October [1942], the Jap was no longer dive-bombing steeply; he was coming down at around 45 degrees. It may be that most of his good dive-bombing pilots were gone.

Captain Joe Foss, a Marine Corps ace, discusses his actions at the Naval Battle of Guadalcanal, where Japanese and U.S. battleships fought it out by night and American aviators came in by day to finish the job.

We arrived in October of 1942 at New Caledonia and flew our fighters, which were new— Grumman F4F [Wildcats]—off the carrier to the island of New Caledonia.

ABOVE: The trees ringing Henderson Field failed to hide this SBD scout-bomber, still smoldering after a raid by Japanese aircraft. The constant air and sea attacks took a heavy toll on aircraft and on the nerves of the pilots. But more aircraft could always be flown in and pilot losses tended to be light during these bombardments. The most important target is at the right—aviation gasoline barrels, without which the airmen of the Cactus Air Force could not maintain their command of the air that kept the vital sea lanes open during the critical months of October and November.

JOE FOSS

RIGHT: Japanese Daihatsu landing barges sunk along the Lunga River shore by U.S. aircraft before the Marine landings at Guadalcanal. The wooden-hull craft came in several sizes, and these are the common, 46-foot model that was heavily employed throughout the Southwest Pacific. Japanese use of landing barges with "draw-bridge" ramps predated the American Higgins boat by roughly a decade, and most Daihatsu types were armed with a 25mm gun similar to the 20mm Oerlikon.

None of our pilots had much experience doing anything. With exception of the C.O. of VMF-121, Major [Leonard K.] Davis, and myself, the executive officer, no one was really qualified to land on an aircraft carrier. We got a little bit of flight time and then we flew back aboard the carrier and headed for Guadalcanal. We were 360 knots [nautical miles] from Guadalcanal when an enemy submarine popped up around the ship [probably the USS *Wasp*]. They got us up in the middle of the night and we catapulted off the ship one by one. You know, there were two catapults on the ship. The skipper took off first, and he told me to take off last, and see that everything got well done. We were in a battle over Savo Island, flying at 12,000 feet to draw fire. Half the Japanese Fleet was look-ing up at my flight of eight airplanes and began blasting away [at] it. Then we peeled off one at a time and dove down.

We had 100-pound bombs, which was like hunting an elephant with a flyswatter. It was great because we drew the fire. In the initial action, I was just flying over the fleet and then diving down one by one. I almost hit the superstructure on the ship. I got so interested in seeing the pom-pom guns that were blast-ing away at us. And I couldn't figure out why they were missing me.

And then [Captain] George Dooley and his TBF squadron [Avenger torpedo bombers] came around the island and managed to hit the battleship [probably the *Kirishima*]. George got two hits on the stern—and that was all she wrote for that ship. All the old battlewagon could do was go in a circle [the Japanese eventually scuttled the *Kirishima*]. We'd made it too interesting for them with the real dive-bombers and the torpedo planes. We ended up losing some of the dive-bomber boys, but I don't recall losing any of the fighters.

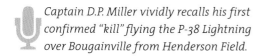

Captain D.P. Miller vividly recalls his first confirmed "kill" flying the P-38 Lightning over Bougainville from Henderson Field.

I was assigned to fly top cover with one wingman at 18,000 feet, and there were a few other P-38s at two different elevations below us. I saw the Japanese planes. There were no American planes anywhere in sight. I don't know what happened to the others, but they'd been milling around and so forth. It was no use staying up there at 18,000 feet, so down I went after rocking my wings and signaling my wingman, after the three Japanese planes—which were flying in a loose string, maybe 200 or 300 yards apart—and I got down there after the tail-end Charlie [the last plane of the formation] of the three Japanese planes and looked around and there was no wingman behind me. I couldn't see him anywhere. So therefore, and perhaps for more prudent reasons, when the tail-end Charlie started a slow turn to the left, I realized that he had seen me and was going to make a beam attack on me. So instead of pressing on and shooting down the number one and number two planes, which I probably could have done—certainly if my wingman had been with me to take care of this tail-end Charlie—I had to prudently turn and meet the attack of the number three plane, tail-end Charlie Japanese.

I was going to take advantage of my concentrated firepower and fire when I was out of range and gradually drop the sight. So I lined up one engine diameter above his engine at about 600 yards, and then I started firing when I was 450 yards, maybe 500 yards out, gradually dropping my sight down into his engine. But this, of course, took only a very few seconds. And he burst into flames when he was still beyond 300 yards; to be precise his right wing near the root burst into flames, and that wing dropped down a couple of feet, which may have put him into slight turn to the right and he lost about 150 feet of altitude, and I was able to stay right on my course, without deviating a fraction of a degree, and I watched him pass underneath my left wing burning, and watched him slowly turn over. He was obviously killed or injured and plunged into the sea.

BELOW: *Enterprise* ordnancemen prepare to insert a 500-pound bomb into the swinging cradle of an SBD Dauntless on August 7, 1942. The cradle ensured that ordnance swung clear of the prop during dive-bombing, and could handle up to 1,000 pounds. The aircraft was launched against Japanese targets on Tulagi, which would serve as a forward naval anchorage for the battles off Guadalcanal and up the Slot.

Over the course of the next five months,
six more major naval battles and at least nine
more land battles occurred—with air combat
occurring daily. After critical and punishing
naval battles in November, the American Army
and Marine forces resumed their offensive to
chase the Japanese off Guadalcanal for good.
By the time the campaign ended in early 1943,
the land-based Japanese 11th Air Fleet was
decimated, the IJN no longer had any veteran
carrier aviation pilots left to speak of, and the
IJA withdrew from Guadalcanal in humiliation.
American losses were no less severe—Nimitz,

at one point, was down to only one operational
aircraft carrier in the entire Pacific. However,
the Americans could afford those losses and
the Japanese could not. Too, the Americans
learned from their mistakes.

*Lieutenant Junior Grade Charles Melhorn
was assigned to Motor Torpedo Boat
Squadron Three aboard PT-44. He had a
"balcony seat" for the climax of the three-day
Naval Battle of Guadalcanal and participated at
the end. Here he discusses that experience and
his subsequent operations interdicting Japanese
shipping bound for Guadalcanal on the "Tokyo
Express."*

There were lots of people on Tulagi, and
everybody was looking that night [the night
of the battleship engagement]. We went
down the following night, which was the
night of November 13 [1942]. The PT squadron
to which I had just reported, this MTBRON 3,
was the only firepower that we had left there
at the time, and another Japanese battleship
task force was expected that night. Admiral
Lee was around, Willis Lee, someplace with
his battleships, *South Dakota* and *Washington*.
But they didn't know whether or not he was

going to make it. The skipper of *McFarland* [a damaged destroyer in Tulagi Harbor] briefed us as to what we would do that night. The briefing amounted to: "There is a Japanese task force due in about midnight, and we may have a battleship task force due in about midnight. Go out and get the Japs." And that was the extent of the briefing.

About ten o'clock [p.m.] we pushed off… we put out that night certainly no more than five boats, because the rest of them were down for mechanical [problems], or they'd been hit. I know one of the first things I saw when I went to the PT base was this PT boat sitting up with its bow out of the water and the whole bow had been absolutely shredded, exposing the head [the toilet]. The toilet bowl was right up in the forepeak of the ship and

all the plywood planking had been splintered and torn away, leaving this porcelain throne up there exposed for everybody. It apparently hadn't been touched but it really must have taken a shell hit right up forward. This was the culminating battle of the three-day engagement of the Battle of Guadalcanal and left the sound [between Tulagi and Guadalcanal] still in our hands. By all odds, it was the crucial sea battle of the Guadalcanal campaign, because the Japanese threw everything they had left at us and we turned aside the attack.

From then on, we just settled down to protect Guadalcanal—this was our job—and to interdict any Japanese forces that might be coming down. Our work was strictly at night. We never went out in the daytime

ABOVE: A Dauntless dive-bomber flies over "Iron Bottom Sound" as smoke rises from a pair of beached Japanese troop transports and a land target in November 1942. This carrier aircraft is probably land-based at Henderson Field.

So the Japanese submarine [I-3] surfaced right in front of him, and Jack [Lieutenant JG Searles] fired four torpedoes into him and that was the end of that, for which Jack got the Navy Cross and everybody else on the boat got the Silver Star.

—Lieutenant Charles Melhorn

BELOW: Guadalcanal was run on a shoestring on both sides, and the *Kinugawa Maru*, heavily damaged by U.S. aircraft on November 15, 1942, and beached west of the Marine perimeter, provides a stark example of this. The Japanese efforts to resupply and reinforce their forces led to desperate measures. Sometimes they would simply run their ships aground at night and have everyone swim ashore rather than attempt to sail them back up "The Slot," given the attendant loss of manpower if Allied bombers found the ships in the daytime. On other occasions, the ships were simply too damaged to go any further.

because we were fair game then for any hostile aircraft that might be in. So we would set up interdicting patrols the length of the coast of Guadalcanal from the Tassafaronga up past Savo [Island], up past Cape Esperance, and down to Kokumbona and down to Coughlin Harbor.

It was about this time that we began getting these "ultras" which were the code intercepts from Admiral Nimitz's headquarters...one came in one night that said there was a Japanese submarine expected to surface off Lunga Point and gave the coordinates at such and such a time. The message read, "There is a SOB aboard, X-ray, get him, X-ray." In other words there was some VIP coming in. So we sent a boat out under [Lieutenant Junior Grade] Jack Searles, who was there at the appointed time at the appointed place, and right on the dot this submarine surfaced

right in from of him—probably heard the noise of the PT boat's engines and figured those were the engines of his own surface boat coming out from the Japanese-held coast there...to make a transfer. So the Japanese submarine [I-3] surfaced right in front of him, and Jack fired four torpedoes into him and that was the end of that, for which Jack got the Navy Cross and everybody else on the boat got the Silver Star.

The next big action was the battle of Tassafaronga, which I believe was on the thirtieth of November, 1942. We were set to go out that night. There was a very able Japanese admiral, [Raizo] Tanaka, who had been really a thorn in the side of the U.S. endeavor down there with his persistence and his skill in handling destroyers. We found out after the war that he had spent a lot of time before the war training his ships in night tactics, and they

were very good at it—particularly torpedo work. We were set to go out on this night, because we were always having brushes, little firefights, with Tanaka's destroyers, and we were told very grandly that we could stay in that night, to stay out of the way, that "the first team" was arriving and would take care of these people [Tanaka's "Tokyo Express"]. So we stayed in. About two o'clock in the morning we [were] ordered frantically out to go to the assistance of "the first team," Admiral Wright's cruiser squadron.

By the time we got out there, *Northampton* had sunk, *Minneapolis* had her bow blown clear to the number one turret and was dragging the bow, *New Orleans* had her bow blown off past the number two turret, and *Honolulu*

was nowhere to be seen. We spent the rest of the night trying to get survivors in and shepherd these stricken cruisers into Tulagi. What had happened was that Tanaka had come along and without firing hardly a shot had let go a spread of torpedoes and practically wiped out our cruiser line. I think we got one destroyer that night—it was hardly a trade. The third ship to be very badly hit was *Pensacola*. She had taken a hit under her mainmast. I remember her coming into Tulagi Harbor and her mainmast was completely scorched, and they unloaded bodies off of her that almost filled up a tank lighter [a tank landing craft] and these corpses were all charred. It was just like taking cordwood off, for temporary burial over there in Tulagi.

ABOVE: Sailors aboard the cruiser USS *Minneapolis* begin the dangerous work of shoring up the remnants of her bow at the Tulagi anchorage. A Japanese torpedo had blown the bow away during the November 30, 1942, night battle off Guadalcanal's Tassafaronga Point. In all, four U.S. cruisers were either sunk or grievously damaged by a flotilla of Japanese destroyers that lost only one of its own ships.

BELOW: The USS *Pensacola*, alongside the fleet repair ship USS *Vestal*, undergoing repair of torpedo damage received during the Battle of Tassafaronga on November 30, 1942. Fires blacken the after half of the ship and there is a large shell hole in her side, below the mainmast.

In response to a request by General George C. Marshall on how the U.S. military might do better, Sergeant D.L. Golden of the 164th Infantry observed.

The biggest thing I have learned since I hit Guadalcanal is that the Japanese camouflage is miles ahead of ours. Their individual can camouflage himself a lot better than ours. Every man should [also] be equipped with a compass, and must know how to use the compass. The dumbbells who don't know how to use one have to be helped instead of being able to help themselves. I have been on twenty patrols in the last forty days, and in most all of these patrols we went out from 2 to 5 miles. Getting communications back to [our artillery] is an awful problem.

Lieutenant Colonel John A. Bemis, U.S. Marine Corps, describes the second major Japanese attack at Guadalcanal and some general observations about Japanese operational flexibility.

The second Jap attack came on September 14–15. It was a five-pronged affair, not well timed or coordinated. This was the Battle of Raiders Ridge, where artillery fire was adjusted by "rudimentary flash ranging" and by the human ear. The enemy abandoned a large quantity of arms and ammunition when he withdrew on this occasion.

INSET: The stern and starboard side of the heavy cruiser *New Orleans* after the Battle of Tassafaronga. The ship ends abruptly forward of the superstructure because the bow was blown away by a Japanese torpedo on the night of November 30 – December 1, 1945. With her power unable to be restored for several days, the cruiser was a "sitting duck" in Tulagi's harbor, so the ship was moored near the PT boat tender *Jamestown* a mile up Florida Island's McFarland Channel to help hide it from Japanese aircraft. Both the *New Orleans* and destroyer *Maury*, which supplied electricity and steam (and whose mast is visible just beyond the cruiser's stern), were draped in camouflage nets and chopped-down trees. A coconut-log barrier was laboriously rigged to help plug the blunt stump of the forward hull before the ship sailed to Sidney, Australia. There it was given a "proper" false bow for its long voyage back to the United States for extensive repairs.

According to our experience with the Jap, he has the pronounced tendency to carry through persistently with a single inflexible plan. It seems difficult for him to alter his plans to fit the exigencies of a situation.

—Lieutenant Colonel John A. Bemis

ABOVE: Rear Admiral
Daniel Judson Callaghan.

BELOW: The heavy cruiser
USS *San Francisco* showing
shell hits from the opening
engagement of the
November 14–15 Battle of
Guadalcanal. Three areas
along the starboard hull
originally believed to be
shell holes were soon
determined to have been
made by large splinters
from near misses, and
were scratched off.

The *San Francisco* was
littered with hits from a
variety of ships, including
the Japanese battleship
Kirishima. Although the
cruiser survived, Admiral
Callaghan and most of
his staff were killed when
the flag bridge was hit
by shells. The Navy lost
over 15,000 killed from
August to February in the
Guadalcanal campaign.
When the wounded are
added, the Navy had the
highest losses for any
single campaign of the
war to that point. These
casualty rates would not
be exceeded again until
the kamikazes attacked
off Okinawa in 1945.

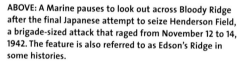

ABOVE: A Marine pauses to look out across Bloody Ridge
after the final Japanese attempt to seize Henderson Field,
a brigade-sized attack that raged from November 12 to 14,
1942. The feature is also referred to as Edson's Ridge in
some histories.

According to our experience with the Jap, he has the pronounced tendency to carry through persistently with a single inflexible plan. It seems difficult for him to alter his plans to fit the exigencies of a situation. The Jap has a habit of attacking on Saturday or Sunday night, apparently in the belief that the white man is most likely to be caught napping at those times—and Japanese troops bunch up at night. While these tendencies have corroboration elsewhere, it is never safe to underestimate the Jap or try to predict him definitely.

Admiral Raizo Tanaka, the tenacious Japanese commander of the infamous "Tokyo Express," commented in his summary of the entire campaign.

The greatest pity was that every Japanese commander was aware of all the factors [that contributed to their defeat], yet no one seemed to do anything about any of them. We stumbled along from one error to another while the enemy grew wise, profited by his wisdom, and advanced until our efforts at Guadalcanal reached their unquestionable and inevitable end—in failure. It was certainly regrettable that the Supreme Command did not profit or learn from repeated attempts to reinforce the island. In vain they expended valuable and scarce transports and the strength of at least one full division. I believe that Japan's operational and planning errors at Guadalcanal will stand forever as [a] classic example of how not to conduct a campaign.

Admiral Matome Ugaki, Yamamoto's chief of staff and later the architect of Japan's punishing kamikaze tactics in the last year of the war, was somewhat more wistful in his regrets over the disaster at Guadalcanal in this December 31, 1942, diary entry.

The year 1942 is going to pass tonight. How brilliant was the first-stage operation up to April! And what miserable setbacks since Midway in June! The invasions of Hawaii, Fiji, Samoa, and New Caledonia; liberation of India; and destruction of the British Far Eastern Fleet have all scattered like dreams. Meanwhile, not to speak of capturing Port Moresby, but the recovery of Guadalcanal itself turned out to be impossible.

RAIZO TANAKA

ABOVE: Rear Admiral Raizo Tanaka was among the most competent Japanese admirals of the war, and a superb combat leader. He defeated superior American naval forces on several occasions and literally ran the "Tokyo Express" that kept the Japanese in the fight so long for Guadalcanal. Once he was relieved, the Japanese Army's days on Guadalcanal were over. After the war he was a scathing critic of both the Japanese Army and the Navy's conduct of the campaign.

ABOVE: Senior U.S. commanders confer on a mountaintop observation post, January 21, 1943. Within little more than two weeks, all the Japanese forces that could be withdrawn by swift Japanese destroyers in the dead of night had escaped north. (Left to right) Secretary of the Navy Frank Knox; Major General Alexander M. Patch who succeeded Marine Major General Alexander A. Vandegrift as the commander of U.S. forces on Guadalcanal; Commander in Chief Pacific and Pacific Ocean Areas, Admiral Chester W. Nimitz; Commander South Pacific Area, Admiral William F. Halsey; and 25th Division Commander, Major General Joseph Lawton Collins.

WATCHTOWER
Task 2 and 3

The same sort of attritional jungle battle was taking place hundreds of miles to the west on the huge island of New Guinea. Although the Japanese offensive along the Kokoda Trail had run out of steam, the mostly Australian counteroffensive operated under the very same severe conditions that plagued their antagonists. By November, the Australians—with American support—had captured Kokoda and now concentrated on capturing the three key seaside towns on the northern coast: Buna, Gona, and Salamaua.

Captain Alfred Medendorp, U.S. Army, remembers the rigors of the march overland through jungles and mountains of Papua New Guinea to the Gona and Buna battlefields.

The troops had no trail discipline. The hills were steep. Footing was insecure. Leeches and insects began to be a nuisance. The trail was strewn with cast-off articles: leather toilet sets, soap, socks, and extra underwear told a tale of exhaustion and misery. Upon reaching streams, the men would rush to them and drink, regardless of the fact that upstream some soldier might be washing his feet. The trail was filled with struggling individuals, many lying on one side panting for breath. The medical officer bringing up the rear, reached the bivouac [temporary camp] that night with a platoon of limping and dazed men. There were no stragglers, however, for it was feared through the march that stragglers might be killed by a Jap patrol.

First Sergeant Paul R. Lutjens remembers the final stages of the march across the Owen Stanley Mountains to Buna.

I could hardly describe the country. It would take five or six hours to go a mile, edging along cliff walls, hanging on to vines, up and down, up and down. The men got weaker; guys began to lag back, and an officer stayed at the end of the line to keep driving the stragglers. There wasn't any way of evacuating to the rear. Men with sprained ankles hobbled along as well as they could, driven on by fear of being left behind.

The Australians were responsible for Gona and Salamua, but the Americans were assigned Buna, which was a Japanese fortress in the midst of a tropical, fetid swamp. The fighting here was done by improperly equipped, green U.S. Army troops under Major General Edwin F. Harding. When his assaults were massacred amidst the swamp, MacArthur—who never went to the front here—replaced Harding with the talented and tenacious Lieutenant General Robert L. Eichelberger. MacArthur told his old friend to "take Buna, or not come back alive." Even with new leadership, the going was hard and an Army amphibious landing was virtually trapped up against a nearly impassable mangrove swamp after storming Buna's beaches. Fortunately, the Australians captured Gona on December 9, 1942, and were able to assist the American effort and Buna fell in early January 1943. The Japanese garrison had virtually died to the last man, a grim portent of the fighting yet to come.

BELOW: A smoke screen obscures the drop zone from prying Japanese eyes during the 503rd Parachute Regiment assault in support of the 9th Australian Division's September 4, 1943, landings at Lae, New Guinea. The paratroopers and a battery of Australian artillery secured the Nadzab Airfield so that the 7th Australian Division could be landed behind Japanese lines to prevent their escape into the Markham Valley.

ABOVE: American and Australian soldiers cross a footbridge connecting Buna Mission to Musita Island. The narrow structure, built by soldiers from U.S. 23d Engineer Regiment, greatly facilitated the capture of the heavily fortified Government Gardens area and Mission buildings that finally fell on January 2, 1943, after more than two weeks of heavy fighting.

Colonel Harry Knight, an Army military observer, was part of a concerted effort to document lessons learned in this new style of warfare in the southwest Pacific. Here he recalls some lessons from the Battle of Buna.

The fact that our troops did not see the enemy who was shooting at them, and the further fact that they could not definitely locate where the enemy fire was coming from, had a most demoralizing effect on morale. I had soldiers all up and down the line tell me that they "sure did wish they could see the yellow bastards so they could shoot them." The first Jap I saw was a dead one, and I followed only about 100 yards behind the assault wave in the attack on December 18 [1942]. I had been all along the front lines for three days before then and I was looking for them!

Soldiers must be taught to realize that their sole reason for being on the battlefield is to kill Japs. Airplanes, tanks, artillery, mortars, and machine guns have the function of keeping down the fire of the enemy, and enabling the infantryman to get close to his enemy. He must keep going until he can get to where he can *see* the enemy, and then he must kill every one of them he can. This determination to close with the enemy, and the desire to kill as many of [them] as possible, must be instilled in every soldier.

Lieutenant Robert H. Odell of the 126th Infantry Regiment recalls the arrival of Lieutenant General Eichelberger at the front lines during some of the most intense fighting around Buna.

The lieutenant general explained what he wanted, and after a brief delay, I brought up the company and deployed accordingly. First Sergeant George Pravda was to take half the

Buna fell in early January 1943. The Japanese garrison had virtually died to the last man, a grim portent of the fighting yet to come.

—Paul R. Lutjens

company up one side of the trail, and I the other half on the other side. We were given ten minutes to make our reconnaissance and to gather information from the most forward troops we were to pass. It was intended that we finish the job—actually take the village [Buna]—and [it was thought] that we needed little more than our bayonets to do it. Well, off we went, and within a few minutes our rush forward had been definitely and completely halted. Of the forty men who started with me, four had been known killed, and eighteen were lying wounded. We were within a few yards of the village, but with…no chance of going a step further…. Pravda was among the wounded, and casualties were about as heavy on his side.

🎙 *Major General Edwin F. Harding, in command of the 32d Infantry Division and later relieved by MacArthur, related difficulty training his National Guard division for combat in the jungles of New Guinea.*

Unfortunately, we had no opportunity to work through a systematic program for correcting deficiencies in the division's training. From February, when I took over, until November when we went into battle, we were always getting ready to move, on the move, or getting settled after a move. No sooner would we get a systematic training program started than orders for a move came along to interrupt it.

BELOW: An M3 Stuart light tank of the 2d Battalion, 6th Armored Regiment pulls another Stuart free from the sodden ground near Buna on December 27, 1942. Valuable support by this unit during the latter stages of the battle for Buna saved many Allied lives.

BELOW: With the help of a microphone and powerful speakers, an Army instructor orchestrates a company-sized charge straight up a volcanic ridge at the Jungle Training Center, Hawaii, in 1943. Infantry trainees are clothed in a wide assortment of cast-off uniform shirts and trousers, and lug World War I-era Springfield rifles tipped with their distinctive 16-inch bayonets. Smoke pots add a touch of realism, and machine guns fire live rounds over the top of the ridge.

Lieutenant Odell describes a night assault on Buna.

As soon as it was dark, preparations began. When these were completed, we each grasped the shoulder of the man in front and slowly shuffled forward in the pitch-black of the night. Our only guide was the telephone wire leading to the jump-off point, and the troops in the foxholes along the way who had been holding the ground recently captured. There was no trail and consequently several hours were required to travel as many hundreds of yards. We all had bayonets. Rifle fire was forbidden until after the attack was well underway. Japs encountered along the way were to be dealt with silently.

Tanks also played a role in the battle for Buna and Gona. Lieutenant Colonel Alexander McNab remembers the use of M3 Stuart light tanks by the Australians around Cape Endaiadere.

The tanks completely demoralized the Japs [who] fought like cornered rats when they were forced into the open when the tanks broke through their final protective line. There were few holes knocked in the bunkers, except where the tanks stood off and blasted them at short range with their 37mm guns.

Major General Kensaku Oda, commanding the Japanese troops around Sanananda, remembers their condition just before being ordered to withdraw.

Most of the men are stricken with dysentery. Those not...in bed with illness are without food and too weak for hand-to-hand fighting. Starvation is taking many lives, and it is weakening our already extended lines. We are doomed. In several days, we are bound to meet the same fate that overtook Basabua and Buna. Our duty will have been accomplished if we fight and lay down our lives here on the field. However, this would mean that our foothold in [eastern] New Guinea would be lost and the sacrifices of our fellow soldiers during the past six months will have been in vain. [I] urge that reinforcements be landed near Gona at once.

One of the benefits of the Buna-Gona Campaign was the acquisition of the Dobodura airfield in the region. Dobodura later became a 5th Air Force staging base for General George C. Kenney's heavy bombers used for much of the intense air operations of the Southwest Pacific campaign. Here army observer Colonel H.F. Hardy discusses early Japanese air attacks against Dobodura and the response by Army air defense measures.

Among Air Force personnel, I often heard the expression: "God bless the small ack-ack [antiaircraft guns]." On November 26 [1942], the Zeros discovered our newly prepared and undefended landing strip at Dobodura, and proceeded to riddle one transport plane on the ground and shoot down another which was taking off. Three Zeros and three dive-bombers attacked there for about fifteen minutes on November 30. Our AA machine guns [.50 caliber] opened up. The longest burst I heard them fire was about five seconds. An eyewitness reported seeing two dive-bombers and one Zero go down in smoke. Whether these were hit by ground machine guns or by Allied fighter planes could not be determined for there was considerable aerial combat throughout the area. Except for a transport plane which overran the field and crashed [no casualties] while trying to escape a Zero, damage was limited to half a dozen bomb craters along the side of the runway. There were no 40mm [the famous Bofors AA guns] at Dobodura at this time.

🎤 *Colonel Hardy goes on to discuss how, at this early stage of the war, senior officers often had to man equipment or be prepared to engage in close combat in the lethal environment of the Southwest Pacific.*

One brigadier general and one colonel, both ground officers, have had occasion to man machine guns of aircraft while in flight. I know several officers who prefer to accept the additional weight and carry a sub-machine gun instead of a pistol [and] I have observed general officers carrying hand grenades in the combat area. I recommend that stress be laid on giving all officers an appropriate amount of training with hand grenades and with all automatic weapons and small arms.

With a firm footing on the north shore of New Guinea, General MacArthur's campaign to achieve the neutralization or capture of Rabaul was back on track. The pattern established here, as at Guadalcanal, was to secure the ground followed by the air forces moving in to establish local control of the air and seas, providing an umbrella for further offensive operations.

Far to the north, a deadly sideshow played itself out as a sequel to Japan's successful occupation of the Aleutian Islands of Kiska and Attu. Typically, the U.S. Army and the Navy elements were at loggerheads with each other and with their superiors about what to do. Nimitz wisely avoided committing any substantial resources to retaking these islands, although he did try to cut off Japanese supply lines with his naval forces under Rear Admiral Robert A. Theobald. Theobald, however, was too abrasive and Nimitz replaced him with Rear Admiral Thomas C. Kinkaid, a much better administrator and a veteran combat leader. In March 1943, a cruiser force under Kinkaid's subordinate, Rear Admiral Charles H. McMorris, fought a long-running daylight surface engagement near the Komandorski Islands in the north Pacific with a superior force of Japanese warships under Vice Admiral Boshiro Hosogaya. McMorris' flagship USS *Salt Lake City* was badly damaged and it looked as if the Navy was about to absorb another humiliating

OPPOSITE: Wounded American soldiers on native-built bamboo stretchers receive treatment at an aid station south of the Buna Mission battlefield on December 28, 1942. Already badly weakened by disease, their recovery would be slow. Both the 1st Marine Division on Guadalcanal and the 32d Infantry Division on New Guinea started combat with roughly 11,000 men each, and had received almost no replacements during the fighting. The division on Guadalcanal saw 13,081 hospital admissions for disease over its four months of combat, while the one on New Guinea saw 7,125 over its first two, with nearly half of all admissions for malaria. When the 32d Division's sickness rate from October 1942 to February 1943 was averaged, it was found that the unit attained a rate of 5,358 cases per 1,000 troops from malaria, dengue, and fevers of undetermined origin.

LEFT: The heavy cruiser *Salt Lake City*, damaged by Japanese shellfire, starts losing speed prior to going dead in the water during the Komandorski Islands battle southeast of the Soviet Union's Kamchatka Peninsula. Accompanying destroyers lay a smoke screen to help shield it from the Japanese gun directors. The *Salt Lake City*, light cruiser *Richmond*, and four destroyers had intercepted a Japanese force intending to resupply its garrisons in the Aleutian Islands. The subsequent fight was exclusively a gunnery duel, and the Japanese were forced to retire.

surface defeat when the Japanese turned away, giving the Americans a victory of sorts.

By early May 1943, the Americans were ready to retake Attu. Here the Japanese commander did not contest the landings. Most of the fighting centered around the key area appropriately named Massacre Valley. It was a bloody slog amidst ice, snow, and fog for the Americans and Japanese. As usual, the Imperial troops fought almost to the last man. One American divisional commander was relieved and the island was not secured for two weeks. As at Buna, the fighting on Attu was a chilling preview of things to come, with the Japanese defenders pulling into the interior and selling their lives dearly.

Brigadier General William E. Lynd was the Army Air Corps officer assigned to Admiral Nimitz's staff during the time of the Attu operation. Here he recalls the difficulty of providing air support to ground operations at Attu.

The planes were based at Amchitka, a distance of 300 miles away. These people, the ground forces, would want air support on some

particular target. When the planes came out to attack, you wanted it [the air support] up here [at Attu]. So all the operations were merely this: When you could get planes off Amchitka, and they could come to make an attack, they came. But these people would keep howling for support all the time and wondering why they didn't get it. You can't convince a ground officer that you can't furnish him ground support when he can see clear weather [on Attu]—he can't visualize what's 300 miles away [on Amchitka]. They don't know the people are sitting back here in solid fog.

Captain Danforth P. Miller of the Cactus Air Force marveled at the reliability of the Australian lookouts scouring the skies from their island hideouts.

A coast watcher usually was helped by a few natives, and sat up on hill overlooking Bougainville or some other Japanese operation; or perhaps just out on some lonely island where he was in the air lanes, so to speak. We had rudimentary radar equipment, and the radar gave us about thirty-five minutes warning. Pretty damn good, long enough to scramble the Corsairs [F4U fighters], which would climb up, and long enough for everybody else to select his foxhole and so forth.

But when the Australian coast watchers gave us warning, we'd have over an hour warning, sometimes an hour and half's warning. They'd say, "About eighteen coming your way, about 18,000 feet, should be down there in an hour and a half," or something like that, "on such and such a course," and these guys were right every bloody time.

The first Navy-piloted aircraft arrived on August 24, just as the Battle of the Eastern Solomons was ending. Flying off of the carrier

Cactus Air Force

The dire situation on Guadalcanal in 1942 led to the creation of the first-ever "joint" air force. As the only fixed-wing airfield for hundreds of miles around, Henderson Field—named after a Marine Corps aviator killed at the Battle of Midway earlier that summer—became the crucial patch of real estate for most of the campaign. The Marine, Navy, and Army aviators that flew from Henderson eventually became known as "the Cactus Air Force" after the radio call sign "Cactus" assigned to the burgeoning airbase.

Using Henderson to maximum advantage, the Cactus Air Force kept the Japanese Navy at bay in its efforts to completely cut Guadalcanal's supply lines through the contested seas surrounding the island. This was essential to supply support until the U.S. Navy, severely defeated at Savo Island and other naval battles, built up enough combat power to run the Imperial Navy off for good. The Cactus Air Force also provided close support to the Marines and soldiers on the ground, which helped blunt the numerous Japanese attempts to recapture the airfield.

The Japanese, ironically, began the construction of Henderson Field in the early summer before the Americans arrived—if they had not, then there may have been no Guadalcanal campaign at all since the original American plan had only envisaged the seizure of the harbor and seaplane base on Tulagi Island, just north of Guadalcanal. The Marines captured the airfield without a shot on August 7, 1942, as the workers, mostly Koreans, simply ran into the jungle and graciously left their bulldozers, which the Marines and the Seabees (Navy engineers) used to finish the runway.

The importance of having a continuous air presence was emphasized later that day when the Japanese launched the first of seemingly unending series of air raids from their main base at Rabaul on New Britain Island. Fortunately, Navy carriers under Admiral Fletcher were there and shot down many of the approaching bombers, but some still made it through. Late the next day, after interdicting several other bomber raids, Fletcher left to refuel his destroyers in safer waters to the south. That night, a Japanese cruiser force essentially destroyed the naval surface group that was providing cover for the Marines. The following day, Admiral Turner—bereft of any warships to defend himself—pulled the rest of the naval shipping out of the area, which left the Marines with no support either on the sea or in the air.

The first aircraft soon arrived at "Cactus" and operations ran on a shoestring until after the great naval, land, and air battles of mid-November solidified American dominance in the area. The first plane to use the barely operational field was a PBY-5 Catalina that landed on August 12. However, the first permanent elements of the Cactus Air Force—consisting of a squadron each of Marine Wildcat fighters and Dauntless dive-bombers—arrived on August 20. They flew in from the escort carrier *Long Island* (CVE-1). The next day, the Marines shot down their first Zero fighter.

Initially, it was an all-Marine outfit, but events soon conspired to add sailors and soldiers to the mix. Army planes and five Bell P-39 Airacobras of the Army's 67th Fighter Squadron arrived on August 22, but because the Airacobras were seriously outclassed by the Zero, they would often be given ground support missions. The Wildcats were somewhat better and soon the tactic evolved of launching them as soon as the Australian coast watchers "up the ladder" in the Solomon Islands reported that Japanese aircraft were

ABOVE: Bell P-39 Airacobra's on Guadalcanal, circa late 1942–early 1943. Although this Army Air Force fighter performed adequately against the Zero and—with its 37mm cannon in addition to six machine guns—was a much appreciated ground support aircraft, it was superseded by the Republic P-47 Thunderbolt after the mid-war Guadalcanal, Aleutian, and New Guinea campaigns.

OPPOSITE, BOTTOM: PBY pilots lounging on Guadalcanal outside their tent near Henderson Field. This shot was taken as the Solomons Campaign was moving up "The Slot" in 1943, but gives one a good feel for the spare jungle conditions these men served in. Extra planks of tent matting and Marston matting from the runway are used to cut down on the mud they track into their tent after the rains. The airmen, left to right, are Lieutenant Norman Pederson, Lieutenant Clem Wilkes, Lieutenant William Pack, Lieutenant Fred Hockelman, Lieutenant Cyrenus Gillette, and Lieutenant Jim Kilke.

on the way. The Wildcats would then climb to the highest possible altitude and try to use superior speed and surprise to defeat the Zeros escorting the bomber raids. Because the Zeros were at the maximum limit of their operational range, these tactics often proved effective.

Enterprise for a night strike on the fleeing Japanese, six Navy Dauntless aircraft under Lieutenant Turner Caldwell found that they were too low on fuel to return at night to the damaged carrier and diverted ("bingoed") to Henderson Field. These valuable planes and pilots were to remain with Cactus for over a month.

The Cactus crowd had more than just bombers and Zeros to fear. There were snipers in the jungles and cruisers and battleships at sea whose rifles—or big naval guns—could ravage the airfield, especially at night when air operations were virtually impossible. Replacing damaged or destroyed airplanes and repairing the damaged operations center (nicknamed "The Pagoda") became routine. Rear Admiral John McCain, the Commander, Air Forces South Pacific, flew into Cactus at the end of August and got to experience one of the nightly Japanese Navy bombardments first hand. He wrote a prophetic message to Admiral Nimitz stating, "Cactus can be a sinkhole for enemy air power and can be consolidated, expanded, and exploited to the enemy's mortal hurt." Not long after, Admiral Nimitz sent

the following cryptic message about the air situation at Guadalcanal to his boss in Washington, Admiral King, one of the fathers of carrier aviation:

All aircraft that can be spared from *Enterprise* and *Saratoga* [are] being transferred to ComSoPac for use present campaign...Employment carrier aircraft and pilots [to] shore bases necessary because lack of suitable Army type planes for Guadalcanal fighting, but such use carrier pilots is most uneconomical.

Key to the effort would be unity of command, and Brigadier General Roy S. Geiger, commander of the 1st Marine Air Wing, arrived at Guadalcanal on September 3 to assume command of all the air elements at Cactus. In the meantime, more Marine squadrons arrived and, as the naval battles raged, more Navy squadrons, low on fuel or whose carriers had been sunk, continued to use Henderson as a "divert field." Accordingly, they were added to the air order of battle and remained for weeks and even months.

The most notable addition in this regard was Air Group 10 from the *Enterprise*, which flew into Henderson in its entirety and operated from the land base during the seesaw battles around Guadalcanal November 13–16.

Meanwhile, there was hard fighting, and equally difficult logistical challenges, ashore. In September, Cactus Airacobras were used to assist in the defeat of the Japanese at the Battle of Bloody (Edson's) Ridge. The single worst moment for Cactus came on the night of October 13–14 when Vice Admiral Takeo Kurita (of later Leyte Gulf fame) brought down two battleships in an attempt to finish off Cactus after a series of punishing air raids. When Kurita was done, he could smugly look on at the sea of flames that had once been the airbase.

Nearly a thousand 14-inch shells had been pumped into the perimeter, centered on the airfield. The radio station was destroyed and the runway pockmarked by shell holes but, miraculously, only forty-one troops were killed. However, the real disaster was the destruction of almost all of the aviation fuel. There were only five Army aircraft that survived, along with just seven dive-bombers to use against the major effort the Japanese were making to reinforce the island. By this time, Cactus included a separate fighter strip, which most of the Japanese shells missed, so most of the fighters survived—but they would need gasoline.

The situation was so desperate that aviation fuel was delivered aboard Navy submarines due to the danger from prowling Japanese warships and attacking carrier- and land-based aircraft. When the gasoline was available, the waters around Guadalcanal were just as dangerous by day for the Japanese ships, especially those carrying the troops whose landing was essential to the recapture of Henderson. Somehow, despite continued bombardments from both the sea and the air, fuel was pushed through and Cactus hung on.

By late October, Japanese air power was a spent force, although some very hard fighting continued on land and at sea. Nevertheless, it was the air power from Henderson Field that helped the Navy, Marines, and Army forces to maintain the initiative and defeat the Japanese on Guadalcanal.

BELOW: Black smoke pours from fires raging on the USS *Wasp* after a trio of Japanese submarine torpedoes struck it on September 15, 1942. Just three weeks earlier, damage inflicted on the *Enterprise* forced it to be withdrawn for repairs, and the same fate befell the *Saratoga* on the last day of August. With the sinking of the *Wasp*, the U.S. Navy had only one operational carrier left, the *Hornet*. To help fill the gap, the HMS *Victorious* was sent to the Pacific where it flew a mixed U.S.-British air group during the invasion of New Georgia.

No sooner had we hit the water than the Japanese machine guns really opened up on us...It was painfully slow, wading in such deep water. And we had 700 yards to walk slowly into that machine gun fire, looming into larger targets as we rose onto higher ground. I was scared, as I had never been scared.

—Robert Sherrod, *Time* correspondent

Chapter Five

ISLAND HOPPING

A s the battles on Guadalcanal and New Guinea were winding down, the Allied leaders were meeting in Casablanca to discuss the next steps in the global war against the Axis powers. One of the items for discussion involved the completion of the offensive against Rabaul on the eastern end of New Britain in the Bismarck Archipelago. General MacArthur was supposed to take overall command for this task. However, Admiral King reinserted himself into the discussions and tried to renege on the Navy's promise to give MacArthur overall command. Through a very complicated series of negotiations, the Joint Chiefs of Staff (JCS) essentially agreed to underwrite offensives for both MacArthur and Nimitz—what has become known as "the dual advance" was born from this arrangement.

Essentially, JCS was unwilling to give the reeling Japanese a breather in order to concentrate solely on the Germans. Nimitz would retain command of any Navy forces not specifically assigned to MacArthur and so began to prepare for an operation based on the pre-war "Orange Plan" to begin island hopping in the Gilbert Islands in late 1943. Meanwhile, MacArthur retained overall strategic direction over the forces under his

command as well as the nominally independent South Pacific forces of Admiral Halsey. In
this manner, broad pressure would be applied
against the Japanese defenses, preventing
them from massing against any single offensive. The first phase of this dual advance
became more generally known as "island hopping." Once the admirals and generals realized
that they need not take every island along the
two axes of advance, they began "hopping"
around and over many of Japan's most formidable strongholds, driving ever and ever deeper
into the maritime empire that the Japanese
had seized so quickly.

Operation CARTWHEEL

Fortunately, Halsey and MacArthur had a
face-to-face meeting in Brisbane, Australia,
and agreed to cooperate. They came up with a
new plan to take Rabaul, which they submitted
to JCS. It involved Halsey advancing up the
Solomons to protect MacArthur's flank while
MacArthur advanced with American-Australian
forces along the north shore of New Guinea
to seize airfields and jumping-off points from
which to ultimately capture Rabaul. Eventually,

the two offensives would converge at Rabaul.
This plan, submitted in April 1943, was named
CARTWHEEL. In a sense, it was really a minia-
ture dual advance within the larger dual
advance. Halsey retained a large measure of
independence and effectively commanded
his own effort under MacArthur's strategic
oversight.

By this point in the war, MacArthur's air
elements (the 5th Air Force) were led by the
command of a new type of Army Air Corps
officer, General George C. Kenney. Kenney was
practical about the use of air power and became
one of the most effective air commanders of the
war. He used his planes for logistical support,
maritime strike, interdiction, and close support,
as well as the traditional roles of air superiority
and bombing. His efforts, and those of the
air-minded Halsey, would go a long way toward
establishing permanent air dominance in
MacArthur's theater wherever the Americans
set up airbases. They both learned that once an
airfield or anchorage was seized and a secure
perimeter established, they could fight from a
superior defensive posture against the ill-supplied
Japanese ground forces, which had little air cover
of their own. This advantage in the air was also
critical in limiting the ability of the Japanese
surface navy to influence events. In 1943, the
first wave of a huge ship-building program could
finally be seen—the U.S. Navy would only get
stronger and would out-build the Japanese in
every category of ship and airplane.

*Major Jay T. Robbins, one the many aces in
General Kenney's 5th Air Force, discusses
flying the P-39 Airacobra and later the
P-38 Lightning from airfields in New Guinea.*

We were flying P-39s. I had to check out in a
P-39 because I had never flown it before. It
was a good airplane at low altitude, but not a
very good plane at higher altitudes. As long
as we were down below 10 or 12,000 feet, it
could compete with a Zero, but if you were
ever forced to operate at higher altitudes, you
were at a distinct disadvantage. It didn't have
the power or performance that the Zero had,
or speed and movability. I only fought a little
bit of combat in the P-39. Later on they got

CLOCKWISE FROM TOP:
The USS *Hardhead*, just after launching by the Manitowoc Shipbuilding Company of Wisconsin, in December 1943. Named not after a trait of the American character but, like most U.S. submarines, a type of fish, it was one of twenty-eight submarines built by the Great Lakes firm. It sunk nine Japanese ships.

The "new" USS *Wasp* (CV-18), built by the Bethlehem Steel Company's Quincy, Massachusetts, yard, is launched in August 1943 to replace the *Wasp* (CV-7) lost during the vicious sea battles around Guadalcanal.

Progress continues on the 45,000-ton battleship *New Jersey* at the Philadelphia Navy Yard in July 1942.

ABOVE: Ensign Edward J. Ruciniski uses the "new" *Lexington*'s shipboard communications system to describe to the crew how he just shot down three Japanese aircraft. Lieutenant Eugene R. Hanks, who knocked down five, stands grinning to his right. Some seventeen of twenty Japanese planes attempting to raid Tarawa were destroyed during the November 23, 1943, engagement.

OPPOSITE, BOTTOM: This starving Japanese soldier captured in 1942 shows the physical condition of many Japanese troops in the Southwest Pacific after their supply lines were severed.

P-38s, which was a hell of a good airplane. You preferred to operate below 10 or 12,000 feet, certainly no higher than 15,000. It would fly higher than that, but wouldn't operate very well. We had three squadrons: the 35th, 36th, and the 80th.

Because the type of airstrips we were operating off of (usually small), you operated more as a separate squadron than as a group. My squadron would be on the 3-mile and the 35th squadron would be on the 17-mile airstrip. It was just the name of it. There might be in the Port Moresby vicinity as many as five or six airstrips. The advantage, of course, being dispersal. It required less facilities; you could build an airstrip and a few taxiways with pierced metal planking and you were pretty well off. The first mission that I recall was a fighter over the Owen Stanley range in New Guinea, near Lae and Salamaua, primarily a fighter sweep to find

supply barges. We flew in P-39s. The aim was to destroy and disrupt the supply system and any coastal shipping.

About this time, the squadron was in the process of moving to Milne Bay, which is down on the southern tip of New Guinea. We were still flying P-39s down there. After I had been at Milne Bay for a short while, we were on the receiving end of a daylight air raid by the Japanese. Of course we were getting bombed nearly every night and there were a number of raids just for harassment. During this daylight raid, we managed to scramble a few airplanes. We took off while they were bombing. I think four or five of us got airborne. Two of us actually shot down an airplane and both of us thought he had gotten it. When we got back on the ground, and during the debriefing by the intelligence people, we finally flipped a coin to see who got credit for the destroyed enemy airplane and I lost. The first one I thought I really had to my credit and I lost it by a flip of a coin! So we stayed in Milne Bay for a brief while and then went back to Australia and got reequipped with P-38s.

We were down in northern Australia at a place called Mareeba just long enough to get the squadron equipped and get the pilots and maintenance people all checked out in the P-38. Then we went back to Port Moresby. We were there for a while and moved across the island to an airstrip on the other side where we started making raids against Rabaul in New Britain. Most of the time, we were on escort missions where we would be escorting bombers. The policy early on was to stick very close to the bombers and not engage in air-to-air combat unless you had to, because the main objective was to let the bombers through, and do their job, and get them back home without any losses if you could.

Kenney struck the first blow. The Japanese, anticipating another round of U.S. offensives, had begun moving two fresh divisions from China and Korea to New Guinea. In early March 1943, Kenney's air forces—including specially configured B-25 medium bombers—located and massacred a convoy carrying most of the

Imperial 51st Division in the Bismarck Sea. Navy PT boats moved in and mopped up many of the survivors. Japanese General Headquarters over-reacted to this battle by never attempting another major convoy again and routing most of their reinforcements to New Guinea to try and attack Kenney's airfields. The result was even more strain on the already inadequate maritime logistical efforts to their ground forces. Many of the Japanese troops in New Guinea would suffer a slow death by starvation; unsup-ported in isolated jungles, unable to seize or neutralize the all-important Allied airfields.

Admiral Yamamoto attempted to redress the rapidly deteriorating situation by launching an air counteroffensive against Allied bases and shipping that April. He even used his precious carrier pilots in this offensive, but gained little as a result. He lost about as many planes as he destroyed as new U.S. fighters (P-38 Lightnings

ABOVE: Rabaul burns as B-25s of the 38th Bomb Group attack Japanese shipping in Simpson Harbor, New Britain. The wake at lower left leads to a ship that was near-missed (note the bomb-blast's water spout at the bottom of the photo) by the aircraft from which this picture was taken. Although they were not direct strikes, explosions this close to a small ship's hull frequently caused lethal damage. The actual Japanese losses were fewer than the twenty-six ships claimed sunk or damaged, but the November 2, 1943, raid did succeed in sinking two cargo ships, a large oiler, and a mine sweeper. The Japanese air defense downed eight B-25s and nine P-38s at the cost of only twenty of their own planes, but this level of feroc-ity could not be maintained against the U.S. 5th Air Force's grinding pressure.

Yamamoto Shootdown

Admiral Isoroku Yamamoto knew he was running out of time. He had predicted that his forces could put up a "tough fight" in the first year of the war. But now, as the fighting moved inextricably through its second year, he saw nothing to contradict the rest of his statement that he had "no confidence as to what would happen...." if the war was not quickly won. It was in this frame of mind that he conceived the I-Go campaign. It was to be a deliberate air offensive that would reestablish Japanese dominance in the skies of the south and southwestern Pacific. He knew that the key to his ability to fight the Americans would be the neutralization of their air power so he could keep his island garrisons supplied and even launch counter-offensives to retake the initiative.

Yamamoto moved his headquarters to Rabaul and brought ashore with him the bulk of his carrier aircraft and pilots because he did not want to risk losing one of the precious aircraft carriers. He was able, by hook and by crook, to put together a striking force of over 300 aircraft. Yamamoto sent his pilots, mostly young and newly trained, to replace all of the losses of the previous twelve months against the American airfields at Guadalcanal, Tulagi, Port Moresby, Milne Bay, and against Allied shipping along the coast of New Guinea. His pilots came back with exaggerated reports of dozens of enemy planes shot down and numerous ships sunk. Yamamoto unwisely believed these reports and decided to fly to southern Bougainville to personally congratulate his pilots and to boost morale. The Japanese compounded their error by transmitting Yamamoto's upcoming visit over their supposedly secure radios.

LEFT: Admiral Isoroku Yamamoto tips his hat to a young Zero pilot bound for the skies over Guadalcanal in the fall of 1942. Disturbed by the losses during the disastrous Guadalcanal Campaign, he scraped together every plane and pilot he could—including precious carrier pilots who he based ashore—for the futile I-Go air offensive in April 1943 that failed to recapture command of the air over the Solomons.

In Pearl Harbor, Admiral Chester Nimitz was contacted by Captain Edwin T. Layton, his head of intelligence. Layton's cryptographers had intercepted and broken the code that protected a message containing the precise timing of Yamamoto's visit to Bougainville. Nimitz asked Layton if they should try to intercept him with American fighters, and Layton answered the question with a question: "Can the Japanese replace him with anyone better?" Nimitz gave his subordinates the go-ahead to attempt to shoot down the Commander of the Combined Japanese Fleet.

Yamamoto's Mitsubishi Betty bomber took off on the morning of April 18. His chief of staff accompanied him in a separate plane. They were escorted by nine Zeros, but the American airmen were taking no chances. They launched eighteen of the new heavily armed P-38 Lightning fighter aircraft to take Yamamoto down. The ambush was sprung at high altitude over Kahili near southern Bougainville. The Americans dove down into the flock of Japanese aircraft with Yamamoto's bomber peeling off as the Zeros attempted to dogfight. Flight leader Captain Thomas G. Lanphier, Jr., pursued Yamamoto's aircraft with four

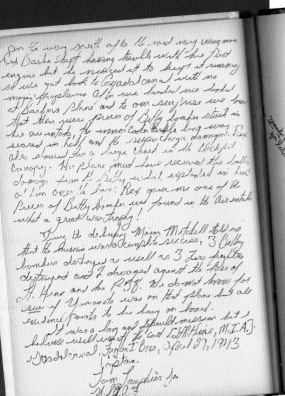

Yamamoto Raid
April 18th 1943

P-38s and fired a burst from his 20mm cannon that caused the old admiral's plane to burst into flames.

The combination of American signals intelligence and air power was mighty indeed, as would be demonstrated repeatedly, and the Yamamoto shoot down would prove to be one of the most perfectly executed tactical attacks based on signals intelligence during the entire war. As a bonus, the Americans also shot down the plane carrying Yamamoto's chief of staff, Admiral Matome Ugaki. Ugaki, however, was only wounded and lived to fight another day as the leader of the deadly kamikaze campaign at the end of the war.

Yamamoto's remains were recovered by the Japanese and sent back to Tokyo where his ashes were buried in a state funeral. The "reluctant" Japanese admiral who had planned Pearl Harbor had indeed reaped the whirlwind—or perhaps more appropriately, he had been struck by lightning from the storm he helped create.

and F4U Corsairs) and better tactics eliminated the advantage his diminishing veteran pilots and superior Zero fighter planes had maintained so far. Yamamoto lost his own life when U.S. code breakers detected an upcoming flight and ambushed it with a squadron of P-38s. At one stroke, the Japanese lost their most inspiring and farsighted naval commander.

The air battles that took place over Rabaul were fierce. Here, P-38 ace Major Robbins discusses the characteristics of the P-38 and the day he shot down five Japanese airplanes.

The P-38 was pretty much a natural for the Southwest Pacific Theater. We did a tremendous amount of over-water flying and flying over jungles. The search and rescue at that time was very marginal. If you ever went down, the possibility of being picked up was not good. The fact that the P-38 had two engines was a big advantage over there.

Also, it had no torque and the firepower was concentrated in the nose. It was a very good gunnery platform. The Japanese Zero was a single-engine airplane, not quite as fast as a P-38, but it had an extremely good turning

LEFT: Entry from the diary of Captain Thomas G. Lanphier, Jr. describing the mission targeting Admiral Yamamoto.

"April 29, 1943—On the way south after the raid my wingman Rex Barber kept having trouble with his port engine but he nursed it to keep it running so we got back to Guadalcanal with no major problems. After we landed, we looked at Barber's plane and to our surprise we found that there were pieces of Betty bomber stuck in his air intake, the inner cooler [. . .] line was seared in half and the supercharger damaged. Rex also showed us a large crack in the cockpit canopy. His plane must have received the battle damage from the Betty, which exploded in front of him over the bay. Rex gave me one of the pieces of Betty bomber we found in the air intake. What a great trophy!

"During the debriefing Major Mitchell told us that the mission was a complete success, three Betty bombers destroyed as well as three Zero fighters destroyed and two damaged against the loss of Lt. Hine and his P-38. We do not know for sure if Yamamoto was on that plane, but all evidence points to his being on board.

"It was a long and difficult mission, but I believe well worth the cost."

[Lieutenant Ray Hine was missing in action and later declared dead.]

OPPOSITE, INSET: Yamamoto during one of the formal "map exercises" that were used to "wargame" naval courses of action to test their feasibility and suitability. The map maneuvers were frequently artificial and scripted, and they did not allow for unexpected enemy moves.

BELOW: A target-rich environment. The November 2, 1943, attack on the Rabaul bastion from the perspective of a Royal Australian Air Force B-25 bomber. Ships fill Simpson Harbor, and in the upper right corner (circle in red), a Zero taking off to intercept the B-25s has yet to retract its wheels. In the foreground on the runway is a Nakajima J1N1-S "Irving" night fighter, perhaps preparing to take off. Along the lower left is a trio of Mitsubishi Ki-25 "Sally" bombers, including one that is partially obscured under camouflage netting. At bottom right is a Mitsubishi Ki-46 "Dinah" reconnaissance plane.

capability and was highly maneuverable. If we got into combat with the Zero or the Zeke Z-13—they were the different types of Japanese airplanes—the Zero could always out-turn us and we knew that. We tried not to get into a turning combat with them. We could usually break off engagement if we had both engines functioning, either in a high-speed climb or a high-speed dive. Then we could out-climb them or out-dive them. We could run away from them, break off combat pretty much when we wanted to depending on the situation. The P-38 had one disadvantage. When it went into a dive, it tended to want to stay in a dive and tuck under. You had to avoid a situation where you were going straight down at high speed. It was pretty rugged. It could take punishment and you always had the advan-

tage of that one engine if something went wrong with the other one.

The P-38 had counter-rotating propellers. Therefore, you had no torque and all your firepower was centered right in the nose of the airplane, rather than being in the wing like it was in a lot of airplanes. There was some point out there at 1,500 feet or so where the fire would converge from the wing guns of a P-47 or P-40, but in the P-38 you had four .50 caliber machines guns and a 20mm cannon. They were all right there in the nose, so that you virtually had a solid cone of fire straight out until dispersion began to take place. I always tried to get in very close before I opened fire. I had seen too many people fail to get hits because they were too eager and fired too soon.

I would try to get within 200 or 300 yards minimum, preferably 200 yards. Once you got that close, then you had a good solid cone of fire and you could pull out your lead. Most of my aerial victories were on deflection shots. I would pull out enough lead and try to hold that lead steady and then gradually walk it right back through the target airplane while he was turning. I would let him fly through the projectiles rather than try to stay on him all the time. I used that technique quite often. Originally we had tracers in our guns to help in aiming. I finally took them out of mine. Tracers light up once you fire them and you can see them from behind, and so could the Japanese pilots you were shooting at. If you happened to pull out a lead in front of him a little bit, he could see the tracers in front of him and knew someone was after him. Then he would go completely wild and half-roll down or do all sorts of wild things. I found that I didn't need the tracers for shooting accuracy. They were more of a disadvantage than an advantage, so I just took them out.

This particular day, we came in with B-25s and got into a big mess of Japanese fighters over Rabaul. There must have been fifty or sixty of them. In my particular squadron, we only go twelve [fighters] over the target, but there would have been other squadrons escorting other waves of bombers. I remember shooting down the first enemy airplane about 300 feet, not too long after he had taken off [Robbins was strafing the airfield].

I came in from the rear quadrant. He was in a left turn when I shot him down. The first one was low and the second one was a head-on pass, fairly high altitude. This was the first day in combat that I could recall a fighter in a head-on pass that was attempting to ram me.

A head-on pass was not too uncommon. I had two or three occurrences where you just happened to get in the same air space with a Japanese fighter and you would both start coming at each other and start shooting and you nearly always both broke one way or the other. This was the first time I could recall

ABOVE: Major Jay T. Robbins shot down twenty-two Japanese aircraft during the war.

BELOW: Republic P-47 Thunderbolts of the 348th Fighter Squadron at Saidor, New Guinea, on March 21, 1943. The other two squadrons of the 340th Group would arrive within a week, and help complete the encirclement of the once key Japanese stronghold at Rabaul.

that the guy was actually trying to fly right into me. Fortunately, I hit him good enough with my guns to make the aircraft pretty much disintegrate, so I only flew through bits and pieces of debris. We were probably a hundred yards apart. It is kind of frightening. During this same mission I tried something I had never tried before, and I never tried again. There were large cumulus clouds in the area and there were a lot of Japanese Zeros.I saw three going behind a big cumulus cloud and my wingman and I followed. I was trying to figure out how I could get close enough behind them to engage them. So I cut through the cloud. I just made a guess as to what kind of bank I would have to be in if they maintained the same heading...

I couldn't have been in the cloud more than thirty or forty seconds. I broke out right behind the tail guy and I must have missed him no more than 2 or 3 feet. That convinced me there must be a better way than that to close on one. It happened so quick, I never got to shoot.

The third kill was a deflection shot from the rear. I picked out the wingman out of a flight of four or five. I picked on the one in the rear.

The fourth victory was back down low again. The fight had worked back down fairly low and we had whipped out over the big bay where all their naval ships were. Here the battleships and cruisers and destroyers were firing away with flak [antiaircraft guns].

They were shooting at B-24s and B-25s and, of course, we were milling around in there, too. As I said, the fourth one was back fairly low. He apparently had been airborne for a long period of time and was trying to get back onto land.

The fifth kill I remember was right after the second head-on pass. I had a good lead on one and was getting good solid hits on it and he flew into a cloud, so I could never get the camera confirmation nor could I get another pilot confirmation, although I am convinced that he went down. I had hit others the same way and had seen the same kinds of hits and seen the airplanes reacting to these hits and this one was throwing out heavy smoke and pieces were flying off of it.

There was a lull in the ground fighting due to the very slow delivery of the precious new amphibious shipping and equipment to both MacArthur and Halsey. They were in direct competition with both Nimitz and the European theater for these assets. As a result, these specialized ships and crafts were slow in coming and their use had to be carefully managed. For MacArthur especially, the dearth of equipment led to an emphasis upon landing at undefended beaches until such time as enough assault shipping was available. Halsey, in contrast, was better equipped and so would adopt tactics that included outright assaults on defended beaches as he did later at Bougainville in the Solomons.

The mutually supporting CARTWHEEL offensives got underway that summer. MacArthur moved against the Trobriand Islands and along the northwest coast of New Guinea to Nassau Bay. Almost simultaneously, Halsey moved against the Japanese airfield at Munda on New Georgia Island in the central Solomons. Most of the landings were unopposed.

🎙️ *Lieutenant George Gay, of Torpedo 8 fame at Midway, was later posted back to the Solomons to help soften up Munda Airfield for Admiral Halsey.*

After Midway and a public relations tour, I joined Torpedo Squadron 11. The Air Group Commander at that time was Commander Ramsey, my squadron leader was Lieutenant Commander F.L. Ainsworth and previous to that he'd been a patrol plane pilot. He had a very difficult job of learning torpedo tactics and torpedo work, and he did a very marvelous job. He was a great skipper. I had asked Admiral Nimitz and Captain [later Rear Admiral, Charles Perry] Mason if it would be arranged so that I could come back and go aboard the *Hornet*—and Air Group 11 was supposed to go to the *Hornet*—but before we could get back out there, she was sunk [during the Guadalcanal campaign]. From Pearl, we went to the Fijis and then on up to Guadalcanal where we did quite a bit of night work on what we call "prowl hops." Strike Command would send us up 300 miles from Henderson Field [Guadalcanal] into the

BELOW: Wounded air crewman Alva Parker is helped from his SBD Dauntless, on board the USS *Saratoga*, after receiving shrapnel wounds during a November 5, 1943, raid on Rabaul. The Japanese, unwilling to risk their valuable aircraft carriers by this point in the war, were operating almost exclusively from land-based airfields. The Allies, on the other hand, operated from both land and sea. This flexibility gave them an inherent advantage in establishing local air dominance and providing Navy fighter escort to land-bound medium and long-range bombers over areas the Japanese thought safe.

ABOVE: The fourteen-ship convoy SO-903 is caught by the 38th Bomb Group off New Hanover Island as it nears Rabaul on February 16, 1944. A squadron of the 345th Bomb Group joined the attack later in the day, and the Japanese lost a sub chaser, an auxiliary sub chaser, and a transport ship towing a midget submarine (which was also believed sunk) to the conventional, low-level bombing and skip-bombing of the B-25s.

A bomb can be seen plummeting toward an unseen ship below the B-25 tail gunner who took this photo, while the strafing by the tail gunner in the following B-25G reaches a CH-28 class sub chaser turning hard to port. In the distance (inset), explosions rock a merchant ship, probably the transport *Sanko Maru*, and the bow of a sinking sub chaser to its starboard, is silhouetted against the spray and foam of escaping air as it goes under. Yet another B-25 can be seen coming in at mast-top level beyond the exploding ship.

Bougainville-Kahili [northern Solomons] area looking for shipping at night. We would drop flares and skip bomb ships. The squadron was told before we left that we had been able to wreak more havoc on the enemy with less casualties to ourselves than any other unit that had been at Guadalcanal, which I thought was a pretty good record.

We didn't lose very many people to the enemy. One radioman was killed on a daylight raid to Bougainville, lost an ensign on a night mine laying, and on a daylight raid we lost another ensign. Of course, we lost the crews with each of the pilots. We were very lucky and had a wonderful squadron.

We were in on the initial softening up [pre-invasion bombardment] of Munda and then came back to the States. Munda had been pounded long before we ever got to Guadalcanal. As a matter of fact, the palm trees and everything up there were pretty well beat up and we'd go up on an average of about twice a day with some forty-eight TBFs [Avengers], loaded with either four 500-pound bombs, demolitions, or 2,000-pound instantaneous bombs or daisy cutters [used to destroy runways], and we'd have some forty or fifty SBDs [Dauntless dive-bombers] with 1,000-pound bombs, and a number of fighters. We'd go up there and just move the dirt over a couple of hundred yards, and then the next afternoon we'd come back again; and we did that nearly every day. Just kept right on pounding them, but it happened that although we thought that it would be easy for the ground forces to walk in there and take the place, the first thing they started crying for when they got there was more air support.

The Japs were dug in, they were all underground, and I think that although you beat on them from the air like the devil, they are going to be hard to take whenever you hit them on the ground. Of course, I am not much of a ground tactician. I don't know much about the ground fighting out there, except that we all thought Munda was beat down to such a state that it would be easy. It turned out that it wasn't. It took them longer than we thought it would. We had to go back up and do it some more.

MacArthur's attack relieved the pressure of a Japanese offensive against the Australian airfield at Wau in Papua New Guinea, bypassing many of their defenses. Halsey's force, on the other hand, came under fierce attack by Japanese land, air, and naval forces. The ground battles bogged down in the face of fierce resistance and one of the divisional commanders of an American National Guard division was relieved. However, by the end of August, the U.S. Army had had secured Munda.

Colonel Franklin T. Hallam, an Army surgeon with XIV Corps, describes the army troops' exhaustion near the end of the New Georgia campaign, including what are now recognized as symptoms of post-traumatic stress disorder.

At least 50 percent of these individuals requiring medical attention or entering medical installations were the picture of utter exhaustion: face expressionless, knees sagging, body bent forward, arms slightly flexed and hanging loosely, feet dragging, and an overall appearance of apathy and physical exhaustion. About 20 percent of the total group were highly excited, crying, wringing their hands, mumbling incoherently, an expression of utter fright or fear, trembling all over, startled at the least sound or unusual commotion, having the appearance of trying to escape impending disaster. Another 15 percent showed manifestations of various types of true psychoneurotic complexes: insomnia, bad dreams, frequency of urination,

BELOW: An American soldier examines a bunkered Type 41 regimental gun on Munda. This 75mm field piece—originally designed as an easily transported "mountain gun"—was widely used by Japanese forces with as many as two dozen fielded per division by the end of the war. Munda, on the Solomon island of New Georgia, had an airfield critical to the success of CARTWHEEL. Halsey's forces found a very tough fight on their hands and got bogged down in jungle combat against determined defenders in bunkers like this one.

BELOW: A tractor driver struggling to bulldoze a road through the New Georgia jungle in October 1943 appears uninterested in smiling for the camera. The soldier, a member of the 65th Engineer Regiment, is being guarded by a squad of infantry because of the danger from snipers.

The Japs were dug in, they were all underground, and I think that although you beat on them from the air like the devil, they are going to be hard to take whenever you hit them on the ground. Of course, I am not much of a ground tactician. I don't know much about the ground fighting out there, except that we all thought Munda was beat down to such a state that it would be easy. It turned out that it wasn't. It took them longer than we thought it would. We had to go back up and do it some more.

—Lieutenant George Gay

irritability, diminished ability to concentrate, and a generally reduced efficiency in the performance of assigned duties.

Throughout Halsey's operations, a number of fierce naval surface battles occurred—Vella Gulf and Vella Lavella, among others—but more and more the Japanese found themselves faced with rapidly improving American naval surface forces that gave as good as they got in some fierce night actions—the kind of fighting that the IJN had clearly dominated before. Halsey's next step was to bypass the Japanese defending the airfield on Kolombangara island and land on the almost undefended Vella Lavella further north, which had a better airfield anyway. Once this field was operational, the threat from the air diminished rapidly and fighters from the Vella Lavella fields could now provide some escort to bombers flying raids against Rabaul. It was about this time that MacArthur decided he need not capture Rabual in order to neutralize it.

MacArthur pushed on toward the Huon Peninsula, which poked like a finger toward Rabaul from New Guinea. Using an airstrip he had built in secret, MacArthur first destroyed the preponderance of Japanese airpower in the area and then landed near the key villages of Lae and Salamaua. His forces also conducted the first operational parachute assault of the war in seizing a nearby airbase. By mid-September 1943, both objectives were in Allied hands. MacArthur, advancing his timetable, then pre-empted a Japanese move to beef up their garrison at Finschhafen, New Guinea, by landing an Australian brigade first. After some very hard fighting, the town was captured and all subsequent attempts to recapture it—including one of the last Japanese amphibious attacks of the war—were defeated.

General George C. Kenney commander of the 5th Air Force comments on the difficulties of providing close air support during this campaign.

As in the Papuan campaign, we will keep on—first gaining local air control...[then] bombing and strafing to kill off the enemy and prevent his getting supplies and reinforcements. This part goes through quite rapidly. Eventually, however, the troops get in close contact in an area so restricted that if we bomb, we kill both our troops and the Japs.

An anonymous captured Japanese soldier's diary entry offered another picture of the effectiveness of close air support bombing by U.S. pilots and accurate artillery fire during the fight for Salamaua.

The shelling and bombing while I was at Salamaua were beyond words. Positions taken up by friendly troops were bombed by the enemy at least twice a day. The number of casualties resulting from enemy shelling and bombing were increasing, but we could do nothing about it. It was entirely impossible for us to do any cooking in the daytime, as enemy planes were coming over to attack us practically the whole time. Even our movements were extremely restricted. Our artillery could not open fire. Several hundred rounds of shells would come over from enemy artillery positions if we fired even a single round. Moreover, our artillery positions would immediately be discovered and become the target for bombing; and our guns would be destroyed by enemy airplanes. Corpses were scattered all over the place.

The final step necessary for MacArthur to land near Cape Gloucester on New Britain, was given to Halsey. In the northern Solomons was the large island of Bougainville with several key Japanese airfields. Halsey was directed to take the island as a precursor to MacArthur's operations. He would not only distract the Japanese from MacArthur's upcoming thrust across the strait to Cape Gloucester, but fighters from the captured bases on Bougainville could escort both Halsey's and MacArthur's bombers in attacks against Rabaul and New Britain. Halsey initially wanted to simply take the islands adjacent to Bougainville and operate from these—thus avoiding the Japanese defenses—but in the end, the airfields on Bougainville were more promising.

To conduct this operation, Nimitz lent Halsey several of his precious aircraft carriers to contest

GEORGE C. KENNEY

RIGHT: The newly arrived 742d Antiaircraft Artillery Battalion (Colored) (Semimobile) sets up its 90mm gun at Finschhafen, New Guinea, in early June 1944. A major staging area for both the isolation of Rabaul and combat operations to the west, Base F contained two harbors, a major airfield, large hospital, and facilities for the assembly of aircraft from shipped-in components. Although Rabaul had been declared "neutralized" months earlier, periodic small-scale attacks by Kate torpedo planes based there necessitated that its airfield complex be "revisited" by B-24, P-39, and P-40 aircraft through the summer 1944, and that units like this be held in place. The 742d was kept at Base F until late November when it was moved forward to Leyte in the Philippines.

the still potent Japanese air forces from Rabaul and in the northern Solomons. The new combined fleet commander, Admiral Mineichi Koga—making the same mistake his predecessor—sent the bulk of his carrier-based air from Truk to contest Halsey's operations and defend Rabaul. The result was a punishing series of air and sea battles that erupted around Rabaul. The Japanese received the worst of it. At one point, it seemed they might successfully attack the American invasion fleet in Bougainville's Empress Augusta Bay, but hard fighting by Navy surface forces pushed them to retire. In a stroke of very good fortune, Rear Admiral Sherman's carrier aviators caught a major Japanese surface strike force in-port at Rabaul and severely mauled it—effectively eliminating any chance the Japanese had of establishing command of the sea around Bougainville under their air umbrella from

Rabaul. In late October, the U.S. Marines and New Zealanders conducted diversionary attacks on the islands around Bougainville. When the main landings came in Empress Augusta Bay that November, they went smoothly. As elsewhere, the Americans learned they need not capture the entire island, just the airfields and enough defensive terrain to extend their air reach.

Nevertheless, the Marines and the Army faced hard fighting and never completely secured the entire island, as they now understood they didn't need to.

Marine Captain Henry "Boo" Bourgeois, a Marine pilot, first with VMF-122 and then with VMF-214 [The Black Sheep Squadron] discusses his experiences flying against Japanese Zeros in the Solomons Campaign.

My first combat was in VMF-122. We were in Guadalcanal flying F4F Wildcats. We didn't have too many airplanes and the experienced pilots got all the combat flights. We had this photographic F4F7, and I flew two or three missions over Munda to take photographs and a couple of times the airplane was riddled with bullets.

Things had gotten more interesting by my second combat tour because we got brand new Corsairs. That was a great airplane—God, it was a thrill—and then back to Guadalcanal. I was flying wing for an escort mission for some SBD dive-bombers to Bougainville. There were about eighteen dive-bombers and I think we had sixteen Corsairs. We arrived over the target during a really big thunderstorm and the Japs were attacking our naval shipping. The ultimate goal was to hit the airfield and as the dive-bombers started to push over for their attack run, about twenty or thirty Japs jumped us. It started a series of dogfights that spread all over the sky—maybe 10 miles by 10 miles. The Japs got on my tail and I went into this cloud to get away. But it came back out—a Zero—right in front of me, maybe 100 yards at the most, just sitting there. I blasted him and then I went back into the cloud because they were after me again. I shot two Zeros down that day.

BELOW: "Launch the Ready!" Marine pilots of the "Black Sheep" Squadron (VMF-214) sprint from the ad hoc ready-room in their parachute rigger's tent to man their F4U Corsairs during a September 1943 alert. From left to right they are: Bill Case (wearing Australian boots), Rollie Rinabarger, John Begert, and Henry "Boo" Bourgeois.

ABOVE: Flaps splayed wide, a "Black Sheep" Corsair touches down on the white coral runway of their Turtle Bay airstrip after a mission during the CARTWHEEL air battles. Located on Espiritu Santo, southeast of Guadalcanal, Turtle Bay was one of numerous fighter strips used by VMF-214 as U.S. forces fought their way up "The Slot."

General Oscar W. Griswold, commander of the XIV Corps, discusses the crowding at one of the small islands used as a logistics staging base just off one of the main invasion beaches at Bougainville.

Puruata Island was so heavily loaded down it was about to sink. All beaches were congested. No long-range supply road system had been planned. Longhand carry [basically manual stevedore work] was the rule, particularly in the Marine division sector for the frontline troops. Forward ration dumps, ammunition and bomb dumps, gasoline dumps, hospital areas and bomb shelters for the same, beach developments, interior supply roads, the service command area itself, a central cemetery, refrigeration,

sawmills, drainage ditches, and a myriad of other things were nonexistent, and not even visualized. Space for all these things had to be carved out of the virgin jungle.

P-38 pilot Captain Perry J. Dahl remembers dogfighting against great odds during the CARTWHEEL air battles and the very high skill—and poor tactics—of some of his Japanese adversaries.

For example, keeping up a high air speed [for the P-38] was something that they found out in the theater. By the time I got over there—which was fairly early in the war, I am thinking about October, I guess, of 1943—we were in Guadalcanal six months before "Pappy" Boyington's [Major, later Colonel, Gregory R.

Boyington] guys got in there, and when we went in there, the enemy order of battle would be like a hundred or more Zeros and we would go in with eighteen P-38s, and they'd have all their dudes airborne too. That's why the guys learned real quick—boy, you've got to keep that air speed up, and you can't turn with a Zero—there is nothing that can turn with a Zero—so you are an idiot to get down and try to do it.

I always swore, and I still think it's true, that if a Zero pilot ever saw you, you'd never shoot him down. What we'd do, we'd sandwich him, and he'd be turning away from one guy and the other pilot would nail him. There were four of us one day that caught one little lone Oscar [Nakajima Ki-43 fighter], and that was the lightest, most maneuverable Zero they made—it only had two .30-caliber guns on it—but we made passes on that Oscar for over forty minutes. I came home with a hole in my prop—we never touched him, and all four of us just gave up and flew back home. And this guy was so sharp. When you'd line up and start to fire at him, he could turn into you, he could dance on the rudders and that airplane could just turn around and fly back underneath itself almost. It was just remarkable they could do inside loops, really a fantastic, maneuverable little airplane.

But they gave up something to get that of course; they gave up armament, speeds, and things like that. They weren't stressed for it. Because when you hit one of those dudes, it blew up. I mean *right now*. If you hit her right, it really went. They had unprotected fuel tanks. Oftentimes you'd hit a Zero and a belt of flames would come out at you, and you'd say, "Oh boy, I got a flamer," you know. But it was only the fuel from that one tank that you punctured, and he'd fly right on. They were very vulnerable.

You'd have to say that the Tony [Kawasaki Ki-61] was the best airplane all around. In my judgment, by the time the Tony came along, their good combat pilots had all been depleted and as a result they didn't perform as well as they should. But I'll tell you, in the early part of the war they had some real, real good pilots, and the reason they lost the war, the air battle—aside from maybe logistics and a few things like that—is that they employed poor tactics. I think they had good pilots, I think

they had good equipment, but their tactics were deplorable.

I couldn't often tell whether it was a flight of Zeros or a flock of buzzards. And what's more undisciplined than a flock of buzzards? Quite often, of course, I saw them fly in formation. And you would go in there, dive through their formation and you'd scatter them to the winds. We never broke them to less than an element and by doing this, of course, we criss-crossed each other's tails, and you could fly through a hundred of those dang guys and keep each other clear and come through unscathed. As a result, in my judgment, they felt that the name of the game was to get into a one-on-one dogfight situation and we didn't play their game. We didn't dogfight with them, and we didn't let them get one-on-one. We maintained our two-aircraft element integrity.

ABOVE: First Lieutenant Perry J. Dahl and crew chief of the 475th "Satan's Angels" Fighter Group. One of the Army Air Force's youngest aces of the war, Dahl piloted P-38 Lightnings and later flew combat missions in both Korea and Vietnam. A "NO STEP" warning has been painted along the starboard side of his cockpit because too much pressure on the edge could warp the thin metal strip making the canopy difficult to slide—a potentially lethal situation.

ABOVE: B-25s drop "parafrag" bombs along a line of Kawasaki Ki-61-I Tony fighters at a Japanese airfield near Dagua, New Guinea, in February 1943. Use of parachutes allowed extremely accurate low-level attacks by slowing the descent of ordnance long enough for aircraft to get clear of their blast. A single bomber's parafrag run would shower shrapnel along a quarter-mile length.

RIGHT: Allied aircraft employ white phosphorus munitions against parked Japanese planes at one of the airstrips around Rabaul. White phosphorus, which burns long and at very high temperatures, is well suited to destroying clustered targets such as aircraft.

With the Japanese fully distracted by Bougainville, General MacArthur launched his assaults across the strait between New Guinea and New Britain in December. He landed at two locations—the small offshore island of Arawe and Cape Gloucester where the veteran First Marine Division of Guadalcanal fame stormed ashore unopposed the day after Christmas. Despite horrendous weather conditions, the Marines and Army moved inland to secure their defensive perimeters and airfields. By February 1944, fighters were flying missions from airfields on New Britain. Kenney and Halsey's aircraft punished Rabaul throughout these operations and by late February, Imperial Japanese Headquarters decided to leave only ground forces to defend the bastion. By April, Rabaul's airfield's were no longer usable or defensible. The allies, secure in their defensive positions, simply left the Japanese ground forces—now without naval or air support—to their own devices. Rabaul was no longer of any importance.

Colonel Frederick Smith recounts a humorous episode and the importance of "being prepared" during the Arawe operation.

So the troops had to wade ashore against little or no opposition, but they had to wade ashore, and they lost clothing since the boats couldn't carry it in and they hadn't planned on packing everything. So I got an emergency message from the commander of this regimental combat team directing me to drop the complete complement of regimental combat team in the clothing allowance prescribed in Army regulations…socks… underwear…I sent a message to him and told him that we would work with the advance supply depot at a town near Buna… and that we would drop what they thought he needed. And now I did a smart-aleck thing; I also dropped a Boy Scout handbook, which that colonel didn't appreciate one darn bit. Anyway, the Arawe expedition did nothing; it just frittered the effort away, sitting on the south side.

Captain Dahl remembers almost being cut in half by a B-24 propeller during the Cape Gloucester, New Britain operation.

We were on an air-to-ground mission over in Cape Gloucester. The Marines were about to get pushed off the landing strip there, so we were strafing the strip. Our forces were on one side and the Japanese were on the other side,

ABOVE: Marines hit 3 feet of rough water as they exit the ramp of their LST on December 26, 1943, to reinforce the American perimeter at Cape Gloucester, New Britain.

BELOW: Soldiers clearing the Munda airstrip take cover beneath a derelict Ki-21-II Sally medium bomber at the end of the runway. Note the M1 Garand rifle and entrenching tools at center bottom. The New Georgia campaign, under Halsey's command, was fought primarily to extend U.S. air power into the central Solomons as the Americans "climbed the ladder" toward Bougainville. The primary target of the 43d Infantry Division that invaded Munda on July 9, 1943, was the seizure of the Japanese airfield that had been used to bomb Henderson Field during the Guadalcanal campaign.

and even the Seabees were fighting. When we came back we got caught in the weather and had to go down very low trying to get underneath the clouds because none of us were very experienced IFR pilots; we didn't have anything but needle, ball, airspeed, and DF [direction finding] steers. We were all sneaking along underneath the overcast, right above the water, and we made a turn. One kid caught his wing tip in the water, and he cartwheeled in.

We went by the landing strip at Cape Gloucester. It was high noon, but it was so dark because the weather was so bad that everybody was going around with lights on the jeeps. This was a strip that the Marines had just taken, and there was one B-24 off on the runway. So I caught a glimpse of the strip. I lost the guy in front of me, I don't know who was behind me. Like I say, we were in snake formation. So I broke left and kept this airfield in sight and as I circled around they had a tower there and they gave me a green light on the tower. So I came around and dropped my gear and landed.

It turned out that the problem was they gave the green light, but they gave the green light to the guy in the B-24 on the runway waiting to take off. So I met him about midway. The water was 6 to 8 inches deep on the pierced steel planking [of the runway]. I saw him—and it was so black and dark, and heavy rain—I saw him just before I hit him, so I gunned one engine because I was going nose to nose with him and I went through his number one and two prop. So I just kept my head down, his prop hit—once in front of the cockpit and once behind it. I was going down the runway backwards and I ran off the end of the runway. There was a gorge and just a deluge of water. I crawled up and jumped off the leading edge of the wing and that airplane just washed out to sea. So I went back and the guy says, "Where is your airplane?" and I said, "I don't know, I lost it someplace." Nobody really cared very much, you know. The flying safety officer never came around. They just gave me a new airplane.

The Central Pacific Drive

Another reason for the Imperial Japanese Headquarters' decision to write off Rabaul was the unanticipated shock of Nimitz's campaign in the central Pacific. The Japanese had been "robbing Peter to pay Paul" and now they needed to pay Peter back. U.S. Navy and Marine Corps planners in the interwar period had foreseen a methodical step-by-step naval campaign that would advance through the Central Pacific island groups of the Marshalls and Carolines. The Carolines were the location of the major Japanese naval and airbase at Truk, one of the pillars (like Rabaul) of the Japanese defense perimeter. Once airfields were captured or built, they would advance to the next island group. Ultimately the plan foresaw a seizure of the Mariana Islands, including the recapture of Guam. It was also anticipated that a major

naval battle would take place somewhere in the vicinity of the Marianas. From there, the U.S. would have several options, including the invasion of the Philippines, Formosa, and eventually Japan. Nimitz had been conducting raids—most famously against Makin Island—but was not ready to begin operations until November 1943. Sideshows like the Aleutians operations had used valuable equipment needed for this offensive and so delayed its execution.

The Japanese had seized the Gilbert Islands from the British at the outbreak of the war. Because the Gilbert Islands were situated on the flank of any advance against the Marshalls, Navy planners felt it imperative to neutralize them prior to the main effort against the Marshalls as well as the Caroline and Mariana archipelagos. Nimitz's first major naval offensive opened with the seizure of the heavily defended islands in the Tarawa atoll of the Gilberts, especially Betio, on November 20. This

ABOVE: "Lady Lex" packs the deck. American SBD Dauntless dive-bombers are parked "nose-to-tail" aboard the USS *Lexington* (CV-16) following a raid on the Gilbert Islands. This *Lexington* had a long operational life, undergoing conversion to a training carrier in the 1960s. Generations of naval aviators remember her fondly, or perhaps not so fondly, as the site of their first arrested carrier landing. She was active in this role until 1992 and is still afloat as a museum in Corpus Christi, Texas.

operation, code-named GALVANIC, was an inauspicious and bloody opening to the campaign. Although the Marines had a sound doctrine for amphibious assault, they had very little practical experience assaulting across the reef-enclosed archipelagos in their path and were short of critical equipment like amphibious tractors (amtracs) that could cross the reefs at high or low tide. Many things went wrong and Tarawa was a slaughter that shocked the American public—and the Marines. However, the Japanese commander defended the beaches and wasted his troops in suicidal banzai charges. Less than a dozen Japanese were captured out of a garrison of almost 5,000; almost 3,500 Marines had been killed or wounded during the ferocious three-day battle.

Time *magazine correspondent Robert Sherrod went in with the Marines to Red Beach on D-Day at Tarawa. Here he describes the terror of wading across long stretches of water from the reef to the beach.*

No sooner had we hit the water than the Japanese machine guns really opened up on us. It was painfully slow, wading in such deep water. And we had 700 yards to walk slowly into that machine gun fire, looming into larger targets as we rose onto higher ground. I was scared, as I had never been scared before. Those who were not hit would always remember how the machine gun bullets hissed into the water, inches to the right, inches to the left. I could have sworn that I could have reached out

LEFT: Marines shelter behind the sea wall as they assist fallen comrades during the confusion and chaos ashore at RED BEACH 3 at Tarawa. Many others simply never made it ashore, especially if they were in a Higgins boat since these vessels could not make it over the reef. Marines then had to wade or swim in their heavy gear through the nearly 1,000 yards of machine-gun covered water between the reef and the beach.

BELOW: Nowhere to hide. Marines going in with cold steel (bayonets fixed) and entrenching tools at Tarawa in November 1943. The Marines suffered nearly 3,500 casualties in three days, their bloodiest battle in history, at this tiny atoll in the Gilberts.

BELOW: Marines scramble atop a bomb-proof Japanese shelter constructed of sand and palm tree logs, and which probably still contains live Imperial Marines. These men of the 8th Marine Regiment's 2d Battalion, including a flame-thrower team near the peak, have formed an impromptu firing line along the crest facing another such structure located just forward of the palm tree nearly hidden by smoke at the center of the photo.

and touched a hundred bullets. I remember chuckling inside and saying aloud, "You bastards, you certainly are lousy shots."

The American amphibious operations in the Gilbert Island group included the assault on Makin Island by the U.S. Army's 165th Regimental Combat Team of the 27th Division, plus some attached combat and combat support units. An anonymous sergeant remembers bringing his tank ashore.

We went forward about 25 yards and hit a shell hole [under the water]. We got out of that and went about 15 yards more and hit another. The water was about 7 feet deep and our tank drowned out. The tank immediately filled with smoke after hitting the second shell hole. My driver said the tank was on fire. The crew dismounted right there with great speed through the right sponson door. I remained inside the tank. As soon as the crew got out of the tank, they were machine-gunned from the shore and, with more speed, they came back inside the tank. Something like an hour and a half later, we were picked up by an alligator [their nickname for the LVT, Landing Vehicle Tracked].

The water was about 7 feet deep and our tank drowned out. The tank immediately filled with smoke after hitting the second shell hole. My driver said the tank was on fire. The crew dismounted right there with great speed through the right sponson door. I remained inside the tank. As soon as the crew got out of the tank, they were machine gunned from the shore and, with more speed, they came back inside the tank.

—An Anonymous Soldier

BELOW: A tank crew awaits a tow for their M4A2 Sherman tank, which has been immobilized by a hidden shell hole just yards from shore. A piece of its 75mm gun barrel has also been shot away. Dotting the reef lie thin-skinned LVT(1)s—victims of Japanese defensive fires—and clumps of debris and fallen Marines who drifted up against a shallow fence designed to keep flotsam off the shore.

LEFT: Tankers viewed from farther along the beach over the bodies of other 2d Marine Regiment infantry who had almost reached the land.

Smoking out snipers that were in the trees was the worst part of it. We could not spot them, even with [field] glasses and it made our advance very slow. When we moved forward it was a skirmish line, with each man being covered as he rushed from cover to cover. That meant that every man spent a large part of his time on the ground. While at prone, we carefully studied the trees and the ground. If one of our men began to fire rapidly into a tree or ground location, we knew that he had spotted a sniper, and those who could see the tree took up the fire. When we saw no enemy, we fired occasional shots into trees that looked likely.

THIS PAGE: Soldiers of the 165th Infantry Regiment, 27th Infantry Division, assaulting Butaritari Atoll's YELLOW BEACH 2, find it slow going in the coral bottomed waters. Japanese machine-gun fire from the right flank makes it even more dicey, but Japanese defenses were much weaker here than on Tarawa. Butaritari is immediately adjacent to Makin Atoll in the Gilbert Islands, and both were assaulted simultaneously with the Marine operation on November 20, 1943.

7TH INFANTRY DIVISION

Amphibious assaults on American territory—the Aleutian Islands of Attu and Kiska—were the 7th Infantry Division's opening actions in the Pacific war in May, then August of 1943. Subsequently, elements of the 7th captured islands in the Kwajalein atoll during a week of fighting beginning on January 31, 1944, while others struck Eniwetok Atoll on February 18. The division landed on the Philippine island of Leyte on October 20, securing airstrips at Dulag, San Pablo, and Buri after heavy fighting. The 7th shifted to the west coast of the island in November and attacked north, capturing Valencia on Christmas Day, 1944. On April 1, 1945, the division stormed ashore on Okinawa against deceptively weak resistance, which was followed by brutal—and extremely costly—hill fighting that raged for fifty-one days on Kochi Ridge, the Shuri Line, and across the southern third of the island.

I worked my way slowly forward, hugging the ground. I could see the muzzle of the gun, projecting beyond the pit, but it did not seem to be manned. I rushed the pit, jumped in and seized the machine gun to swing it around and face it down the connecting trench, but it wouldn't fire. I dropped the machine gun and grabbed my rifle. Three Japs in the trench, a short distance from me, were beginning to stir. They looked as if they had been stunned by an explosion. So I shot them. Then I walked down the trench and came to an object, well covered with palm leaves. I pulled the leaves back and discovered a much-alive Jap soldier. So I shot him also. The rest of the platoon came up and took over.

Admiral Nimitz did not let Tarawa cause him to shy from the task at hand. The lessons learned at Tarawa were used to change tactics and doctrine, and now Nimitz pushed his forces against the Kwajalein atoll in the Marshall Islands for the next "step-by-step" advance. By late January 1944, Nimitz was ready to go against the Marshalls. The 4th Marine division tackled the sand spit-linked islands of Roi and Namur on the northern part of the Kwajalein atoll and the Army's 7th Infantry Division attacked the main island of Kwajalein in the south, for which the atoll is named.

This time, both equipment and doctrine were more than equal to the task and overwhelming sea-based air support was provided by the new fast carrier task forces of Vice Admiral Raymond Spruance's 5th Fleet.

In this part of the Pacific, the land bases were few and far between and often the few airbases the Japanese had could be overwhelmed and neutralized simply by the carrier aircraft aboard Spruance's fleet. The Japanese Navy, bloodied with virtually no meaningful naval air power, barely contested these operations. Too, the naval gunfire support from the escorting surface ships obliterated Japanese beach defenses, cutting down on the casualties of the assault waves. The Japanese soon learned that to defend at the beaches, contrary to the experience at Tarawa, was a virtual guarantee of defeat.

The holes were everywhere. Each one had to be searched from close up. Every spot where a man might be hiding had to be stabbed out [with KA-BAR knives or bayonets]. So greatly was the beach littered with broken foliage that it was like looking through a haystack for a few poisoned needles.

The fire cut the men down came from the spider hole farther up the line. It was the kind of bitter going that made it necessary for the junior leaders to prod their men constantly. The leader of the 3d Squad had been trying to get his men forward against the fire. Private First Class John Treager got up, rushed forward about 10 yards, hit the dirt, fired a few shots with his BAR [Browning Automatic Rifle], and crumpled with a bullet in his head.

BELOW: 7th Infantry Division armor in action on Marshall Islands' Kwajalein atoll in February 1944. The invasion of Kwajalein was a masterpiece of planning and execution, employing many of the lessons learned the hard way at Tarawa. The M10 tank destroyer in the background at left was an ideal "bunker-buster" with its high muzzle velocity, 76.2mm (3-inch) gun that was produced not for island warfare, but for battling German panzers. An M4 Sherman medium tank appears to be just in front of the larger M10, possibly serving to suppress machine gun fire for the infantry and open-topped tank destroyer. The soldier in the foreground is operating an M1919 30 caliber light machine gun.

Somewhat farther along, a bayonet was seen sticking up through a patch of fronds. The Jap crouched within it hadn't room to draw in the whole length of the weapon. Private First Class Edward Fiske fired his BAR at the hole; the dried fronds caught fire from the tracers. At that point, Fiske ran out of ammunition.

Private First Class Julian Gutierrez then took up the fire with his M1 [rifle]. He stood directly above the hole and fired down into it. Then the hole exploded; the Jap inside had turned a grenade on himself. A man's shattered arm came flying out of the hole and hit Gutierrez on the shoulder, splattering blood all over his face and clothing. The arm bounced off and fell to the side. As Gutierrez looked at it, fascinated and horror-stricken, he saw another bayonet rising out of a patch of fronds just beyond the outstretched and still quivering fingers. He yelled to a man behind him. The man relayed a grenade and Gutierrez pitched it with all of his might into the patch of fronds. It erupted in a shower of palm leaves and blood and flesh.

Gutierrez reeled over toward the lagoon to cleanse himself of the blood. Before he could reach the water, in sight of all the other men, he vomited all over the beach. Minutes passed before he could gather himself together again.

While the Army's 7th Division had responsibility for the southern islands in the Kwajalein atoll, the 4th Marine Division had responsibility for the northern islands of Roi and Namur (today just one island, filled in over time to ease airbase and rocket station test operations), Marine Private First Class Robert F. Graf recalls his thoughts on the night before the amphibious landing.

LEFT: Sherman medium tank during the Kwajalein operation with its supporting infantry clearing the way out front. Operation FLINTLOCK, was launched on January 31, 1944, and the island was declared secured four days later.

As I thought of the landing that I would be making on the morrow, I was both excited and anxious. Yes, I thought of death, but I wasn't afraid. Somehow I couldn't see myself as dead. "Why wasn't there fear?" I wondered. Even though I was nervous, it was with excitement, not fear. Instead there was a thrill. I was headed for great adventure, where I had wanted to be. This was just an adventure. It was

"grown up" cowboys and Indians. Thoughts of glory were in my mind that night. Now it was my turn to "carry the flag" into battle. It was my turn to be a part of history. To top it all off, I was going into battle with the United States Marines. Just prior to falling asleep, I prayed. My prayers were for courage, for my family, and I prayed to stay alive.

 Marine Lieutenant John C. Chapin remembers the assault with the 23rd Marines on Roi.

By now everything was all mixed up, with our assault wave all entangled with the armored tractors [LVTs] ahead of us. I ordered my driver to maneuver around them. Slowly we inched past, as their 37mm guns and .50 cal machine guns flamed. The beach lay right before us. However, it was shrouded in such a pall of dust and smoke from our bombardment that we could see very little of it. As a result, we were unable to tell which section we were approaching (after all our hours of careful planning, based hitting the beach at one exact spot!)

I turned to talk to my platoon sergeant, who was manning the machine gun right

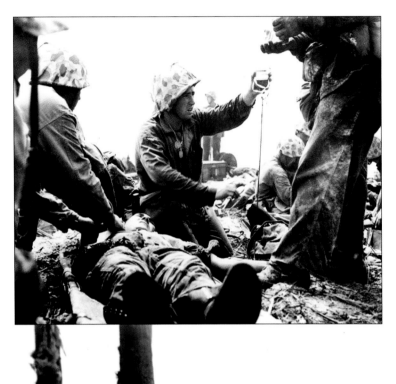

beside me. He was slumped over—the whole right side of his head disintegrated into a mass of gore. Up to now, the entire operation had seemed almost like a movie or like one of the innumerable practice landings we'd made. Now one of my men lay in a welter of blood beside me, and the reality of it smashed into my consciousness.

🎤 *Roi and Namur were linked by a narrow strip of land that separated the two coral landmasses. The 24th Marines were responsible for Namur. Private Graf, now bloodied by combat, recalls his first night on the island.*

Throughout the night the fleet sent flares skyward, lighting the islands as the flares drifted with the prevailing wind. Ghostly flickering light was cast from the flares as they drifted along on their parachutes. Laying in our foxhole, my buddy and I were watching, waiting, and straining our ears trying to filter out the known sounds.

Our foxhole in that sand was about 6 feet long by 2 feet deep, and just about wide enough to hold the two of us. Since I had eaten only my D ration since leaving the ship, I was hungry. D rations were bittersweet chocolate bars about an inch-and-a-half square and were supposed to be full of energy. I removed a

BELOW: "Jungle Jim" turned out to be a somewhat inappropriate name for this Marine Sherman, as there was very little jungle left to crash through during the closing phases of the battle for Namur. Note the thick wood boards cut to fit along the side of the hull to increase crew survivability.

27TH INFANTRY DIVISION
NEW YORK NATIONAL GUARD

Elements of the 27th took part in the capture of the Gilbert Islands' Makin Atoll in November 1943, and Eniwetok Atoll in February 1944. Later that year the division took part in the Marianas Campaign, seizing Saipan's Aslito Airfield in June but was partially overrun during a massive banzai attack on July 7, before organized Japanese resistance was crushed the next day. During the Okinawa Campaign, it assaulted the outer belt of the Shuri Line in mid-April, seized the dominating Kakazu ridgeline south of Machinato, and then captured Machinato Airfield on April 28 after a costly struggle. The 27th attacked from the south end of Ishikawa Isthmus to sweep the northern sector of Okinawa with the Japanese fighting bitterly on Onnatake Hill from May 23 to June 2, before losing the strong point. The division reached the northern tip of Okinawa on August 4, 1945.

K ration from my pack and opened it. K rations came in a box about the size of a Cracker Jack box and had a waterproof coating. These rations contained a small tin of powdered coffee or lemonade, some round hard candies, a package of three cigarettes, and a tin about the size of a tuna-fish can containing either cheese, hash, or eggs with a little bacon. We dined on our rations, drank water from our canteens, and prepared to settle in for the night.

After finishing chow we elected to take two-hour watches, one on guard while the other slept. Also, we made sure we knew where our buddies' foxholes were, both on the left and right of us. Thus we were set up so that anyone to our front would be an enemy.

Kwajalein, despite the intense combat described earlier, turned out to be a masterpiece of military economy and efficiency. Both land and carrier aviation had been softening it

up for more than a month. For the cost of about 800 American lives, Nimitz had secured a major anchorage and operating base in the central Pacific. The success was so overwhelming that Nimitz intuitively moved his timetable rapidly forward and in a follow-on operation seized the important, but lightly defended Eniwetok atoll some 300 miles further west later in February. The assault had originally been scheduled for May. This time, the air support came entirely from Spruance's fast carriers. In order to cover the Eniwetok landings, Spruance pushed west with his fast carriers and their escorts to neutralize the Japanese fleet and air at Truk in the Carolines. The result was a virtual Pearl Harbor in reverse at the same time that the amphibious forces were landing on Eniwetok (February 17). Much of the Combined Fleet had already been pulled back from Truk, but almost 200,000 tons of warship and merchant tonnage were sunk during a punishing series of naval air attacks with more than 270 enemy aircraft destroyed. Truk, like Rabaul, had been neutralized and the Americans decided there was no need to capture it. Thus yet another pattern was established for the remainder of the central Pacific drive: punishing carrier air attacks followed by naval bombardments just prior to a strong amphibious assault.

Much of the success in the central Pacific can be explained as a happy consequence of the sustained offensives in 1943 by MacArthur and Halsey. When Nimitz and Spruance struck in the central Pacific, the Japanese were unprepared defensively with much of their combat power already fighting in the south and southwest. Similarly, as the Japanese reacted to Nimitz in the north, they had to withdraw and retrench in the south—actions that rendered Rabaul and Truk irrelevant.

🎙 *Marine Second Lieutenant Cord Meyer, Jr., wrote home about his experience during the capture of the Eniwetok Atoll by the 22d Marines.*

We were hard hit there, and with terrible clarity the reality of the event came home to me. I had crawled forward to ask a Marine where the Japs were—pretty excited really and enjoying it almost like a game. I crawled up beside him, but he wouldn't answer. Then I saw the ever-widening pool of dark blood by his head and knew that he was dying or dead. So it came over me what this war was, and after that it wasn't fun or exciting, but something that had to be done.

Fortune smiled on me that day, or the hand of a Divine Providence was over me, or I was just plain lucky. We killed many of them in fighting that lasted to nightfall. We cornered fifty or so Imperial [Japanese] Marines on the end of the island, where they attempted a banzai charge, but we cut them down like overripe wheat, and they lay like tired children with their faces in the sand.

That night was unbelievably terrible. There were many of them left and they all had one fanatical notion, and that was to take one of us with them. We dug in with the order to kill anything that moved. I kept

ABOVE: SBD Dauntless dive-bombers have finished their April 29, 1944, mission against Japan's Param Airfield in the Truk Atoll, and are headed for home. These aircraft are from Admiral Raymond Spruance's fast carriers that were used to neutralize the massive Japanese base at Truk in much the same way that Halsey and Kenney used land-based airpower to neutralize Rabaul. The Japanese lost an incredible amount of logistical shipping during Spruance's 1944 raids on the stronghold.

watch in a foxhole with my sergeant, and we both stayed awake all night with a knife in one hand and a grenade in the other. They crept in among us, and every bush or rock took on sinister proportions. They got some of us, but in the morning they all lay about, some with their riddled bodies actually inside our foxholes. With daylight it was easy for us and we finished them off. Never have I been so glad to see the blessed sun.

The time has come to manifest our knighthood with the pure brilliance of the sword. It is our duty to erase the mortifications of our brothers at Guadalcanal. Attack! Assault! Destroy everything!

—Lieutenant General Haruyoshi Hyakutake, commander of the Japanese forces on Bougainville

Chapter Six

THE DUAL ADVANCE CONTINUES

By early 1944 Japan was on the horns of a strategic dilemma, only in China and Burma were her military efforts still successful—but even in these two vast theaters she was still not ultimately victorious. Should she attempt to knock Great Britain out of the war by capturing India? Should she resume offensive operations in China and finally conquer that country? Or should she gamble on a decisive naval victory that would bring the Americans to their senses and the negotiating table? The Japanese Army argued for knockout blows in both China and India. The Imperial Navy, not surprisingly, argued for a single decisive victory in the defense of the Marianas Islands, which would surely be the Americans' next objective. Typically, the Japanese decided to attempt all three.

The Americans, too, were faced with difficult choices—both in the European Theater and in the Pacific. The American leaders were already looking beyond New Guinea and the Marianas, which were both expected to finally fall in late 1944, to the invasion of either Formosa or the Philippine Islands in 1945. In this way, Japan's sea lines of communication to her new conquests in Southeast Asia and Indonesia would be cut once and for all. As these debates raged, Japan's Pacific Empire seized with

WHEELER B. LIPES

PREVIOUS PAGES: Deck crewmen were unsung heroes of the carrier battles that raged across the Pacific, often working 18 to 20 hours a day arming, refueling, moving, and maintaining the aircraft critical to carrier operations. Here, ordnancemen rearm an SBD Dauntless and, at lower right, work on its bomb-release mechanism while other deck crew grab some shut-eye in the shade of nearby aircraft.

With a maximum speed on only 255mph in level flight, the Dauntless was vulnerable to enemy fighters and carried a rear gunner operating twin 30-cal Browning machine guns to help even the odds. The 30-cal, however, had a low rate of fire. So low, as this photo shows, that the red-tipped tracers are placed every other round instead of every fifth as on machine guns with a higher rate of fire. Note the tie-downs attached to the ring at the base of the aircraft's tailhook.

RIGHT: An appendectomy performed by Pharmacist's Mate Thomas Moore aboard the submarine *Silversides* was very similar to the one performed by the *Seadragon*'s Wheeler B. Lipes. Pharmacist's Mates were the de facto doctors on the hot, cramped subs prowling the vast reaches of the Pacific. The photographs were taken with the only camera on board the *Silversides*, a Kodak Medalist.

little cost, was now being recaptured at great cost. Her naval aviation was emaciated, her other air forces dwindling, her veteran pilots dead or cut off in remote bases, and hundreds of thousands of ground troops were isolated and slowly starving on literally dozens of bypassed islands—the largest of which was their garrison at Rabaul. The Americans, though, much like the Japanese, continued offensive operations on both fronts—although Nimitz's Central Pacific drive seemed to get the balance of the resources.

Vice Admiral Shigeru Fukudome discusses the difficult position of the Japanese Navy as it battled against multiple Allied offensives across the southwestern and central Pacific.

In November, as Bougainville landing operations commenced, he [the new Combined Fleet Commander Admiral Mineichi Koga] was forced to send his air strength to Rabaul. As it turned out, practically all of them were lost at Rabaul and Bougainville. Consequently, the Fleet air strength was almost completely lost, and although the Gilberts fight appeared to be the last chance for a decisive fight, the act that the Fleet's air strength had been so badly depleted enabled us to send only very small air support to Tarawa and Makin. The almost complete loss of carrier planes was a mortal blow to the Fleet since

it would require six months for replacement. In the interim, any fighting with the carrier force was rendered impossible.

In the meantime, the Americans had fixed the problems with their torpedoes and the Pacific Submarine Command led by Vice Admiral Charles A. Lockwood, Jr., was conducting the most successful unrestricted submarine campaign in history. Part of Lockwood's success was his direction to his sub skippers to go after enemy escorting destroyers first and then, once the shepherd was gone, to go after the sheep. By early 1944, more than three million tons of Japanese merchant shipping had been sunk, the majority of it during the submarine offensive. By the end of the war, U.S. submarines had sunk over five million tons of Japanese shipping. The Japanese would soon be without a merchant marine to maintain their far-flung empire.

Pharmacist's Mate Wheeler B. Lipes, aboard the submarine USS Seadragon, *recalls an appendectomy at sea during a patrol in September 1942.*

I had been up on the watch and when I came down to the after battery section of the submarine—the crew's compartment—I found Darrell Rector. It was his nineteenth birthday. He said to me, "Hey Doc, I don't feel very good." [Both Navy Corpsman and

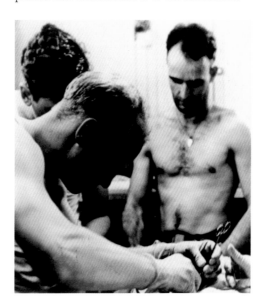

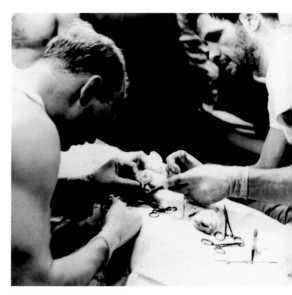

Pharmacist's Mates often went by the nickname "Doc" as they were often the only medical personnel in their units.] I told him to get into his bunk and rest a bit and kept him under observation. His temperature was rising. He had the classic symptoms of appendicitis. The abdominal muscles were getting that washboard rigidity. He then began to flex his right leg up on his abdomen to get some relief. He worsened and I went to the CO [commanding officer] to report his condition.

The skipper went back and talked to Rector explaining that there were no doctors around. Rector then said, "Whatever Lipes wants to do is okay with me." The CO and I had a long talk and he asked me what I was going to do. "Nothing," I replied. He lectured me about the fact that we were there to do the best we could. "I fire torpedoes every day and some of them miss," he reminded me. I told him that I could not fire this torpedo and miss. He asked me if I could do the surgery and I said yes. He then ordered me to do it.

When I got to the appendix, it wasn't there. I thought. "Oh my God! Is this guy reversed?" There are people like that with organs opposite where they should be. I slipped my finger down under the cecum— the blind gut—and felt it there. Suddenly I understood why it hadn't popped up where I could see it. I turned the cecum over. The

ABOVE: A 345th Bomb Group bird of prey named *Near Miss* zooms low over Japanese antiaircraft gunners taking cover during its late fall 1943 strafing attack on Rabaul. In an effort to give the dual-purpose, 75-mm guns additional elevation they have been placed on a low hill in the garrison, but far too many of the dual-purpose guns were crammed into the small area thus making them more vulnerable to a concentrated attack. Because of the reconfigured nose on *Near Miss*, this B-25C/D resembles a G model at first glance.

appendix, which was 5 inches long, was adhered, buried at the distal tip, and looked gangrenous two-thirds of the way. What luck, I thought. My first one couldn't be easy.

I detached the appendix, tied it off in two places, and then removed it after which I cauterized the stump with phenol. I then neutralized the phenol with torpedo alcohol. There was no penicillin in those days. When you

think of what we have…today to prevent infection, I marvel. We had some [sulfa] tablets that I ground into a powder and then put in the oven to kill any spores. This was all I had. I had given this kid a 3-inch incision, yet he healed well and was back on duty in a few days. In fact, the ship's cook said, "Doc, you must have sewed him up with rubber bands, the way he eats."

LEFT: Two sub aces—Morton (right) with his first executive officer, Lieutenant Richard H. O'Kane, on the bridge of *Wahoo* circa February 1943. Morton and his crew went on to sink over 55,000 confirmed tons of shipping during four war patrols, making *Wahoo* among the most famous subs of the war. Tragically, *Wahoo* was probably depth charged and sunk with the loss of all hands during a passage of the dangerous La Perouse Strait north of Hokkaido in September 1943. A postwar analysis of Japanese records points to the boat sinking an additional 13,000 tons on her last patrol, but this cannot be confirmed. O'Kane had already left *Wahoo* in July 1943 and went on to sink twenty-four Japanese ships. Captured in October 1944 when his sub, the *Tang*, was sunk off the Chinese coast, O'Kane served out the war as a POW and received the Medal of Honor after he was liberated.

BELOW: Another one for Davy Jones' Locker. Here we get a periscope-eye view of the cargo ship *Nittsu Maru* as she goes down in the Yellow Sea, another victim of Morton and the deadly crew of the *Wahoo.*

ABOVE: MacArthur aboard the light cruiser *Phoenix* with the Commander of the U.S. Seventh Fleet, the intelligent and cooperative Thomas C. Kinkaid (left), during the daring invasion of the Admiralty Islands and the bypassing of Rabaul. The commanders are observing February 28, 1944, pre-invasion bombardment of Los Negros Island from the cruiser's flag bridge. Kinkaid was only half-jokingly referred to as "MacArthur's Admiral," and his Seventh Fleet as "MacArthur's Navy." The general always maintained excellent relationships with both the admirals who served under him, as well as the Commander of the Pacific Fleet, Chester Nimitz.

Hit 'Em Where They Ain't

With the neutralization of Rabaul, General MacArthur continued his audacious campaign of amphibious and air operations, consistently bypassing or outflanking Japanese strong points. In part, MacArthur was driven by the knowledge that, to the JCS, his theater had become secondary to Nimitz's for planning and resource allocation. This was because the Mariana Islands, especially Saipan and Tinian, could provide bases for a strategic bombing campaign using the new long-range B-29 Superfortress against Japan and at a much earlier date. MacArthur was worried that Nimitz might end up in the Philippines before him!

MacArthur's advance became the great southern blade of a seemingly relentless American advance slicing along two axes to cut Japan's line of communications to her newly won strategic resources in Indonesia and Malaysia. MacArthur optimistically hoped to invade the Philippines by early 1945, but his next objective—after the partial invasion of

New Britain—was the Vogelkop Peninsula on the northwest tip of New Guinea. From there, General Kenney's air forces could provide cover and the Navy logistical support for an invasion of the southern Philippines. MacArthur's first move, typically, was to secure his northern flank against Japanese air attacks.

Acting on incorrect intelligence, MacArthur decided to seize Los Negros Island in the Admiralty Islands for its airbases and bypass the major Japanese defenses on New Ireland at Kavieng. Elements of the 1st Cavalry Division executed an amphibious assault in late February, carried aboard ships of MacArthur's new 7th Fleet commander, Vice Admiral Thomas C. Kinkaid. After some hard fighting, the Americans had secured the entire island group and its airbase by mid-March 1944. At the same time, the Japanese were wasting their dwindling combat power in trying to recapture Bougainville. The Japanese attacking at Bougainville were outnumbered two to one by the American defenders and suffered much the same fate as they had at Guadalcanal— total defeat—all to no purpose.

Captain George Frederick was an Army pilot assigned to coordinate Allied air support for the 1st Cavalry Division operations on the Admiralty Islands. Here he describes his efforts to coordinate close air support by the Royal Australian Air Force (RAAF) for the 7th and 8th Cavalry regiments on Manus Island, including his risky and courageous actions in positioning smoking pots beyond the front lines to mark the American front lines while the bombing was already underway.

March 25 at 0530, left for Lorengau with Lieutenant King, two men and [Squadron Leader] Hannigan of the RAAF. Arrived at the front line of 7th Cav at 0745 and gained contact with "Wingpoo" [RAAF Wing Commander Stoege] who was leading flights [Allied aircraft]. All went according to plan. Twelve bombers [arrived] at 0800 with smoke pots marking our line when planes said okay. I was ahead of the smoke pots to make sure the planes were doing okay. One bomb hit 200 yards short of the objective [Japanese front lines], about 200 yards from me. At 0815, twelve more dive-bombed (our troops withdrew 500 yards prior to bombing, so planes could hit front lines). Planes returned again and dive-bombed. Permission was given by Colonel Bradley, CO of 8th Cavalry, who were to attack through 7th Cavalry, to have planes use all their ammo to strafe the objective. This delayed the artillery. All this time, General Mudge [CO of the 2nd Cavalry Regiment] and Colonel Chandler [were asking] whether it was over so they could shoot artillery. Finally at 1035, I said okay and planes stopped

strafing while troops moved forward under artillery fire which at times fell short and wounded two men. It was one-and-a-half hours before our troops reached the line they had evacuated from even though there was no opposition. This was due to General Mudge's stubbornness; insisting on artillery fire after the bombing and strafing. They sure need practice working with the air.

Captain Frederick was killed not long after during a Japanese counterattack.

ABOVE: At dawn, an infantry-armor team roots out Japanese who infiltrated the defensive perimeter around the U.S. airstrips on Bougainville. The March 8–13, 1944, Japanese offensive against the 27th Infantry and 37th Infantry divisions was beaten back with very heavy losses. U.S. forces had seized the airfield area in November of the previous year. Despite being outnumbered two to one, Japan continued to waste combat power fruitlessly attacking the well dug-in Americans.

1ST CAVALRY DIVISION

A task force of the 1st Cavalry Division landed on Los Negros Island on February 29, 1944, seizing Momote airstrip while nearby islands in the Admiralty chain were taken by other elements of the 1st Cav in April and May. Next, the division took part in the invasion of the Philippines, fighting a grueling series of actions on Leyte from October through December 1944. The division invaded Luzon at Lingayen Gulf on January 27, 1945, and fought its way to Manila by early February 1945, where it liberated military and civilian prisoners at Santo Tomas University and Bilibid Prison. It seized crossings over the Marikina River and secured the Tagaytay-Antipolo line in March. Then elements pushed south into Batangas Province and the Bicol where the division fought until July 1945. Following the surrender of Japan, the 1st Cav was the first American division to enter its capital, Tokyo.

We must fight to the end to avenge the shame of our country's humiliation on Guadalcanal...
There can be no rest until our bastard foes are battered and bowed in shame—till their blood
adds luster to the badge of the 6th Division. Our battle cry will be heard afar.

—Lieutenant General Masatane Kanda

Lieutenant General Haruyoshi Hyakutake, commander of the Japanese forces on Bougainville, exhorted his troops by recalling the defeat at Guadalcanal.

The time has come to manifest our knight-hood with the pure brilliance of the sword. It is our duty to erase the mortifications of our brothers at Guadalcanal. Attack! Assault! Destroy everything! Cut, slash, and mow them down. May the color of the red emblem of our arms be deepened with the blood of the American rascals. Our cry of victory...will be shouted resoundingly to our native land. We are invincible! Always attack. Security is the greatest enemy. Always be alert. Execute silently.

Lieutenant General Masatane Kanda, the 6th Division commander, added an even coarser message for the Japanese assault troops.

We must fight to the end to avenge the shame of our country's humiliation on Guadalcanal... There can be no rest until our bastard foes are battered and bowed in shame—till their blood adds luster to the badge of the 6th Division. Our battle cry will be heard afar.

Unlike most of their men, Generals Hyakutake and Kanda survived the war and surrendered to the Australian II Corps. Kanda's ceremonial sword now resides at the Australian War Memorial Museum in Canberra.

An anonymous writer describes the cooperation between artillery and close air support in helping repel the Japanese offensive on Bougainville in March 1944.

When enemy forces came within range of our medium artillery, we used smoke shells extensively and effectively in designating targets to our aircraft. When the [air] strike became airborne, it established radio communication with the division fire direction center and called for smoke rounds on the targets. Previous arrangements were made with the artillery, and the targets were located by map coordinates and given numbers for the day. It was found that artillery had to smoke a target about eight times for a hundred-plane strike.

With his bold seizure of the Admiralty Islands, MacArthur now had both a base and the air cover he needed for a far larger outflanking operation toward his objectives at the tip of western New Guinea. Although he was unable to augment his air forces with Nimitz's big carriers, MacArthur struck well in advance of JCS timetables, bypassed the entire Eighteenth Japanese Army of General Hatazo Adachi, and seized Aitape Airbase far to the rear on April 22, 1944. A second, larger force under Lieutenant General Robert Eichelberger moved against lightly defended Hollandia, with its airbases and wonderful anchorages in the aptly named Operation RECKLESS.

MacArthur's forces had fooled the Japanese by heavily bombing Wewak—which General Adachi believed was the main objective—from both the air and sea. The deception worked beautifully and many of the Japanese defenders at Hollandia, mostly rear area service troops, fled into the surrounding jungles. Adachi counterattacked ferociously at Aitape but was repulsed, and by the end of July, his army had been rendered combat ineffective for the remainder of the war.

In the summer of 1944, MacArthur's bold
moves along the New Guinea coast in
order to set himself up for the invasion
of the Philippines provoked a violent Japanese
counterattack toward the new operating bases
being developed at Hollandia. Here Colonel
Edward M. Starr, commanding the 124th Infantry,
made these observations following the repulse
of General Adachi's offensive against U.S. forces
defending Aitape.

My first priority was to cut off the line of
Japanese retreat, where it was, as well as the
supply route of the enemy forces. Second priority was to destroy all enemy forces en route [to
the Aitape defense line along the Driniumor
River]. I was convinced that any one of the
four battalions under my control could take

care of itself until support arrived if it became
isolated or cut off. If properly handled this is a
sound principle, but considering the obstacles
of terrain and weather, and the absence of a
supply line and evacuation route, it was open
to question.

Colonel Starr's concerns were echoed by
his operations officer, Major Edward A.
Becker, who wrote the following about
the dense jungle east of Driniumor River.

We discovered, after leaving the Driniumor,
that the only features that could be recognized on the map were the river, the coastline, and a trace of Niumen Creek; the rest
of the operational area was just a mass of
trees. Because of this, we knew we would

ABOVE: Following the first
wave in, troops of the 41st
Division's 162d Infantry
Regiment pile onto shore
at Aitape, New Guinea, on
April 22, 1944. Little resistance was encountered here
or at Hollandia, 140 miles
to the west, which was
stormed simultaneously by
the 24th Infantry Division.
The landing completely
bypassed the Imperial
Second and Eighteenth
Armies in their strongholds
at Madang, Hansa Bay, and
Wewak, and gained the
superb harbor of Humboldt
Bay for the continuing
drive toward the
Philippines.

have to find other means of identifying our location. We found the answer by using two methods…Twice a day, the [artillery liaison] plane would fly over our position and contact… [the artillery liaison officer who] would let the pilot know when he was directly over us. The pilot would then fly to the Driniumor, turn around and fly directly [east]; as he passed over us he would give us the distance [from the river]. To check the above method, the pilot would circle our position and get the concentration number from the [artillery] intersection towers located on the coast. The whole area was dotted with artillery registrations [impact points] which had previously been fired and plotted.

MacArthur's juggernaut offensive plowed on, superbly supported by Kenney's airmen. By late May, MacArthur had seized terrain on which to build heavy bomber bases that could reach the southern Philippines from Biak. The Japanese reacted fiercely, including committing their precious armor in one of the rare tank-versus-tank battles of the Pacific War. The American tanks outclassed the Japanese in every respect and the battlefield was soon littered with their burnt-out carcasses. The Japanese had planned a major naval, air, and ground counterattack, but were forced to call it off when Admiral Spruance struck suddenly in the Marianas that June, for the first time invading Japan's pre-war Imperial territory.

The Biak Landing, particularly in the area of the Mokmer Airfield, was not without the confusion of war. Here the commander of the 186th Infantry, Colonel Oliver P. Newman, writes about the difficulties of getting much-needed ammunition and supplies ashore.

I personally was at the beach, with my [logistics officer]. We had given Division Headquarters flashlight recognition signals, but evidently these were probably not communicated to the boat group commander. They [the boats] did not reply to our signals and proceeded on down the coast before returning and sending in the LVTs [amtracs]. Failure to properly coordinate signals and over-caution on the part of the boat commanders was apparently responsible [for the confusion].

Brigadier General Ennis C. Whitehead, General Kenney's deputy commander of the 5th Air Force, wrote the following assessment of the criticality of air support to operations on Biak.

I am convinced that the ground forces' efforts to capture the Biak airdromes will drag on indefinitely unless we blast a path for Fuller's [Major General Horace H. Fuller, the landing force commander] troops to move to the east end of Mokmer Airdrome… where these troops will have some space for maneuvering. At the present time, our heavy bombers…can, when weather permits, attack the Biak area only between the hours of 1100 and 1230. The Nips have figured out this pattern. It is very essential that we keep the pressure on them by two or three heavy bomber strikes a day. The plan I have outlined would do this. I am convinced that the Nip troops cannot stand up under frequent attacks with 1,000- or 2,000-pound bombs.

32D INFANTRY DIVISION, MICHIGAN AND WISCONSIN NATIONAL GUARD

In September 1942, the 32d Infantry Division was deployed by plane and ship to Port Moresby, New Guinea, to help blunt a Japanese offensive. It fought its way over the 10,000-foot-high Owen Stanley Mountains and served alongside the Australian 7th Division to seize the Japanese Army's beachhead on the northern coast at "Bloody Buna" during November and December 1942. A drive up the coast culminated in a January 1943 victory over the Japanese at Sanananda, and elements of the 32d repelled fierce counterattacks after landing at Aitape in April 1944. During the liberation of the Philippines, the 32d smashed the Yamashita Line on Leyte and helped stamp out Japanese resistance in the upper Ormoc Valley. From there, the division moved to Luzon in late January 1945 and, after more than 100 days of fighting, helped seize the Balete Pass and open a gateway to the Cagayan Valley.

ABOVE: Charles Lindbergh (right) is welcomed to Biak Airfield by Major Thomas McGuire in late June or July 1944. The trans-Atlantic pioneer was in the Southwest Pacific to share his navigational techniques and unique knowledge of how to extend an aircraft's range through a variety if in-flight procedures, but it was not long before his work with the Marine and Army air units led him to "accompany" them as an "observer" on more than fifty missions. While flying a P-38 Lightning on a July 28 strafing mission in the Philippines, a Japanese pilot made the mistake of taking on the civilian non-combatant, who handily dispatched his adversary. During a September 1944 bombing mission, Lindbergh carried a record 4,000 pounds of ordnance on an F4U Corsair. Major McGuire shot down twenty-five Japanese aircraft and was killed in action in January 7, 1945.

In 1944, legendary aviator Charles Lindbergh visited the Pacific Theater and even flew combat missions. Lindbergh had been sharing his wisdom on aircraft design with various corporations and the U.S. government, and he was sent out to share some of his knowledge and techniques about airmanship with the Navy, Marine, and Army pilots in the Pacific. Here Captain P.J. Miller remembers Lindbergh's visit to Hollandia in New Guinea.

Mainly what Lindbergh showed us was how to get far more miles out of a gallon of gas. The most important thing here is to get the drag down to a minimum, and that means getting the speed of the aircraft down to a minimum consistent with mission requirements. If you are in no hurry to get the target, then you leave earlier and you fly at the most efficient air speed, which happened to be for that model of P-38 about 175 miles per hour, without [fuel] tanks. Now with tanks—because the weight of the tanks required a different attitude of the aircraft to carry them at a given elevation—185 miles an hour. So the first requirement was to fly 175 without and 185 with, and instead of flying at 2250 RPM cut the RPM back to 1900 (or even lower), and push the manifold pressure up

to whatever it took to get you the desired cruise air speed. And this would not foul the spark plugs. And yet we had crew chiefs—every time we came back—taking [the spark plugs] out to see. They couldn't believe it, you see. Anyway, I am indebted to Lindbergh. He probably saved a few of us through the exposition of that principle.

He came back to us when we were stationed at Biak. It was there that he developed facemasks. He was a gracious man, was almost never profane. The only time I heard him swear was when he said, "That little son of a bitch tried to ram me!" talking about a Japanese plane. That was on a flight out of Biak into the Ambon area. We were ostensibly escorting B-25s. There were some B-25s along on that occasion...bombing oil refineries down in the Ambon-Ceram area. We watched the bombing and took a look at the refineries and were coming on back when we heard three air-planes, of the 9th Fighter Squadron I believe, calling that they were low on ammunition and unable to shoot down a Japanese plane that eluded them. Some other P-38s had gone on home because of shortage of fuel, leaving it to these three to chase the Japanese aircraft.

Colonel Charles H. MacDonald, group commander, 475th Fighter Group heard these three planes calling to each other. So he called, "Where are you? Where are you?" And they refused to answer. They didn't want anybody muscling in on their kill. However, MacDonald is a pretty shrewd guy, and he figured out where they probably were and he went over that way. I was on his wing, Lindbergh was leading the second element, and Joe Miller, his wingman. And, sure enough, there was the Japanese plane, the other three P-38s long since gone. MacDonald made a great big U-turn and gradually began to overtake the presumably unsuspecting Japanese. But this Japanese had already been alerted by eight P-38s, and was by no means unsuspecting and he might have been watching MacDonald's guns, because it seemed that it wasn't until he fired that he broke left. The Japanese broke left very abruptly, but his maneuver put him head on with Lindbergh, the number-three man in the flight, it seemed to me that they were both firing, Joe

Miller behind Lindbergh said that he saw the Japanese firing at Lindbergh.

I saw what could have been the Japanese guns going off or Lindbergh's cannon shells exploding near the leading edge of wing. In any event, the Jap appeared to try to ram Lindbergh. Lindbergh yanked back in the last fraction of a second and they were so close that Lindbergh felt a violent bump on his tail surface due to the disturbance of the air by the Japanese aircraft. I had seen explosions of the Japanese plane, and Lindbergh got the credit for the victory.

With Biak in hand and Japanese attention momentarily focused on Admiral Spruance, who seemed the far greater threat, MacArthur opportunistically seized the remainder of his objectives near the Vogelkop Peninsula. Noemfoor's airfields fell in late July and shortly after, on September 15, MacArthur seized the island of Morotai just 300 miles south of Mindanao in the Philippines. MacArthur had turned his sideshow into a main event and was now able to argue for his strategic view

on what should be done next from a position of strength. The next step for MacArthur was obvious—invade the Philippines.

One task force after action report noted that the promise of war booty drove the hard fighting of the troops involved in the seizure of Noemfoor Island as much as did élan and a desire to be done with the operation.

As the troops left the area in which they had chased [Colonel Suesada] Shimizu [commanding the 219th Japanese regiment] so relentlessly, their disappointment was not so much at their failure to capture Shimizu the man, nor even capture the regimental colors of the 219th. It was rather that they missed their chance of retrieving the colonel's 300-year-old saber [samurai sword], which prisoners said he still carried when last seen. When the operation officially closed on August 31, this same saber was still inducing the most vigorous patrolling by the 1st Battalion, 158th Infantry [Regiment].

ABOVE: P-39 Airacobras of the 15 Fighter Group stand ready at the newly constructed Butaritari Airfield flightline on Makin Island in late December, 1943. At this point in the war, the unit was flying missions against Japanese positions in the Gilbert Islands. The 15th also flew P-40 Warhawks, and transitioned to P-47 Thunderbolts, and eventually P-51 Mustangs on Iwo Jima.

The Turkey Shoot

June 1944 was a very bad month for the Axis Powers. On June 6, the largest amphibious operation to that date occurred at Normandy, France, sounding the death knell for the Nazi reign of terror in Europe. Meanwhile, the greatest land offensive of the war began on the Eastern front. Starting on June 10 and continuing for the remainder of the month and into July, successive Soviet offensives exploded against the hard-pressed Wehrmacht. The front collapsed and the Soviets literally destroyed the German Army Group Center that had been holding Belorussia (White Russia). In the Pacific in June, MacArthur had seized Biak, which opened the possibility of an early invasion of the Philippines—a move that would cut

Japan's lines of communication to its critical fuel resources in the East Indies. The final disaster for the Japanese occurred in the Philippine Sea, where Admiral Spruance arrived with a juggernaut of his own.

For almost eighteen months, the Japanese had been attempting to rebuild their carrier force to a level that they felt might be able to challenge the naval air machine that Nimitz had created. Operation A-GO, the defense of the Marianas, was believed to provide the ideal opportunity to turn the tables on the overconfident Americans and not only repulse their amphibious forces, but also regain command of the sea with one great naval battle.

Admiral Jisaburo Ozawa was put in charge of a new entity, the Mobile Fleet, consisting of most of Japan's large, medium, and light carriers, including the new supercarrier *Taiho*.

Japan had been carefully husbanding its naval aviators and managed to gather up almost 425 carrier-qualified pilots for the upcoming battle. Not since Midway had the Japanese gathered a carrier force of such size. However, TF-58 under Vice Admiral Marc A. Mitscher, Spruance's carrier commander, had over 950 aircraft embarked on fifteen aircraft carriers. They were supported by seven new "fast" battleships that could keep up with the speedy flattops. The American pilots were mostly veterans with recent combat experience, whereas the Japanese pilots had—at most—six months training in the carrier environment.

The Japanese plan was simple in concept. They would rely on their submarines, as always, to provide them the latest intelligence on U.S. movements and to whittle down the American carrier and amphibious task forces through attrition by setting up a screening line well east of the Marianas. They also deployed the cream of their Army and Navy land-based air power to Guam, Saipan, and Tinian—more than 200 aircraft. These were to be augmented

to more than 500 by flying in additional aircraft from other bases. These planes would attack Spruance's carriers and sap their strength even further. Admiral Kakuji Kakuta commanded this effort and it was imperative that he relay to Ozawa the success of his forces in accomplishing this mission before the Mobile Fleet was committed.

Finally, Ozawa would move in with his carriers for the kill, using his longer-range aircraft to strike the Americans while remaining beyond the range of their aircraft. In part, he would do this by launching at extreme range, recovering his aircraft in Guam, and refueling them there before bringing them back. They could make strikes both coming and going. Once the Americans' carriers had been neutralized, the big battleships and cruisers would move in to help finish off the stragglers, sink amphibious and logistics ships, and help the defenders ashore. The Japanese land defenses had not been neglected either, with a complex defensive system in place, especially on Saipan. In addition to defending at the beaches, the

ABOVE: A Grumman F6F-3 Hellcat fighter returns to the USS *Lexington* during the "Turkey Shoot" phase of the June 19–20, 1944, Philippine Sea battle. In the foreground, 5-inch and 40mm guns are manned and ready as are a string of 20mms along a starboard gun gallery. Additional 40mms below them extend from the hangar deck, and individual 5-inch guns are across the flight deck at port stern. The square structure aft of the big guns is a backdrop that enables the sailor guiding in approaching aircraft to be seen more clearly by the pilots. Both the searchlight platform from which this photo was taken and the 20mm gun galleries at the tip of the starboard stern were removed in a May 1945 refit to make way for additional whip antennas.

Japanese had a second line of fortifications in the mountainous interior of these volcanic islands that, it was hoped, would allow them to wipe out the Americans beyond the visual supporting range of the naval gunnery if the beach positions collapsed. Unfortunately, many of the reinforcements, especially the artillery, for this strategy had been sunk by U.S. submarines prior to the invasion. The Japanese preparations were not nearly as complete as they would have liked.

Everything that could wrong, did go wrong for the Japanese defense of the islands. First, they did not expect Spruance to strike the Marianas until late June or July at the earliest. On June 14, Admiral Nagumo—the overall commander of Midway infamy—was still predicting that attack was weeks away. In part this was due to the Japanese fixation on Truk, which the Americans had continued to pound with Army bombers flying out of new bases in the Marshall Islands and Bougainville. Not until June 11 did the Japanese even have an inkling that Spruance was on his way when Mitscher's

aviators began their first raids on Kakuta's airfields. However, they interpreted this strike as another of the many American raids occurring from Wake Island all the way to Truk. Thus, they were shocked when on June 15, 1944, Spruance's ships—carrying 127,000 troops under Vice Admiral Turner—arrived and began the invasion by landing at Saipan.

Mitscher's TF-58 ravaged the local airbases as well as those farther away at Iwo Jima and Chichi Jima. Additionally, Spruance employed an aggressive hunter-killer anti-submarine effort against the Japanese submarine screen that not only protected his fleet, but denied the Japanese critical intelligence about his offensive. Finally, it was a U.S. submarine that picked up Ozawa's main forces in the San Bernardino Strait as they transited the Philippines en route to the Marianas. The Americans had achieved strategic surprise and the Japanese, who had hoped for a surprise of their own, were now known to be coming.

Admiral Kakuta compromised the Japanese plan by deliberately lying to Ozawa about the course of the air battle, leading Ozawa to believe that Kakuta had crippled Spruance's air forces. In fact, the situation was reversed. Kakuta barely had an air force left, since Mitscher's fighter sweeps had destroyed anywhere from 150 to 200 of his planes in the pre-invasion air battles. Spruance, a cautious and careful commander, decided to stay close to the Marianas and conduct a close defense against the Japanese just west of Guam with Mitscher's TF-58, leaving several cruisers and old battleships to guard Turner's ships supporting the troops ashore.

On June 18, the Japanese carrier forces suffered their first loss from U.S. submarines that sank the large carrier *Taiho*. It was harbinger of

things to come. The next day saw Ozawa launch long-range strikes against U.S. naval forces that resulted in the so-called Marianas "Turkey Shoot." Between them, American aviators and the antiaircraft guns of the battleships, cruisers, and destroyers annihilated Ozawa's inexperienced pilots. Barely fifty remained. While the fierce air battle was underway, the American submarines struck another blow, and sunk the Pearl Harbor veteran carrier *Shokaku*.

Chief Yeoman C.S. King was aboard the new aircraft carrier USS Hornet *off the Marianas during the Battle of the Philippine Sea, where he witnessed the perilous recovery of U.S. aircraft returning from a long range strike, and an impromptu "victory" celebration afterward.*

The [battle] that stands out is the "Turkey Shoot." That's one that really stands out in my mind, because it was a spectacular thing from the spectator's viewpoint. I remember very vividly when they were out there…mixing it up with the Japs, and we'd get these fragmentary reports in [over the intercom system]: splashed two, splashed three, and so on. It

BELOW: Stranded airmen soon to be rescued by Lieutenant Commander Richard H. O'Kane and the submarine USS *Tang*. Critical to the American effort to maintain the edge in carrier aviators were the extensive efforts made to rescue the airmen who had run out of gas on their way back from the long-range strike on the Mobile Fleet. Lieutenant John A. Burns' Vought OS2U "Kingfisher" floatplane, from battleship *North Carolina* was too heavy to lift off after recovering nine downed airmen (two are inside) from the April 29–May 1, 1944, raids on Truk. Guided to the spot, the *Tang* surfaced and Burns taxied his Kingfisher over to transfer the men.

INSET: O'Kane, at center, poses with the twenty-two very happy airmen that *Tang* rescued while serving as a lifeguard submarine off Truk during her second war patrol.

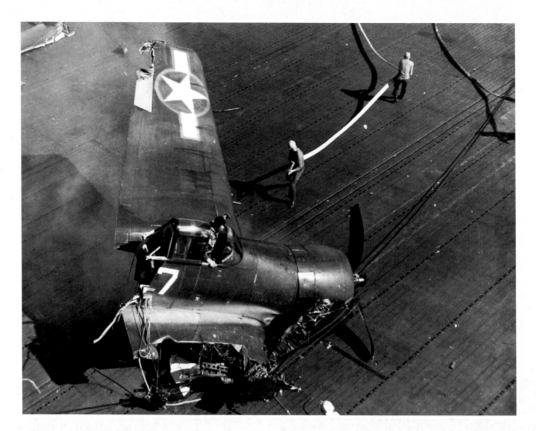

just seemed like this was what we went out there to do. We were shooting up the whole damn Japanese Navy. It just seemed like that was the greatest thing in the world.

The next day, it was high feeling and emotion about the distance our planes had to go in trying to intercept the Jap fleet as it steamed away. I was just close enough that I could sense that this was a big damn decision, about whether to send them off or not—and the distance involved, and all that kind of thing. I remember all the suspense involved in that.

That night, when [our planes] came back in, I was up topside, at my battle station. It was a memorable evening, because there were planes landing all over the place [after the attack]. It didn't matter what carrier they were from. The minute anybody flashed ready deck, somebody landed on it. Almost every landing was some kind of deck crash. They were running on fumes. There were planes going in the water everywhere. That's when [Admiral Marc] Mitscher lit up the fleet: searchlights—the whole damn thing—to help the planes land.

ABOVE: As a radio operator/rear gunner attempts to climb from the canopy, his mortally wounded B5N2 "Kate" torpedo-bomber is only seconds away from hitting the waters of Truk Atoll and exploding. The "Kate" had been the backbone of the Imperial force that struck Pearl Harbor and was responsible for the sinking of several American carriers in 1942. But by the time this photo was taken on July 2, 1944, the now-obsolescent aircraft was on the verge of being pulled from front-line duty.

LEFT: Navy aviators prepare to depart their "ready room" to man up their aircraft during the invasion of Saipan.

ABOVE: U.S. Marines on the beach during the invasion of Saipan. The Marines faced a tough fight ashore, but June 1944 was the "blackest month for the Axis" of World War II as it saw the successful D-Day landings at Normandy, the landings on Japan's "sacred" pre-war posses-sions in the Marianas, American forces overrun-ning Rome in Italy, and the huge Soviet BAGRATION offensive on the Eastern Front, which destroyed the Nazi Army Group Center.

[Normally, the fleet ran "lights out" at night to avoid submarine detection]. It was just a spec-tacular, memorable occasion.

I remember on the *Hornet* they passed the word to throw over anything that would float—wooden orange crates, anything. These guys out in the water—there were just people every-where. It was just an extremely dramatic occa-sion. I just couldn't believe what was happen-ing. When it was all over, that's when we went down to chiefs' quarters and said, "Boy, this is it. We're going to break three or four regulations." Somebody had some booze of some kind. [Alcohol consumption aboard ship was against regulations.] We gathered in the compartment I shared with several other chiefs. So we all had a drink of some kind. A good friend of mine named Duke Helms was the chief photograph-er's mate. He'd often wanted to take a picture of my tattooed feet. He said, "We're going to make this a real occasion. I'm going to take a picture of your damn tattoos." So he had me take off my shoes and socks, and took a picture.

Navy doctor Lieutenant Walter B. Burwell remembers the Japanese air attacks off Saipan.

I recall one very narrow squeak off Saipan one night. Our radar had picked up a bogey some miles out. You could hear reports of the action on our PA [speaker] system. "He's 15 miles out, 10 miles," and so on. As the plane approached, our spotters actually saw him release a

torpedo, which came straight for us. I was at my battle station in the forward battle dress-ing station, which was at the waterline, and I heard the torpedo strike the side of the ship and then glance off. You could hear it bounc-ing off throughout the length of the ship—glunk, glunk, glunk, glunk. It never exploded. The explanation was that the pilot released the torpedo so close to us that it didn't have time to arm before it struck. I remember when we got back into dry dock, seeing the scars along the starboard side of the ship where the torpedo had scraped from front to back.

During these actions Admiral Spruance had kept his distance, remaining close to the Marianas to perform his primary mission to defend the invasion fleet and support the ground forces battling the Japanese ashore. On June 20, he took a calculated risk and launched a huge strike of more than 200 aircraft against the Japanese carriers over 300 miles away in the late afternoon. This strike succeeded in sink-ing a carrier and damaging three others. The Japanese embarked naval air arm was eliminated for the remainder of the war as an effective fighting force—although the Americans did not know this. The cost, however, was steep as Spruance lost nearly half of the strike aircraft when they ran out of fuel on the way back. However, most of the precious aircrew were rescued to fight another day. Spruance was much criticized for not following the Japanese more aggressively on the previous day, but he had actually won a victory on the scale of Midway in terms of its importance to the Pacific War.

Ashore, the fighting was fierce. The Japanese had 30,000 outnumbered troops to defend Saipan who sold their lives dearly against overwhelming odds, although they still wasted their men needlessly in the occasional banzai attack. The fighting on Saipan was particularly difficult and the commander of the Army National Guard division assigned to the center of the island, arguably the worst terrain, was relieved by the overall Marine commander, Lieutenant General Holland "Howlin' Mad" Smith. But the outcome was never in doubt. By July 9, Saipan had been secured at the cost of more than 14,000 American casualties.

Guam, and then Tinian, were invaded not long afterward. Both proved tough fights, but not quite as hellish as Saipan. At Tinian, a feint had drawn away many defenders and the island was secured, except for the mop up, within eight days—not every Imperial soldier need be killed to operate the airfields. Guam, the biggest

island in the group, was more difficult to secure. Its population was also the most pro-American and had been used by the Japanese as slave labor to improve and construct the island's critical airfields, especially at Agana. The Japanese launched fierce counterattacks that wasted their combat strength against the 3d Marine Division. Army-Marine cooperation on Guam was in stark contrast to that on Saipan, and by August 10, this 30-mile-long island had been secured.

The commander of the reconnaissance platoon, Marine Lieutenant Victor Maghakian of the 24th Regiment, describes action by his reconnaissance company against the Japanese on Tinian.

After getting the men in position, I went on a reconnaissance. I spotted a large enemy patrol coming down the road with a scout out in front. After seeing that they moved into position in a cane field about 50 feet from my platoon, I crawled back and told Captain Key

BELOW: A group of Japanese civilians wait for a body to wash up close enough to the shore that they can retrieve it, while Marines, nearly obscured at lower right, look back up at the cameraman. The photo was taken near Mount Marpi's "Suicide Cliff" and south of Marpi Point's "Banzai Cliff," circa July 9, 1944. It was at locations in this area that American troops watched in horror as several hundred local civilians—thoroughly indoctrinated as to what would befall them if captured by the bestial Americans—either committed suicide or were forcefully thrown off these cliffs to their deaths on the jagged rocks below by fanatical Japanese troops. "At times," said the Army history of the campaign, "the waters below the Point were so thick with floating bodies of men, women, and children that naval small craft were unable to steer a course without running over them."

By the middle of the Saipan operation, considerable evidence existed of Imperial soldiers killing civilians with grenades when they committed ritual hara-kiri. As the major fighting came to a close in early July, Marines witnessed even mothers with children being shot down when they tried to reach American lines. Before the Marpi Point area was secured, 4th Division Marines observed numerous instances of armed Japanese soldiers forcing people, hesitant to end their lives, over the cliffs. Chamorro islanders largely avoided becoming victims by keeping well away from the soldiers, as did many Korean laborers who took the opportunity to separate themselves from the Japanese troops when they found the chance.

The Japanese, when you got them corralled or penned up, they would perform a banzai attack. And what they do is...anywhere from 1,000 to 3,000 men and they pick one spot in the line that they think is the weakest and they just keep coming. If you're on the other end of the line and you're firing at them, you can only fire so long before you run out of ammunition and then they overwhelm you. That's the idea behind it. But they kept forgetting that sometimes we have other weapons also that we can use against them like the 37mm tank gun and the things like that you know, mortars, to slow them down. We had a banzai attack on Tinian and they just came near a lake there. They came right through the lake! They kept coming! We were picking them off like ducks as they got swamped down in the water. It was just a massacre, really. As a consequence, the rest of the battle was just a piece of cake—more or less.

Marine Combat Photographer Cyril J. O'Brien recounts his experience covering the invasion of Guam.

I was a combat correspondent, which means that my job was not to shoot. My job was to tell about the enlisted men and junior officers. And when there'd be a battle, we'd go near it. I had been with infantry on Bougainville in the Solomon Islands. Then I landed here with the third assault wave on Guam. Usually our RR [rest and recuperation] spot was Guadalcanal, but prior to Iwo Jima, it was Guam. On Guam we were active in combat as well, and even after the campaign we were still fighting. The reason we were fighting after the battle was that 10,000 Japanese were still there. It was hazardous. They were raiding Chamorran [Guamanian] homes and, in one case, they kidnapped a girl and took her as a comfort girl with them and they all got killed except her. I was on patrol all the time.

Guam was the first invasion I was writing about. All of a sudden, mortar rounds started to come in from everywhere like rain. I said, "damn mortar" as if it was an inconvenience because I was writing. But then, of course, when it got very intense you had to get onto the ground or you'd be cut in half.

ABOVE: Chamorro children of the local inhabitants of Guam play in front of Captain Edward Steichen in March 1945. The population of Guam, a U.S. territory, had been cruelly oppressed by the Japanese during the war. The Chamorrans were forced to build a coral airfield on the plateau above Agana with their bare hands and given no food other than the tree bark from the surrounding jungles to survive on. Those who did not die of exhaustion often starved to death. In addition to this, the locals were also cruelly persecuted for hiding a U.S. Navy signalman in the jungles for the entire war until D-Day in the summer of 1944.

[commanding the division reconnaissance company] what I planned to do. In the meantime, the Japs were digging in and were making a lot of noise talking and did not suspect that we were so close. I passed the word down the line to open up and fire, rapid fire, into the cane field, knee-high grazing fire. Upon my signal, we opened up and let them have it as fast as we could pull our triggers. They began screaming and making awful noises. Then after a few minutes I ordered my platoon to fall back to the division lines because I was afraid that maybe our own division might fire on us. After falling back, I reported what happened, and our troops opened up with mortar and machine gun fire. Next morning I took my platoon back to the road junction and the cane field and found between thirty-five and forty dead Japs in that area. I did not lose a man that night.

John Sbordone was the executive officer of Company F, 2d Battalion, 24th Marines in the 4th Marine Division. He remembers Japanese banzai attacks during operations on Tinian in the Marianas.

With the conclusion of the Marianas operations, the dual advance across the central and southwestern Pacific was effectively over, but no one yet knew that. MacArthur was now poised to invade the Philippines ahead of schedule and Nimitz, at King's urging, was eyeing Formosa [Taiwan] as a possible next target. However, the Americans had now arrived on the doorstep of inner defenses of the Empire, an area the Japanese were sure to defend to the last round, last man, last woman, and last child. The disasters visited on Japanese arms were so severe that the Tojo government, in charge since just before the war, fell that July when Hideki Tojo resigned as atonement for disappointing the emperor. A new prime minister, Kuniaki Koiso, was appointed, but the Japanese Army and Navy had no intention of quitting the fight and began planning for a final decisive battle. More ominously, the U.S. Army Air Corps could now begin the long-awaited strategic bombardment of Japan using B-29s from Saipan and Tinian. The Japanese would soon reap the whirlwind.

ABOVE: Marines fire their 75mm howitzers directly into caves on Tinian to clear fanatic Japanese defenders from their subterranean defenses. Some Japanese soldiers and units did not crawl out of the jungles for many years, and it wasn't until 1972 that the last known holdout, Corporal Shoichi Yokoi, was captured on Guam.

LEFT: One of the 252 Japanese soldiers taken prisoner on Tinian. Although most were only captured because they were too seriously injured to commit suicide, this man appears to have been enticed into surrendering with the help of a proffered Yankee cigarette. The rest of the 9,000-strong garrison died on the island, including an unknown number of civilians. A captured Japanese warrant officer from the 56th Naval Guard Force boasted that 1,000 "loyal citizens" on Tinian had "allowed" the military to blow them up.

Logistics

RIGHT: Antiaircraft artillerymen manhandle steel Marston matting—used to quickly create crude all-weather aircraft runways—into a gap bulldozed through Iwo Jima's high-banked shore so that they can off-load their half-tracks and guns.

BELOW: Steel 5x5x7-foot pontoons provided beach and harbormasters with much-needed flexibility for the wide variety of supply challenges they faced. Arranged in strips up to thirty-two pontoons long, they were transported, one-each, along the hulls of LSTs to be joined side-by-side for a causeway wide enough for vehicle traffic. These were, in turn, constructed end-on-end to attain whatever length was required to bridge gaps between a reef's edge and shore. As this September 1944, photo at Angaur shows, they could also be formed as powered or unpowered barges, and even wide auxiliary docks.

RIGHT: The USS *Pennsylvania* undergoing maintenance, probably on her hull and screws, inside one of the Navy's seven massive Advanced Base Sectional Docks (ABSDs), on October 1–12, 1944. The battleship had sailed to the anchorage site near Espiritu Santu southeast of the Solomon Islands between bombardment missions at Pelieu and Leyte. Drydocks like this one were towed in ten sections across the Pacific, reassembled in remote anchorages, then displaced forward as U.S. forces closed in on Imperial Japan. The ability to perform major repairs of all sorts at forward bases, thus saving Navy ships valuable steaming days, was of incalculable value in maintaining, and sustaining the fleet thousands of miles west of Pearl Harbor, and enabled the Pacific Fleet to employ maximum, unrelenting pressure on the Japanese.

Literally thousands of logistics-related ships and craft of all types were also involved in this effort—tenders, repair and stores ships, salvage vessels, oilers, tankers, tug boats—as well as dozens of other types in a dizzying array of classes. The Japanese had counted on the wide expanses of the Pacific, plus lack of Allied bases near the fighting, to severely impede the American advance across the Pacific. That the United States was able to very quickly produce and man this support structure came as a profound shock to the Japanese who found themselves forced onto the defensive far sooner than expected.

By the grace of Almighty God, our forces stand again on Philippine soil consecrated in the blood of our two peoples. We have come, dedicated and committed to the task of destroying every vestige of enemy control over your daily lives, and of restoring upon a foundation of indestructible strength, the liberties of your people.

—Douglas MacArthur, General of the Army

Chapter Seven

RETURN...WITH INTEREST

General Douglas MacArthur had promised "I shall return" when he left the Philippines. Now that time was at hand. It did not come easily. Throughout the spring and summer of 1944, the strategic councils were divided on which step to take next. The debate centered on two personalities and two locations. The Chief of Naval Operations Admiral Ernest King wanted to bypass the Philippines and strike closer to Japan by seizing Formosa to support an invasion of the Ryukyu Islands (especially Okinawa) as a stepping-stone to Japan. This course of action might support later combat operations in China using airfields in Formosa, as well as provide additional bases for the strategic bombing of Japan.

MacArthur was adamantly in favor of an invasion of the Philippines, arguing it was the United States' sacred duty to keep his promise to return. Eventually, in a meeting with Nimitz and FDR at Pearl Harbor, MacArthur prevailed. Both Nimitz's and MacArthur's bold operational strokes had advanced their invasion timetables to late 1944, perhaps as early as October. The decision was made to land in the central Philippines on the island of Leyte, with a follow-on invasion of the main island of Luzon not long after. MacArthur made claims of a quick campaign that turned out to be grossly overoptimistic. However, the invasion of the Philippines might

PREVIOUS PAGES: LVTs burn as 1st Division Marines, under heavy fire from the direction of the Japanese airbase on Peleliu, take stock of the situation, September 22, 1944. Appropriately named STALEMATE, the operation's objective was the seizure of this and other islands in the Palau archipelago on the flank of the Philippine invasion route. During his raids prior to the Philippine invasion, Admiral Halsey had recommended that Admiral Nimitz cancel the operation. The little-known battle became one of the most casualty-intensive fights of the Pacific War. Seizing Peleliu resulted in 7,368 Marine dead, missing, and wounded, with Navy casualties—principally among medical corpsmen and doctors—totaling 700.

RIGHT: With most of the USS *Houston's* crew having abandoned ship, a damage control party conducts a burial at sea. The sailor was killed when the cruiser was torpedoed off Formosa on October 14, 1944. This photo was taken the following day when the ship was under tow, and she was hit in the starboard quarter (just aft of where this photo was taken) by another aerial torpedo. The original cruiser's namesake had been sunk early in the war by the Japanese and this second *Houston* was one of only a handful of Allied warships to sustain damage during the Third Fleet's punishing raids against Formosa. The Japanese mistakenly believed that the struck warship constituted an entire fleet sinking, and trumpeted a great (but false) air and naval victory to their war-weary populace.

end the war since their capture by the Americans would sever the Japanese Home Islands from the strategic resources of the East Indies. The Japanese were well aware that the Americans were coming and devised the SHO (Victory)—1 through 4 plans to address any number of American invasions, from the Philippines all the way to the Japanese Home Islands.

Precursor Operations

Admiral Nimitz was assigned the mission of seizing key islands in the Palau archipelago and then the huge atoll and anchorage at Ulithi. Additionally, Admiral Halsey would take over Spruance's ships (renamed the Third Fleet while under Halsey's command) to conduct a series of naval and air raids against the Philippines, Formosa, and the Ryukyus. These precursor operations, much like those conducted during the dual advance, would seize critical airfields and logistics bases while at the same time neutralizing the ability of the Japanese air forces to contest the Leyte landings.

In early September, Admiral Halsey sailed with TF-38, consisting of more than fifteen fast aircraft carriers and numerous escorts, for his first series of raids. The Japanese held back their air reserves in response to Halsey, whose aircraft flew with impunity and damaged large numbers of Japanese aircraft on the ground. Halsey's reconnaissance found light defenses and he recommended to the JCS that the timetable for the Philippine invasion be moved up to late October. He also recommended that the invasions of Peleliu, Yap, Mindanao, and Morotai be cancelled. The plans for Mindanao and Yap were cancelled but Morotai and Peleliu went on as planned in mid-September.

Willard Ransom, a Third Class Gunner's Mate, served aboard the cruiser USS Houston. Here he remembers the Japanese air attacks during Admiral Halsey's strategic raids, which stimulated the premature activation of the SHO plan.

I was on the *Houston* off the coast of Formosa when the ship was attacked by Japanese airplanes. We were at battle station up on the superstructure right behind the captain. It was at night and the Japs threw down parachutes with flares that lit the area as if it were daylight. The ship took two torpedo hits almost simultaneously, the first hit the forward magazine section and the second hit the engine room, which stopped the ship completely. After about ten minutes the captain gave the order to abandon ship; the main deck was underwater; waves were 14 feet high. Four destroyers boxed the *Houston* in to rescue those overboard. I was in the water about thirty minutes when my waist flotation device came unhooked. I swam to the USS *Boyd* and climbed aboard using the netting over the side of the ship. The *Boyd* delivered us to a troop transport ship, which brought us back to Mare Island, California. I was forever grateful to the ship and decided at the time of

rescue that my first male child would be named for the USS *Boyd*, as it turned out my son followed the tradition and also named his son, my grandson, after that ship.

Peleliu turned out to be a charnel house, and one of Nimitz's rare missteps during the Pacific War. Landing uncontested on September 15, 1944 (the same day MacArthur's forces landed at Morotai), the 1st Marine Division soon encountered fierce resistance from the Japanese defenders, who had prepared a cave system with supporting artillery fire among the coral ridges dominating most of the island. The new Japanese strategy was simply to bleed the Americans, and it worked, with a nearly one-to-one ratio of American-to-Japanese casualties during a two-month nightmare battle—all for an objective that could have been bypassed in the first place.

BELOW: A tank-infantry team of the 1st Marine Division moves into the crazy-quilt of steep ridges, draws, and sinkholes in Peleliu's Umurbrogol Mountain region, September 1944. At left, a tank almost completely obscured by smoke leads the way as a platoon of Marines jumps off in another assault. Until this maneuver blocked its line of fire, the 37mm gun at right shot at Japanese targets along the draw.

> **Our amtrac was among the first assault waves, yet the beach was already a litter of burning, blackened amphibian tractors, of dead and wounded, a mortal garden of exploding mortar shells.**
>
> **—Robert Leckie**

BELOW: Marines take what shelter they can under an amphibious DUKW-353 on Peleliu as amtracs burn along the beach.

The Japanese moved veteran troops from Manchuria [Manchukuo] to bolster their garrison on Peleliu. Here a Japanese regimental commander outlines in notably patriotic language his plans for a fanatical defense.

All the officers and men carried in mind the meaning of our sacred war, and the leaders, burning with the will to be "Breakwater of the Pacific," and feeling the obligation of this important duty, and being a picked Manchukuoan regiment that does not expect to return alive and will follow to the death an Imperial order, devoted themselves to the endeavor of being the type of soldier who can fight hundreds of men. Using all wisdom especially while acquiring our anti-landing training, we will overcome the hardships of warfare and under the battle flag, which displays our battle glory, we vow with our unbreakable solidarity we will complete our glorious duty and establish the "Breakwater of the Pacific."

Marine grunt Robert Leckie remembers his arrival on Peleliu.

Our amtrac was among the first assault waves, yet the beach was already a litter of burning, blackened amphibian tractors, of dead and wounded, a mortal garden of exploding mortar shells. Holes had been scooped in the white sand or had been blasted out by the shells, the beach was pocked with holes—all filled with green-clad, helmeted Marines.

Major E. Hunter Hurst describes how an antitank ditch helped in the Marines' frantic efforts to find safe ways to communicate and move around Peleliu.

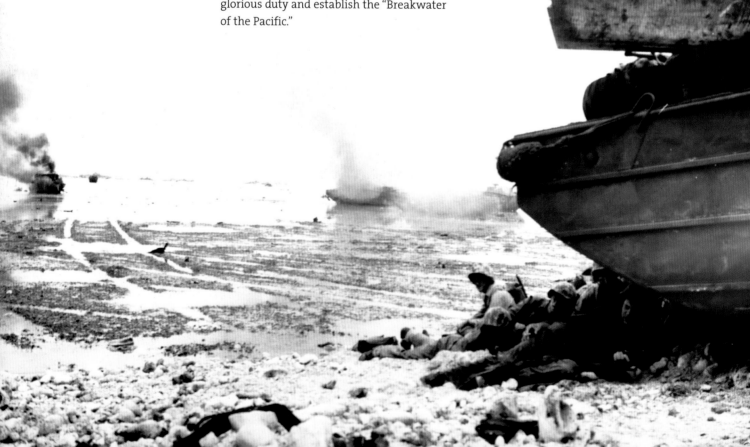

Once officers were able to orient themselves, it [the antitank ditch] proved an excellent artery for moving troops into the proper position for deployment and advance inland since it crossed the entire width of our zone of action approximately parallel to the beach. With respect to the battalion CP [command post], I am convinced that it enabled us to join the two principal echelons of CP personnel and commence functioning as a complete unit at least an hour earlier than would otherwise have been possible.

Lieutenant Colonel Lewis W. Walt describes tank-versus-tank action on D-Day at Peleliu.

Four Sherman tanks came onto the field in the zone of action on the south end of the airfield and opened fire immediately on the enemy tanks. These four tanks played an important role in stopping the enemy tanks and also stopping the supporting infantry, the majority of which started beating a hasty retreat when these Shermans came charging down from the south. They fought a running battle and ended up in the midst of the enemy tanks.

The first day at Peleliu resulted in over 1,000 Marine casualties killed and wounded. The Japanese, on the other hand, were quite pleased with what they had accomplished as attested in this somewhat misleading report by their commander, Colonel Kunio Nakagawa.

By 1000 hours, our forces successfully put the enemy to rout. At 1420 hours, the enemy again attempted to make the perilous landing on the southwestern part of our coastline. The unit in that sector repulsed the daring counterattack, and put the enemy to rout once more. However in another sector of the coastline near Ayame [Beach, ORANGE 3], the enemy, with the aid of several tanks, were successful in landing, although they were encountering heavy losses inflicted by our forces. Our tank unit attacked the enemy with such a cat-like spring at dusk, that they were able to inflict heavy damages on the enemy.

Meanwhile, Nimitz's amphibious forces, now under Admiral Theodore S. Wilkinson, easily seized the critical Ulithi atoll on September 23. Halsey sortied from this new base in mid-October to pound Formosa and the Ryukyus prior the Philippine invasion. The Japanese mistakenly believed that an invasion was underway and activated the SHO-2 plan for the defense of Formosa, feeding their carefully conserved airmen—including precious carrier pilots—into the "meat grinder" of TF-38's carrier air. The rookie Japanese pilots did manage to damage two cruisers, but they so amplified their damage reports that the Japanese concluded that they had sunk major portions of Halsey's fleet and shot down hundreds of his aircraft. The Japanese believed they had won a great victory, when in fact they had lost hundreds of valuable pilots. No one knew it at the time, but the premature activation of SHO-2 had doomed any hope the Japanese had of succeeding in a naval defense of the Philippines.

LEWIS W. WALT

BELOW: A Marine examines the remains of a Type 95 Kyu-Go light tank and its crew on Peleliu.

Leyte Gulf and the Philippines

The American forces that sailed toward Leyte Gulf were the most powerful assemblage of ships and embarked men in history. MacArthur had appointed Lieutenant General Walter Krueger as commander of the Sixth Army (200,000 troops). These soldiers were embarked on 738 ships of Vice Admiral Kinkaid's Seventh Fleet. Kinkaid's force included six old battleships as well as three escort carrier task forces (known as Taffys) to provide air support. Finally, Nimitz sent Halsey's Third Fleet to provide carrier protection with the powerful TF-38, which included seventeen aircraft carriers, six new battleships, and over eighty cruisers and destroyers. These forces, with the exception of land-based air support, were even more numerous and powerful than those involved in the Normandy landings the previous June. Only Kinkaid and Krueger were directly under MacArthur's command. Halsey, under Nimitz, was in support but had orders to destroy the Japanese Fleet if it appeared—a critical error in command and control. On October 20, Krueger's forces landed on Leyte. By October 21, over 163,000 troops were ashore and many of the vulnerable transports and amphibious ships had departed.

 Colonel L.A. Sprinkle recalls the difficulties of landing troops at Leyte.

All ships were unloaded by 1900 hours. The landing over the beach was very difficult due to landing craft being unable to get near enough ashore to get out of deep water. Most troops and vehicles landed in water 4 to 5.5 feet deep. This resulted in practically all vehicles being temporarily drowned out— the engines flooded with seawater. Those that would run were used to tow others ashore. No road of any consequence whatever existed along the shore. Bulldozers and blades were put to work at once clearing a path, which eventually became a road. Units dug in where they were to remain overnight.

The Japanese were stunned by the early appearance of the U.S. invasion fleet and SHO-1 was activated. The emperor personally scuttled the plan to make the main fight in Luzon and ordered the Army and the Navy to make Leyte the decisive battle that would bring the United States to the negotiating table. It involved four parts. First, land-based Japanese aircraft (including secret kamikaze aircraft) would attack American ships while at the same time providing air cover for the main fleet. The kamikaze effort was in its infancy and involved suicide tactics. If the Japanese could not hit the Americans with bombs or torpedoes, they would simply dive at high speed against the Navy ships. The other parts of the plan involved the convergence of three powerful naval forces upon the American landing beaches in Leyte Gulf—designated Northern, Center, and Southern Forces.

The Northern Force consisted of the pitiful remains of Japan's carrier force, plus a few battleships and was to serve as a decoy to lure Halsey's powerful forces to the north. The main effort was the Center Force under Vice Admiral Takeo Kurita and consisted of five powerful battleships and numerous cruisers and destroyers. The Southern Force was somewhat smaller than the Center Force and consisted of two separate surface task forces that would combine with each other prior to penetrating through the Surigao Strait to the south of Leyte Gulf. They were to join with Kurita in order to ravage the American landing beaches.

The Americans discovered Kurita's force when submarines ambushed it as it transited north from Singapore. Kurita lost three heavy cruisers in this action. Then, on October 24, Halsey's TF-38 aircraft located the Center Force in the Sibuyan Sea. Fierce air battles raged throughout the day, but the Japanese got the worst of it, losing numerous aircraft and the super battleship *Musashi*. Kurita seemed to turn away and Halsey assumed the threat from this quarter was over. Halsey did lose one light carrier, the USS *Princeton*, to a lucky hit—but he could afford this loss much more than could the Japanese.

That night, the Southern Force tried to penetrate the Surigao Strait and were ravaged by a layered defense of PT boats, destroyer squadrons, and finally the old battleships from Pearl Harbor under Rear Admiral Jesse Oldendorf. Both of the

OPPOSITE, TOP: The torpedoed battleship USS *West Virginia*, refloated and headed for a Pearl Harbor dry dock on June 9, 1942.

OPPOSITE, BOTTOM: The *West Virginia* in July 1944 after extensive modernization. At first glance, the old battlewagon—laid down just two years after World War I—could easily be mistaken for one of the new "fast battleships" of the *South Dakota* class. Sporting not only a rebuilt superstructure and eight twin 5-inch mounts to replace its miscellaneous secondary armaments, it now carried ten quad 40mm mounts; 58 single, one twin, and one quad 20mm antiaircraft guns, plus the latest radar. Although the *West Virginia* and many of her other Pearl Harbor mates were assigned to the Seventh Fleet for shore bombardment, they exacted their revenge at the Battle of Surigao Strait during the Leyte invasion against the battleships of the Japanese Southern Force under Admiral Nishimura. The "interwar" battleships had finally been used in the role originally envisaged for them in, ironically, what was to be history's last big-gun duel between battleships.

Japanese battleships and most of their escorts were sunk in this action. Meanwhile, Admiral Ozawa, in command of the Northern Force, had finally attracted Halsey's attention with a feeble air attack and radio transmissions. Once Halsey heard that there were Japanese aircraft carriers to the north, he proceeded at high speed after them. Halsey had fallen for the bait. Worse, Kinkaid and Oldendorf wrongly believed Halsey had detached his fast battleships to keep Kurita from sailing through the San Bernardino Strait.

The intrepid Kurita, under cover of darkness, reversed course and penetrated the San Bernardino Strait unopposed. Rear Admiral Clifton Sprague's Taffy 3 only had small escort carriers, destroyers, and destroyer escorts to oppose Kurita. In an incredibly heroic action, he sacrificed his ships in order to slow Kurita down. Kinkaid, meanwhile, frantically tried to recall both Oldendorf and Halsey who were both too far away to do any good. Then the real "miracle" of the Pacific War occurred.

Kurita, baffled and bloodied by suicidal destroyer torpedo attacks and harassment by Sprague's tiny, but highly aggressive air groups, came to believe he was actually up against Halsey. Several of his cruisers were sunk and Kurita's nerve broke. The Japanese admiral broke off the action and turned away, within sight of his objective—the beaches of Leyte Gulf. Sprague had lost three of his gallant escorts and one of his small carriers. However, even if Kurita had pressed on, the Americans had already unloaded more than a month's worth of supplies. It is unlikely that any damage Kurita could have inflicted would have defeated the forces ashore before Halsey came back to finish Kurita off. With the defeat of the Japanese Fleet, the sea lines of communication with Japan were severed.

On October 25 we had gone to general quarters at dawn. After being released from general quarters, I had had breakfast and gone back to my stateroom to take a shower. Our captain announced on the PA system that the whole Japanese fleet was attacking Taffy 3 to the north of us. I looked out on the forecastle and sure enough it looked like there were a hundred ships on the horizon. At that point, general quarters sounded and I had to go below to my battle dressing station in the forward part of the ship. It was one deck below the main deck—two or three below the flight deck. We were just about at the waterline.

There was nothing unique about the battle dressing station; it contained twenty-five to thirty bunks, and medical supplies stored in lockers, and was just below and aft of the catapult engine room. There was an open deck one deck above so you could look out on either side. This was ordinarily used as a barbershop and had a couple of barber chairs there. Many times during general quarters I would sit in one of those barber chairs because it was the most comfortable thing I could find.

Shortly thereafter, we were hit by the first kamikaze. Our sister ship, the [escort aircraft carrier] Santee [CVE-29], was actually hit first, but nineteen minutes later, another kamikaze managed to get through all the antiaircraft fire and crash into our flight deck about amidships and penetrate to the main deck. This attack did not do nearly as much damage as the second attack the next day.

On the morning of the 26th, we had maybe twenty-five wounded in the forward battle dressing station from the action of the day before. And we had things pretty much under control by that evening. In fact, we were not even at general quarters. My stateroom was only two decks above our battle

dressing station and I told my corpsman that I was going up there to get a change of clothes and maybe lie down a minute, and that if he needed me to come and get me. For some reason, exhaustion just got the better of me before I even got up there and I crawled into a bunk in an adjoining sleeping compartment just forward of our battle dressing station and fell asleep.

I was asleep when the second attack occurred. The thing that woke me up was the sound of our antiaircraft guns going off. When I heard the guns, I jumped up and started for the dressing station. Just as I got to the doorway there was a terrific explosion and we lost our lights. I went into the dressing station and helped our corpsmen pull the wounded out from under wreckage when there was a second explosion. That one shattered all the bulkheads and broke water mains.

After the first explosion, my corpsman lit out for my stateroom to get me, thinking that's where I was. But when he got up there

ABOVE: Antiaircraft gunners climb up onto the USS Suwannee's flight deck from the smoke-filled 20mm gallery moments after an amidships hit during the war's first wave of deliberate kamikaze attacks, October 25, 1944. An explosion has just occurred amid the fires in the hanger deck below, and sailors who jumped overboard can be seen in the water. The flight deck was patched up and made useable (minus four arrestor cables) in just one-and-a-half hours, but a gaping hole remained in the hanger deck, and the escort carrier received a devastating strike the following day, which put her out of commission for more than three months. There were 169 confirmed dead from this first strike, and the U.S. Fleet would receive far more damage from kamikaze pilots, like the one who struck the Suwannee, than from the immense guns of Kurita's Center Force.

he found that my stateroom had been demolished and thought I was gone. I will never forget how after we got working again, he looked up and saw me and said, "My God, you can't be here." Indeed, he thought I was dead. "I'm so glad I'm not here by myself," he said.

The second explosion forced us to evacuate the battle dressing station. After the first explosion, there was smoke and fire fed by aviation gasoline pouring onto the deck above us. The wreckage in the passageway and ladder to the deck above by bomb and ammunition explosions prevented entrance or exit to or from our dressing station. Up to that point, we could have remained where we were, at least temporarily.

BELOW: A kamikaze in its death dive at upper left streaks toward the USS *Suwannee* on October 26, 1944, as smoke rises from the carrier's gun galleries and the first of two TBF Avengers enters the frame at lower left. (Inset top) The suicider strikes the *Suwannee*'s forward elevator area, containing ten recovered aircraft, as a second Avenger enters the frame and the first is almost out of the picture. (Inset bottom) The blast billows upward as the second Avenger flies helplessly by.

These photos were taken from the USS *Sangamon*, which had been struck by a kamikaze the previous day. Although the first Avenger's flight (as well as the second's) was level throughout and appear to be passing the Suwannee's stern diagonally to starboard, the official Navy caption says that it was preparing to land. This was simply a quick—and false—assumption by the caption writer since the pilot's complete attention when landing would have been on the pitching flight deck before him, and he would have not seen the kamikaze on it 80-degree dive. If he had been landing, his Avenger's tail hook would be snagging an arrestor cable even as the suicider plunged into the bow. The two aircraft are simply transiting the "crowded skies" above the task force on the way to an escort carrier ahead of the *Sangamon*, and their pilots likely never even saw the suicide dive until seconds before impact. There were eighty-five crewmen killed, fifty-eight missing, and 102 wounded as a result of the October 26, 1944, attack.

The second explosion further wrecked our compartment, buckled our bulkheads, and ruptured water mains above and in our compartment, so that we began to flood. As the water level rose to knee height in our compartment, the ship was listing uncomfortably and lying dead in the water without steerage because of destruction of the bridge and wheelhouse. Isolated from the rest of the ship with only the reflection from the gasoline fires above and a few flickering battle lamps for light, I saw my wounded ship partially covered with wreckage and already awash and knew that we had to evacuate.

I think there were about thirty of us, including two corpsmen, two stretcher bearers, and perhaps twenty-five wounded resulting from the action of the day before, mostly consisting of extensive burns, blast and fragmentation injuries, traumatic amputations, compound fractures, and multiple severe lacerations. About half the wounded were able to help themselves to some extent in dragging themselves about, but the remainder required stretchers to be moved.

Though I did not know the extent of damage to the compartments aft of us, I knew that they were unoccupied and sealed off during battle conditions. I informed my corpsmen that I would try to find an escape by this route as it seemed to offer our only hope of evacuation. We opened the hatch to the adjacent compartment, and I was able to get through it and lock it behind me without flooding from our compartment. Feeling my way with the help of a pocket flashlight, I found the compartment to be intact and dry, though without light or ventilation. Then I worked my way aft through several adjacent unoccupied compartments in the same way until at last I reached an open space on the main deck.

Feeling certain that we could make our way out by this route, I returned to my group in the forward battle dressing station. There, with my corpsmen and stretcher bearers, and with the valiant help of some of the mobile wounded, we were able to move our stretcher-bound wounded through the hatches from one compartment to the next, without leaving or losing a single member of our party, to finally emerge on the open deck. From there, we entered the Chief Petty Officers' Mess to find two corpsmen tending to about twenty more wounded. So, we joined forces to organize an amidships dressing station and began to gather additional wounded in that area.

On the deck above, we found about fifteen or twenty more wounded, mostly burns and blast injuries, who had made their way into bunks in the Chief Petty Officers' Quarters. There was no immediate possibility of moving them to our already overflowing and under-staffed amidships station. One of my corpsmen and I gathered up what medical supplies we could carry and made our way up to the Chiefs' Quarters to treat the wounded there. Just as we arrived at the entrance to the compartment, a sailor, apparently in panic, came running along the passageway screaming, "Everybody's going over the side! The captain's dead! Everyone on the bridge has been killed! Everybody's abandoning ship!"

Now, havoc! Now, contagious panic and cold fear! The wounded who had crawled into the compartment began struggling to get out, screaming hysterically, "Where's my life jacket? Who took my life jacket? Turn that loose! G'mme that! No, it's mine!" Some were shoving toward the entrance, fighting and scrambling over one another. My heart sank as I stepped into the threshold to block the entrance and shout over and over, "Get back into your bunks! There's no order to abandon ship! You don't need your life jackets!"

I could see this was only having limited effect; so, with much inward trepidation but outwardly extravagant bravado, I made myself step into the compartment from the threshold, remove my own life jacket and helmet and hang them in clear view on a coat hook near the entrance. Then, I had to consciously force myself to move away from the entrance and the comfort and security of my life jacket and go into the compartment to tend the wounded, fearing that at any moment some panicky sailor might snatch my life jacket and bolt, setting off a wild melee. It seemed to me that time hung in the balance for an eternity, but finally one after

ABOVE: Heroic "tin can sailors" of Taffy 3 being rescued off Samar on October 26, 1944, the day after their furious fight with Kurita's force of battleships and cruisers. Some 1,200 survivors of escort carrier *Gambier Bay*, and destroyer USS *Hoel*, destroyer escort USS *Samuel B. Roberts*, and destroyer USS *Johnston* were rescued during the days following the action.

another of the men quieted down and crawled back into their bunks, so that gradually things began at last to calm down and sort themselves out.

In the meantime, one of our corpsmen tending the wounded on the flight deck saw the plight of those isolated by fire on the forecastle. He came below to report that medical help was critically needed there. It seemed to me that we would have to try to get through to them. So he and I restocked our first aid bags with morphine syrettes, tourniquets, sulfa, Vaseline, and bandages, commandeered a fire extinguisher and made our way forward, dodging flames along the main deck. Along part of the way, we were joined by a sailor manning a seawater fire hose with fairly good pressure, and though the seawater would only scatter the gasoline fires away from us, by using the water and foam alternately as we advanced, we managed to work our way up several decks, through passageways along the wrecked and burning combat information center and decoding area, through officers' country, and finally out on the forecastle.

Many of the crew on the forecastle and the catwalks above it had been blown over the side by the explosions. But others trapped below and aft of the forecastle area found themselves under a curtain of fire from avia-

tion gasoline pouring down from burning planes on the flight deck above. Their only escape was to leap aflame into the sea, but some were trapped so that they were incinerated before they could leap. By the time we arrived on the forecastle, the flow of gasoline had mostly consumed itself, and flames were only erupting and flickering from combustible areas of water and oil. Nonetheless, the decks and bulkheads were still blistering hot and ammunition in the small arms locker on the deck below was popping from the heat like strings of firecrackers. With each salvo of popping, two or three more panicky crewmen would leap over the side, and we found that our most urgent task was to persuade those poised on the rail not to jump by a combination of physical restraint and reassurance that fires were being controlled and that more help was on the way.

Most of the remaining wounded in the forecastle area were severely burned beyond recognition and hope. All that could be done for the obviously dying was to give the most rudimentary first aid consisting of morphine, a few swallows of water, and some words of companionship, leaving them where we found them and moving on to others.

Within an hour or so after being struck in the last attack, power and steerage had been restored, fires were out, ammunition and gasoline explosions had ceased, pumps were working, and ruptured water mains had been shut off. But it was miraculous that we escaped destruction during this period, because we were vulnerable to further air or submarine attack.

By this time, we had done what we could for the wounded on the forecastle, and I moved back to the amidships dressing station. From there my corpsmen and stretcher-bearers were searching out and gathering wounded. By nightfall, we began to run short of medical supplies and I realized that we needed to salvage the supplies left behind in the forward battle dressing station. I was able to recruit a small group of stretcher-bearers to help me and successfully made our way back to the forward battle dressing station.

We found the compartment was still flooded with knee-deep water, but most of our supplies were salvageable in wreckage above this level. We were able to load up our stretchers with plasma, dressings, sulfa, Vaseline, and morphine and haul them out. After two or three trips, we had all our supplies safely out and distributed elsewhere.

The battle ashore was hard-fought. Leyte's interior proved a tough nut to crack and the overall Japanese commander, General Yamashita—obeying the orders of his emperor—moved more troops in to reinforce those already defending Leyte. Mother Nature seemed to aid the Japanese, too, with three typhoons, constant rain, and an earthquake making American operations—especially air support—even more

BELOW: Wildcat fighters are prepared for launch as crewmen aboard the "baby flattop" USS *Kitkun Bay* watch the demise of their sister ship, *Gambier Bay*, lying dead in the water amid towering shell splashes. The *Gambier Bay* is being tightly bracketed by at least two Imperial cruisers and, at the time she capsized, two more and a destroyer also engaged her and the defending destroyers from as few as 9,000 yards. This is one of the very few photos showing Japanese and American combatants in the same frame, and the *Tone* class heavy cruiser firing on the horizon at left is believed to be the *Chikuma*.

difficult. The Japanese fought on, despite being cut off from all support from the surrounding islands and on December 15, MacArthur declared the island secured (although combat would last to April).

Colonel Sprinkle here recounts the difficulties of supplying the troops once they got to the interior of Leyte.

The supply problem was very acute. Roads were scarce, traffic demands were tremendous, and many times troops were miles from any road. Water supply by amphibious truck, LVT, and LCM [Landing Craft, Mechanized; usually a Higgins boat] via the San Juanico Strait facilitated this matter. Airdrop made it possible to get supplies to troops, which were so isolated that all other means including native carrier were inadequate. Air-ground coordination in this method of supply was very difficult. The jungle is so thick that the use of panels [marking areas for airdrops] cannot be considered. Smoke is uncertain. Map coordinates are so unreliable that they are worthless.

The only method that brought satisfactory results was to fly an observer...over the troops in the field artillery liaison plane. After seeing what the terrain looked like from the air and [picking] out a spot to make his drop, put this same observer in the plane that is to make the airdrop. He can then direct the crew of the airdrop plane.

Poor roads, constant rains, and the resultant mud made the operation, maintenance, and upkeep of motor vehicles a very difficult problem. Wear and tear on these vehicles were so great that nearly all will have to be replaced in the very near future.

Lieutenant General Walter Krueger comments on the unique challenge Leyte posed for Fifth Air Force to provide land-based air support to his operations.

The inadequate number of aircraft on Leyte practically ruled out all close support missions and materially restricted direct support missions. In fact, the first air strike by Army planes in support of ground troops was not made until November 26. But even after that date, air strike in close support of troops was very limited.

The failure to provide adequate air strength on Leyte during most of the operation was definitely not the fault of the air forces, however. Fifth Air Force had an ample number of planes available on Morotai and at other bases in rear areas but could not bring them forward until the necessary facilities had been provided for them on Leyte. It was therefore no wonder that Fifth Air Force fighters had all they could do to hold their own against Japanese air raids, and that very few planes were available to keep hostile reinforcements from reaching the island, and practically none for close support missions.

The battle for the Philippines was far from over. While the fighting continued on to Leyte, MacArthur pushed on with his plans to recapture the remainder of the islands, especially Luzon. General Eichelberger and the Eighth Army took over on Leyte as General Krueger and the Sixth Army redeployed for an invasion of Luzon. The forces, at least in terms of ground troops, were evenly matched—280,000 for MacArthur and about 287,000 for Yamashita, who decided not to contest the beaches, but rather to continue the new strategy of drawing the Americans into attrition battles in the mountainous interior.

Sonarman First Class Jack Gebhardt, a crewmember of USS Pringle *(DD-477) remembers his first exposure to kamikaze attacks during MacArthur's Philippine campaign in late 1944 and early 1945.*

The only way to stop a suicide-piloted plane was to shoot it down before it hit you. Now there could be no margin for error. Prior to the kamikaze attack style, we would shoot at the Japs and they would bomb us; sometimes everybody missed! It was horrifying to try and comprehend someone intentionally diving through a hail of deadly antiaircraft fire with the sole purpose of killing themselves in a blinding explosion.

The first kamikaze attack against the *Pringle* occurred [on November 27, 1944] the day after arriving at Leyte Gulf. As the Japanese planes approached our anchorage area, the antiaircraft fire from U.S. picket ships [warships posted in outlying rings to protect the main force from Japanese air attacks] intensified and a continuous stream of red tracers [bullets that leave a trail of fire or smoke to aid in aiming a weapon] could be seen as our ships hurried to circle or steam away to avoid the attack. The Jap planes seemed to be everywhere and the noise of gunfire, explosions, and yelling was intense as we manned our battle stations.

A light cruiser came under persistent attack by about a dozen planes and all were shot down without hitting the ship, but then

suddenly a lone Jap plane dove out of the clouds and struck the ship. The explosion was ear-shattering and smoke and flames were soon belching from the stricken vessel as she maneuvered to avoid further hits. The frequency of enemy air raids over the next several weeks at Leyte Gulf was intense and many times the *Pringle* crew remained at battle stations for several hours. The human stress level from the constant air attacks rose, and fear could be seen in the eyes of every man, [however] showing fear was not a sign of cowardliness.

The *Pringle* was assigned to antiaircraft patrol in the Philippines area and was constantly in the thick of the air attacks. Finally, the *Pringle* was ordered to Pamoc Bay on the western side of Leyte Gulf for fire support duty covering our ground troops moving along the

ABOVE: Jeeps and fully loaded two-and-a-half-ton trucks head for the invasion of Leyte aboard an LST (landing ship, tank). The vehicles have been jammed tightly along the center of the ship's weather deck to both increase stability and provide gunners manning the outboard 20mm Oerlikons maximum freedom of movement. Cracking open even one door on some of these vehicles is out of the question, but their canvas- or open-topped cabs allow drivers to clamber over hoods and supplies to reach their seats. Upon grounding, the LST's massive bay doors were swung open and a vehicle ramp near the bow allowed their exit.

Captives Freed in Lightning Strikes

U.S. operations on Luzon were conducted with such speed that the Imperial Army was unable to move to Japan all of the prisoners it held. Intelligence gathered by Filipino guerrillas revealed that the already-wretched conditions in POW camps—only marginally better at the overcrowded civilian detainee compound in Manila—were deteriorating rapidly. American forces from MacArthur on down were already determined to rescue as many prisoners as possible and were further spurred by the discovery that some 150 POWs on the Philippine island of Palawan had been herded into an air-raid shelter where they were doused with gasoline and burned alive.

Although the Japanese had managed to move most of the captives beyond reach, guerrillas confirmed that roughly 500 survivors of the Bataan Death March remained at the infamous Cabanatuan POW camp, a tantalizing 25 miles from U.S. lines. A daring night rescue mission was quickly organized and conducted by the 9th Ranger Infantry Battalion with critical support from the area's large, well-organized guerrilla force and elements of the Sixth Army's "Alamo Scouts" intelligence unit.

The U.S.-Filipino force moved undetected behind Japanese lines to the camp with its 150-man Japanese garrison and secured it in a precisely timed assault on the night of January 30, 1945. The emaciated prisoners were brought out—in some cases, literally on the backs of Rangers—with many who were too weak to move ferried along jungle paths on locally acquired carts. During the fighting withdrawal, Filipino units held back Japanese counterattacks of up to 800 strong.

Several days later, heavily armed "flying columns" of the U.S. 1st Cavalry Division burst through Japanese defenses and rushed headlong to the 3,767 POWs held in Manila's Bilibid Prison as well as Santo Tomas University where a similar number of civilian internees were being held in increasingly squalid conditions.

American tanks crashed through the university gate shortly after dark on the evening of February 3, and a perimeter was formed to protect the grounds, still surrounded by Imperial troops.

Most internees at Santo Tomas were freed immediately, but a large number were held hostage in the Education Building for two days by the compound's sixty-five Japanese guards. The commander of the rescue operation, Brigadier General William Chase, immediately entered into negotiations with the Japanese, explaining to a reporter: "Our mission is to save these prisoners, not get them killed." After two days of tense negotiations, an agreement was reached. The guards—still armed—were escorted to Japanese lines flanked by a wary parade of U.S. soldiers, and with an American officer, Colonel Charles E. Brady, in the lead.

LEFT: Three men who led Army Rangers on the mission to free the POWs at Cabanatuan (left to right): Captain Robert W. Prince, commanding officer of the Rangers; Lieutenant Colonel Henry A. Mucci, overall commander of the rescue operation; and Staff Sergeant Theodore R. Richardson of Company C, who led the assault on the prison compound's main gate.

coast. During the transit to Pamoc Bay with another "tin can" [destroyer], a Japanese submarine was sighted on the surface and both destroyers attacked immediately. The gunfire exchange was short but deadly as the sub took a direct hit, exploded, and sank quickly. There was no time to search for survivors as the air attacks had become so frequent that to stop would be very dangerous. The air raids continued in the Leyte Gulf area, but *Pringle* was ordered to make a quick run to Tagoban Island for supplies and mail. Some of the crew got ashore, but the town only consisted of a few tin huts and mud buildings, but it was a safe haven from the Jap air raids.

In December 1944, we participated in the invasion of Mindanao in the [southern] Philippine Islands and escorted several supply convoys carrying men and equipment through the Surigao Straits, southwest past Cebu and Negros islands to Mindanao. The trips took almost four days due to the slow speed of the supply ships and we were attacked frequently, resulting in numerous casualties. The air attacks now involved Jap suicide planes, which made the encounters even more deadly.

The final *Pringle* trip to Mindanao was escorting supply ships, and the Japanese attacked continuously day and night as we steamed through the Surigao Straits, then just north of Mindanao the Japs really hit us hard. A large ammunition freighter got hit and exploded in a blinding flash. When the ship blew up, the pilothouse was blown onto another ship, which exploded and the debris rained down on us almost a mile away from the blast.

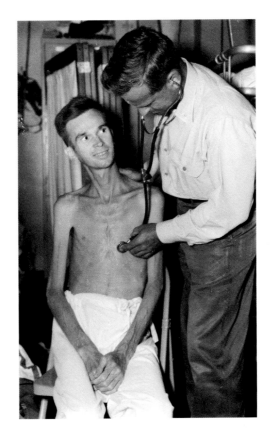

LEFT: Freed POW, Marine Corporal Leopold A. Kulikowski of Muskegon, Michigan, is examined by a Navy doctor V. G. Clark aboard the hospital ship *Benevolence* in Tokyo Bay. Kulikowski was a survivor of Corregidor, Bataan, and the unmarked Japanese "hell ships" that brought POWs from Luzon to Japan, and his physical condition testifies to the horrors of internment by the Japanese. American POWs in the Philippines experienced a mortality rate of 40 percent.

There were no survivors from the ammunition ship, and the convoy never slowed down to search for survivors due to the threat of attack. The raids became fanatical and furious in their attempt to hit us. Sometimes a suicide plane would pass so close overhead we could see the pilot struggling to control his aircraft before it plunged into the ocean and exploded.

There were seldom any survivors among the Jap pilots. The enemy air raids continued and the *Pringle* crew seldom slept or ate with any regularity. Our Marine CAP (Combat Air

AMERICAL DIVISION

Activated in May 1942 on the Southwest Pacific island of New Caledonia, the Americal Division helped defend Henderson Field on Guadalcanal against determined Japanese attacks on October 23–25, then took part in the offensive that ended resistance on the island. It landed on Bougainville, relieving the 3d Marine Division in December 1943, and went on the offensive in March 1944. In early April, the Americal Division drove the Japanese east of Mavavia River and seized numerous hills during the rest of the month. During the liberation of the Philippines, the division first engaged in cleaning out remaining Japanese forces on Leyte, Samar, and other islands. On March 26, the division landed on Cebu and seized its capital city and airfield within two days. Combat teams from the Americal subsequently made landings on Bohol, Negros, and Mindanao, where they cleared out pockets of resisting Japanese through June 1945, then took part in the occupation of Japan.

BELOW: The forward dual-purpose 5-inch guns of the destroyer USS *Pringle* practice target acquisition under the direction of the ships gunnery officers in the director turret atop the bridge. Note that the No. 2 turret's gun is at maximum elevation and that No. 1's is tracking with the Mk 4 radar antenna mounted on the director turret. The OS2U Kingfisher scout plane high overhead was part of a brief experiment to see if a destroyer could effectively handle such aircraft. The *Pringle* was sunk in April 1945 by a bomb-laden kamikaze while operating at a radar picket station 75 miles north-northwest of Okinawa.

Patrol) pilots were extremely heroic as they pursued "Nip" planes right into our antiaircraft fire without any hesitation or thought of being hit by friendly fire. Our luck finally ran out while on patrol in the Philippines area when, while steaming at flank [high] speed, a Japanese airplane suddenly dove out of the clouds and crashed into our aft 40mm [antiaircraft] gun mount killing eleven men and wounding eighteen. Many of the wounded men were burned severely when the fuel tank exploded and one man was killed from jumping over the side to avoid the flames and being run over by the ship.

We buried our shipmates at sea the next day between attacks and there was not even time for prayer as we scanned the sky for enemy aircraft from our battle stations. After the *Pringle* was hit, I walked past the Officer's

Wardroom, where the wounded were being treated, and the smell of burned flesh and cries of pain were overwhelming. The explosion and fire had destroyed a 40mm [anti-aircraft] and a 5-inch [main battery] gun mount so we were ordered to the Admiralty Islands, north of New Guinea, for repairs. The ship tied up between a heavily damaged cruiser and a destroyer tender performing the repairs. In less than a week the destroyer tender crew had cut several holes in the deck, removed the damaged guns, and replaced them with salvaged guns from the sinking cruiser.

On January 9, 1945, the Americans surged ashore at the same location on Luzon's western coast the Japanese had landed at some three years earlier. Yamashita abandoned Manila shortly thereafter, although Japanese naval troops—not under Yamashita's command—went on a rampage of rape and murder in the city, killing perhaps 30,000 Filipinos in the process. By February 3, the first American patrols had

reached Manila. However, the naval troops had decided to turn Manila into the Stalingrad of the Pacific and much of the city was leveled in the fighting that followed. The JCS wanted MacArthur to end his operations with the neutralization of Japanese forces in Luzon and then prepare for the invasion of Japan, but MacArthur launched numerous other amphibious operations across the rest of the Philippines. MacArthur never did completely subdue the islands, and Yamashita held out until after the atomic bombs had been dropped.

Kamikaze aircraft were not the only suicide units in the Japanese inventory. Here Navy Lieutenant (junior grade) J.F. Brown, Commanding Officer of LCI (M) 974, remembers how his craft was sunk by a suicide boat during the landings at Lingayen Gulf on January 9–10, 1945.

After the army had started inland from the beach area, we retired to the seaward,

ABOVE: A "Murderers' Row" of Third Fleet carriers at anchor in Ulithi atoll, shortly after the Battle of Leyte Gulf, as photographed from a USS *Ticonderoga* plane on December 8, 1944. First row, front-to-back are carriers *Wasp, Yorktown, Hornet, Hancock, Ticonderoga,* and battleship *New Jersey*. Second row, front to back are a *Fletcher*-class destroyer, a *Cimarron*-class fleet oiler, battleship *South Dakota* (nearly invisible in this photo due to its all-blue camouflage), and a hospital ship. Third row, front to back are an *Independence*-class light fleet carrier (anchored somewhat forward of the row's center-line), and the bow of the battleship *Iowa*.

The Divine Wind—Death from Above

The brutal attrition of men and machines in the skies above the Solomon Islands and New Guinea, coupled with the disastrous defeats at Midway and the Marianas, had cost Japan nearly all of its best pilots by the fall of 1944. Desperate to stem the tide of the relentless American advance across the Pacific, the Japanese began to employ the "divine wind"—suicidal kamikaze tactics—as a last-ditch alternative to conventional bombing attacks.

A novice pilot willing to die for his emperor could fly an obsolescent aircraft into a warship infinitely more easily than he could aim a bomb at it, and sheer momentum would frequently carry a damaged, burning aircraft to its target even after its pilot had been killed. More experienced airmen, deemed too valuable to sacrifice, were to provide fighter cover or to fly conventional strikes.

At first, suicide attacks were organized on an ad hoc basis from Nichols Field in the Philippines, and on October 13, 1944, the aircraft carrier USS *Franklin* was apparently the first target of a kamikaze one week prior to official authorization of the 13-aircraft Shimpu Tokubetsu Kogekitai (Divine Wind Special Attack Corps) unit of volunteer suicide pilots. First blood was drawn on October 25–26, when a five-plane raid sank the escort carrier *St. Lo* and damaged three similar flattops.

This prompted many more young fliers to volunteer, and on October 30, a kamikaze attack damaged three large fleet carriers so severely that they had to be pulled back to the Ulithi anchorage for repairs. Within days, another large flattop fell victim, as did three more toward the end of November. This stunning disruption of carrier air power

spelled the loss of 10 Liberty ships and tank landing ships (LSTs) as well as six destroyer-type vessels during the opening days of the Leyte invasion, and had a pronounced effect on the conduct of the subsequent ground campaign.

Buoyed by their successes—some real and some only imagined—the Japanese honed their tactics and massively expanded their suicide units to deal with the next American landings. When the blow fell on Okinawa on April 1, 1945, they flung themselves at the invaders in a series of attacks that stretched well into June. Exactly 400 warships and large landing craft were struck, including thirty-two that were sunk outright and more than forty so heavily damaged that they had to be scrapped, plus more than sixty others knocked out of the war while undergoing extensive repairs.

桑田軍曹　国分少尉　磯谷少尉

BELOW: One of the very few operational Japanese aircraft in the western Caroline Islands, a Nakajima B6N "Jill" torpedo bomber, flies through a storm of antiaircraft fire in a futile effort to sink an American warship on January 31, 1945. This photo may be the kamikaze strike of the same date that inflicted insignificant damage on the escort carrier *Manila Bay* near Ulithi anchorage as it headed back to San Diego for battle damage repairs. The ship had been badly struck off Luzon on January 5, with fourteen men killed and fifty-two wounded.

consolidated our ammunition with other LCI(M)s, and remained at anchor for call fire on special targets [fire missions requested by the Army troops ashore on designated targets]. We were not called on to come in during the

rest of the day for any special assignment so we remained at anchor until late in the afternoon, up to the time for laying a smoke screen. Then we proceeded just to seaward of the transport area with other LCIs and anchored approximately 6,000 yards from the beach in about 20 fathoms of water, and then we laid smoke screens [using smoke to conceal the movements and location of friendly ships, somewhat like heavy fog] until approximately dark. We remained at anchor during the night and at about 0400, a small enemy speedboat sneaked in and hit us on the port [left] side.

There were quite a few other ships around. I believe there was an army boat close by that sent over some sort of a dinghy and

then later some other ship, probably an APA [attack transport], sent over an LCVP [landing craft]. I had my full quota of mortar ammunition which was approximately 20 tons, after I had consolidated with another LCI. I also had a full magazine of 20mm [antiaircraft gun] ammunition. We were very fortunate in not having any...internal explosions, or any fires on the ship, because where the [suicide boat's] explosion occurred was underneath the fuel tanks, and the diesel fuel men who were below in the compartments where the diesel oil was, the fumes were quite bad and it was all mixed with the water that came in...the ship sank in about six minutes, which was a very short time.

All the power was knocked out and it was in complete darkness, the battle lamps were all jarred loose, and of course the flashlights were hard to find in all the confusion, and by the time the injured men got out, it was time to abandon ship.

BELOW: After breaking into Manila's Rizal Stadium, 1st Cavalry Division troops move cautiously across right field. An important Japanese supply dump was located under the bleachers, and a deep, 15-foot-wide drainage ditch on the other side of the facility limited tank access to the area. These soldiers are attempting to attack the "back door" of the fortified ballpark, but Imperial Marines had fortified the infield and waited until troops had entered the enclosed space before firing from the dugouts-turned-bunkers and concrete-lined stairwells in the bleachers. The 1st Cavalry used tanks, satchel charges, and flamethrowers to reduce the defenses on February 16, 1945. After the Japanese had taken control of Manila in the waning days of 1941, American civilians and foreign nationals had been processed for internment at the stadium, and it was used as a U.S. supply dump after its costly seizure.

ABOVE: A Nakajima Ki-43 "Oscar" peels off after making an apparently unsuccessful attack against the undefended belly of the photographer's B-25. The other bombers in formation are a B-25C/D (left) and B-25J.

Where is TF-34? The World Wonders.

ABOVE: Admiral William F. Halsey on the bridge of the USS *New Jersey*, flagship of the U.S. Third Fleet, in December 1944.

The Battle of Leyte Gulf was the last major fleet action in history between two large industrial navies. The battle was full of drama, incredible heroism, and controversy. On this last score, the confusion and uncertainty that reigns in a modern sea battle was encapsulated by what happened when the flamboyant and pugnacious Admiral William F. Halsey took the bulk of his Third Fleet, Task Force-38 (TF-38), north to engage Vice Admiral Jisaburo Ozawa's Northern Force—a group of carriers whose sole mission was to act as a decoy. As a result, he uncovered the San Bernardino Strait for Admiral Kurita's battleships and drew down a firestorm of judgment and implied criticism forever after, tarnishing an otherwise brilliant naval career.

The roots of Halsey's and the Navy's misfortune can be traced to several causes, chief of which was the divided command structure for the U.S. Navy forces supporting General Douglas MacArthur's invasion of the Philippines in October 1944.

MacArthur's primary naval support was provided by Vice Admiral Thomas C. Kinkaid's Seventh Fleet, which was composed primarily of amphibious shipping, older battleships, cruisers, and a host of smaller combatant vessels. He controlled very few aircraft carriers, so most of his naval aircraft providing fighter cover, anti-submarine patrols, and close air support, were based on escort carriers, or CVEs. Halsey, on the other hand, worked for the Pacific Theater Commander, Admiral Chester Nimitz, whose headquarters was thousands of miles away at Pearl Harbor.

Halsey was tasked to provide carrier protection for the invasion with the powerful TF-38, which included seventeen medium-to-large aircraft carriers, six new battleships, and over eighty cruisers and destroyers. Of particular importance were Halsey's new fast battleships under Vice Admiral Willis Lee of Guadalcanal fame. Halsey was given contingency orders to separate Lee's battle wagons from his carriers as a new task force, TF-34, at his discretion. Everyone from Nimitz on down to Kinkaid and MacArthur assumed that Halsey would do just that if he needed to move his carriers out of the vicinity guarding the San Bernardino Strait. Unfortunately, Halsey's orders also included an additional paragraph that specified that if Halsey was offered the opportunity to destroy the main Japanese carrier force that was to become his primary mission.

This paragraph had probably been added as an afterthought because of what had happened months earlier at the Philippine Sea when Vice Admiral Raymond Spruance was perceived to have let the bulk of the Japanese carrier force escape due to his excessive caution. In reality, the Japanese carrier force was no longer a credible force, and Japanese battleships were now the main threat to U.S. naval operations.

At first, things went well enough for TF-38. Kurita was discovered on October 25 and pounded by Halsey's aircraft in the Sibuyan Sea as it sailed east toward the U.S. beachhead. Halsey's dive- and torpedo-bombers sank the super battleship *Musashi* and Kurita's battered force turned back to the west. As night settled in, so did confusion about just how badly the Japanese had been defeated. When other forces under Admirals Shoji Nishimura and Kiyohide Shima tried to take the southern route late that night and were turned back, a false sense of relief and overconfidence set in. However, Halsey was convinced that the main effort had not yet been made, the one he expected from the remnants of Japan's once mighty carrier-based naval aviation.

Meanwhile, Admiral Ozawa in command of the Northern Force obliged Halsey's misconception. He broke radio silence in an attempt to attract Halsey's attention in order to lure him away from his guard station off the San Bernadino Strait. Ozawa finally succeeded when he launched a feeble air strike that finally attracted the Americans. Halsey immediately executed what he thought were his primary orders, to destroy the "main" Japanese fleet. In speeding north, he took his battleships with him, since Ozawa's force was reported to have several battleships in company (it had two).

As Halsey moved north he notified Kinkaid of his plans, but neglected to inform Kinkaid that he had not formed TF-34 to watch the strait in his absence. Thus, while Halsey assumed that Kurita was heading away from the battle,

Kinkaid assumed that TF-34 was watching the strait just in case Kurita turned around. Kinkaid proceeded blissfully along in his ignorance as his own older battleships of the Seventh Fleet pursued the beaten remnants of the Japanese Southern Force ships.

Reality intruded when Kurita's Main Force, suddenly appeared and began attacking the weak escort carrier groups covering Leyte Gulf off Samar Island. By this time, Halsey was almost 400 miles away obliterating Ozawa's decoy force. Kinkaid lost his composure and sent a message asking Halsey to send Vice Admiral John McCain's carrier task group to the rescue, but there was no chance at all that McCain would arrive in time to salvage the situation.

Halsey continued to pursue Ozawa's decoy fleet. At the same time, the frantic messages being transmitted across the radio waves were being monitored by Admiral Nimitz in Hawaii. Once Nimitz found out that Kurita was attacking off Samar, he sent Halsey a message asking, "Where is Task Force 34?" Unfortunately, this message had what was called "padding" attached to it for communications security purposes. When the message was decoded at Halsey's end, the padding,

which decoded to "the world wonders" was attached to the rest of the message that was handed to Halsey.

What Halsey received seemed like a slap in the face from the boss in Hawaii, "Where is Task Force 34? The World Wonders." Halsey reportedly broke out in tears and threw his cap on the deck. He then terminated his pursuit and turned his force around; too late to catch the wily Kurita, who had slipped back through the San Bernardino Strait after prematurely breaking off his attack.

In the aftermath of the battle, Halsey's poor run of luck continued when he led his fleet into a major typhoon and suffered even further ship losses and more criticism. Nevertheless, the Japanese were soundly defeated and Halsey was never officially reprimanded for a decision, which admittedly, was as much due to his opponent's skill and the fog of war as it was to the Admiral's own judgment.

BELOW: The battleship *Musashi* and escorting destroyers under attack in the Sibuyan Sea on October 24, 1944. Bereft of meaningful air cover, the battleship was overpowered by masses of American carrier aircraft, yet it took seventeen bomb hits and a remarkable nineteen torpedoes blasting her hull before the *Musashi* finally capsized. Destroyers *Kiyoshimo* and *Shimakaze* rescued 1,376 of her 2,399-man crew.

There were three shock waves from the Hiroshima weapon. The first one was a good jolt....There was, and I was quite aware of, a brilliance in the airplane....Simultaneously with that, I tasted it...I tasted that thing [the bomb] just as clear as could be.

—Colonel Paul W. Tibbets

Chapter Eight

REAPING THE WHIRLWIND

With the effective destruction of the Japanese Fleet and the fall of the Philippines imminent, America and its allies were now poised to begin the final destruction of Japan. The debates about how to do this varied depending on which service you talked to. The Navy thought a blockade would starve the Japanese into surrender. The Army Air Corps was just as convinced that a strategic bombing campaign would end the war. Finally, the Army—especially General Marshall—believed that an invasion of Japan would be necessary in order to bring about the Japanese capitulation. FDR, and later President Harry S. Truman, believed the participation of the Soviet Union was also essential as a means to break the Imperial will. As usual, the Americans planned for and executed, until the fateful days of August 1945, all of these options.

The Japanese strategy had become clear—bleed the Americans until public opinion in the United States forced the American political leadership to negotiate a close to hostilities. If this could be accomplished, the emperor would remain in place with Japan unoccupied, and perhaps with most of the land seized in China still in Imperial hands. To this end, the next two great battles of the Pacific War—Iwo Jima and Okinawa—reflect the perfection of this grim strategy.

Iwo Jima

The capture of these islands was essential. Iwo Jima, a volcanic rock some 600 miles south of Japan, had several airfields from which Japanese fighters could attack the B-29s flying from the Marianas as well as warn the main islands of impending raids. The strategic air campaign had first begun from China in the summer of 1944, but the logistics challenge of that offensive was enormous. With Admiral Spruance's capture of the Marianas, the bombing forces relocated to this superior geographic location. Tinian and Saipan would serve as the pillars for the air assault and Guam's Apra Harbor became the linchpin for subsequent amphibious operations.

In late November, the B-29 offensive began against the Japanese Home Islands—a 2,600-mile round-trip with 111 B-29s carrying almost 10 tons of bombs. Major General Curtis LeMay, fresh from China, took over this offensive in January 1945. Iwo was the thorn in the side of his efforts and by January it was decided that it must be captured in order to stage fighter escorts for the bombers heading to Japan. Iwo could also serve as an emergency divert base for bombers damaged over Japan that could not make it all the way back to the far-off Marianas.

 Major General Curtis E. LeMay recalls the air offensive against Japan using the B-29 bomber.

A lot of effort had gone into the B-29. We were operating at high altitudes and ran into strong jet streams, which seriously affected our range. Additionally, the B-29 was in a development status; there were "bugs" in it

and operating at high altitude aggravated our mechanical problems. The weather was very bad in Japan; only three to seven days per month were suitable for visual bombing. At the Marianas, after a few weeks, it became apparent to me that we had to do something. We had to come down under the weather, right down on deck if necessary, to get the job done. I made the decision. If it failed, [General] Arnold could have chosen someone else for my job. The use of firebombs coincided with the initiation of the low altitude attacks. Although the 350 aircraft we then possessed were less than the number desired to do the firebombing job properly, we went ahead with the firebombing. Radar had just arrived but our radar operators, most of whom were former gunners, were very poorly trained. So we set up a radar training school and also trained lead pilots and lead bombardiers. We progressed rapidly, and eventually we could hit a factory in a thunderstorm. With radar, we could bomb in any weather.

Admiral Spruance's Fifth Fleet staff was given the task of capturing Iwo Jima. In addition to the world's most powerful naval force, Spruance would have the V Amphibious Corps under Marine General Harry Schmidt. And so began a campaign to take a tiny volcanic island whose very name came to represent "uncommon valor" and the heroism of the United States Marine Corps. The Japanese commander, General Tadamichi Kuribayashi, crafted his defenses carefully, with interlocking fields of fire for his artillery hidden in mazes of tunnels beneath the volcanic rock, especially the eastern end of the island. Iwo Jima became a battle between the Marines and Navy fire support on the surface and subterranean Japanese troops who had vowed to die to the last man.

The Marines landed on February 16, 1945. Despite an extensive air assault, and a powerful but ineffective naval bombardment, Kuribayashi was as good as his sacred word to his emperor. His 21,000 soldiers burrowed deeper and then emerged from holes and caves to punish the Marines.

An LCVP landing craft, the famed Higgins boat, brought Marine enlisted grunt Jack Lucas to Iwo Jima's deadly shore.

The first three or four waves went in with amtracs. The rest of us went in on Higgins boats. We circled and circled out there waiting for our turn to go in and when we finally went in is when they really, really opened up on us. So the reason the Japanese held back on heavy artillery at first was to allow more Marines to get on the beach, and be able to kill more Marines instead of just trying to pick us off coming in. I mean, it was really heavy shelling.

My Higgins boat operator, he must have been scared to death 'cause he wouldn't even pull up to the land. I guess he was afraid he would get the boat hung on the beach somewhere. So when he dumped us out, we went up to our necks in water. And, unfortunately, I had been assigned a pair of fatigues [pants] that I should have rolled up. When I went in that water and came up on that beach, man, I looked like Charlie Chaplin with that thing flapping over my feet. So I hastily took my bowie knife out and cut the things off. Every time I heard a shell hit near me I said, "God, if I hear it, it had to miss me. If I don't hear it, I ain't got to worry about it." So from then on, I didn't duck down or jump down when the shells came nearby and I just progressed up through the volcanic ash of beach, which was about a 45-degree angle.

 Coxswain Third Class Bill Konop was one of quite a few Seabees at Iwo Jima. He remembers the initial landing.

On the sixteenth of February we left Saipan and arrived Iwo Jima on the eighteenth. I was a runner for the reconnaissance party for C Company, and my role was to carry messages to the platoons on the right flank. We did not think it would be dangerous because they had bombed that island for seventy-two consecutive days and prior to the landing, they had shelled it from the battleships and cruisers, for three or four days. So we thought it would be a piece of cake to walk on the island. But, boy, were we wrong.

On the nineteenth we were awakened at three o'clock in the morning and for breakfast we had bacon, steak, and eggs. At seven-thirty,

BELOW: Amphibious tractors (LVTs) packed with Marines approach Iwo Jima (literally Sulfur Island) on February 19, 1945. Almost completely obscured by smoke from the heavy bombardment, Iwo Jima's Mount Suribachi is just visible at left. These amtracs are part of the force that landed 4th Marine Division troops at the two BLUE Beaches, northernmost of Iwo Jima's eastern landing zones.

The first three or four waves went in with amtracs. The rest of us went in on Higgins boats. We circled and circled out there waiting for our turn to go in and when we finally went in is when they really, really opened up on us. So the reason the Japanese held back on heavy artillery at first was to allow more Marines to get on the beach, and be able to kill more Marines instead of just trying to pick us off coming in. I mean, it was really heavy shelling.

—Jack Lucas

I was summoned to my LCDP landing craft and we disembarked from the ship. We circled about a half a mile off the beach. The artillery fire was just terrible, but finally, about noon, I think, about noon, D-Day we went in. Our landing craft ran up on the beach, but the ramp wouldn't go down on the boat. So several of the Marines started over to the right side of the boat and they all either fell in the water or fell back in the boat shot. So finally everybody started jumping off the left side of the boat, which I did too. The ocean floor drops off so tremendously, and when I jumped off the boat I was up to the back of my neck in water, just like that. But I made it on the beach. Artillery shells and mortar shells were landing all around us. And machine gun and rifle bullets. It just surprised me that we made it onto the beach, but we did. It was a curtain—a curtain of red-hot bits of fragments of shells.

It was a shock, completely a shock. In fact, I watched the second wave come in behind us. When the ramp came down, these Marines were running off the ramp and they were just falling on their faces. I couldn't understand what was going on. Here they were being shot. But I didn't realize it. They were being shot and just falling right down, just like that. It didn't take long for me to know this was not the place to be.

The shells were landing around us, about every ten or fifteen seconds. [The Japanese] had every bit of the beach zeroed in. And, they had Mount Suribachi to our left with its guns. To our right were the high bluffs. To the front were the airfields built up on a higher plane. So we were right down in the hole there and we tried to dig a foxhole into that volcanic ash—it was impossible. It's just like trying to dig in a bed of wheat or grain. It just keeps caving in on you. It was hard—you couldn't hardly move, let alone perform your duties. There was no place to run to—if you wanted to run back, you'd be in the water. The first message I ran I wasn't really running, I was more or less crawling—maybe run a couple steps and dive, and it was more crawling for about 30 to 40 yards. No matter where I was, the situation was bad.

I carried my last message about five-thirty in the afternoon. It was the message to platoon leaders there to my right flank, to maintain present position for the night and they all frowned on that. They wanted to move up, because the beach was just a just a terrible place to be. But I was wounded right after I carried that message—I got shrapnel in the face and back, and a concussion. I didn't feel nothing actually, but first thing you know my buddy was laying alongside me and said, "Your face is all bloody." I knew I was wounded, but I didn't think it was that bad. The blood made it look much worse than what it actually was. I was evacuated to the hospital ship about six o'clock.

That was a million-dollar wound, to get off that darn island. I was out at the hospital ship for about seven days, and they sent me back in because my wounds weren't that bad and they needed the room for the severely injured Marines. I rejoined my outfit, but by then everything was tamed down pretty good on the beach there, so it wasn't that bad. We lived in a foxhole for forty-five days, and after

the island was secured, we began working on the airfields. We had our own hot mix asphalt plant, our own rock-crushing plant. So we worked on the airfields and we built roads. Our battalion, the 133d, we had 1,100 that landed on D-Day, we had forty-two killed and 370 wounded—which is 34 percent casualty rate. Most of these casualties were suffered within the first forty-eight hours. So we had horrific casualties for our battalion. There's hardly a day goes by that I don't think of this invasion and my buddies that were killed on that island.

 Marine John Sbordone remembers the terror occasioned by Japanese tunnel tactics at Iwo Jima.

Well, we knew that they were great for caves and also tunneling, because we had that same thing happen at the other islands. And, of course, this island wasn't any different and it was ideal for tunneling. They come out and they fire at you and then they disappear again. So you put one and one together and you say to yourself they must be either in caves or spider traps or tunnels. So, that's how, eventually we started looking for them.

On Hill 382, what they were doing is that they would fight you from the face and let you come up to them; they would go down in their tunnels and go down behind you, come behind you, and shoot you in the back. In order for them to do that, you had to know that they had to have something like that [tunnels].

We didn't [take] too many prisoners on Iwo Jima. Most of them were dead or killed by the fighting and everything. But on the other island [Okinawa], we did. And the Japanese seemed like they were never, ever taught to not say anything. Once they get captured, they just talk. They just talk, talk, talk. They'll tell you almost anything. And then you question them and they'll tell you about the tunnels and everything.

We were working right on the other side of the airfield. And we got into a target area called Charlie Dog. And the Japanese opened up on us and we all dove into this huge bomb crater. And you're safe as long as you stayed to the forward part of that hole...that crater.

But if you drifted, they could shoot you. And it happened, a couple of guys got wounded. I had the captain, the first sergeant, and we had the radioman, we had a couple run-

BELOW: The ominous mass of Mount Suribachi towers above 5th Marine Division tanks and infantry as they clear the neck of land between it and Japanese Airfield No. 1. This bloody task was accomplished by nightfall on D-Day, February 19, 1945, but it would take three more days of heavy fighting before Suribachi was finally taken. Iwo Jima, which split the distance between the U.S. bomber bases in the Marianas and Japan, was tenaciously defended by an entire division of Imperial troops because of its suitability for airfield development within easy reach of Japanese industrial cities.

ners, and myself. There was about six of us in there. And every time we would stick a helmet up on a rifle, they put a hole through it.

And so we couldn't move. No matter how we tried. So we stayed there for a while. Something possessed the first sergeant to raise up out of the hole and look up over the edge of the hole and a machine gun opened up right through the head. I pulled him down and he was dead already.

He had a .45 automatic, which I copped because he had no more use for it, and 'cause we weren't issued .45s anymore after the Japanese were shooting everybody that carried a .45. After we took Hill 382, we got orders to tie in for the night. So I was setting up the CP and I was telling these men where I wanted them to go. And just as I did, a shot rang out and I could hear it and I grabbed my throat because I thought I was hit.

It went past me and because the [new] sergeant was so tall, it tore his nose off...the shot had to come from a spider trap because of the angle of it. He splattered us all with blood and everything and we all hit the deck. They're around you all the time. You just have to be careful and keep your eyes open. That's all you can do.

The Japanese died virtually to the last man and inflicted over 28,000 casualties on the Americans in the bloodiest month in Marine Corps history. The debate continues to this day over whether seizing Iwo Jima was worth the cost—although no airman would deny how thankful he was that the Marines took it.

Navy Seabee, Carpenter's Mate Valdemar Johansen, remembers when the first aircraft landed at Iwo Jima, before the battle was even over.

We had had a thousand guys doing all they could do, twelve hours a day, seven days a week, working on this project to get an airstrip on Iwo that could be used. And we did it and that turned out to be the big thing—not individual heroism. They figured that we saved a total of 25,000 airmen that wouldn't have made it back if they couldn't have come in. We were only 750 miles from Tokyo, you know, and that's not very far. The huge bombing raids that went from Saipan and Guam to Japan went right over Iwo.

We'd get up in the morning, it would just be one big hum and you'd look up and there'd be B-29s as far as you could see. Just unbelievable. Thousand-plane raids, you know, that's a lotta planes. And then, of course, naturally, someone would get shot up and then they'd come back and come in and that's what Iwo was for. And also we had the Mustang fighter squadrons there that would go up and follow the B-29s up and help 'em out and then come back to Iwo. The first B-29 we brought in there came in on that No. 1 airstrip and that was really something.

[The pilots] come out and they were just tickled to death. Everyone cheered, you know, we really thought, well, ha ha—that made you feel good. Years later I met one of these Mustang pilots at a reunion and he said, "You worked on that No. 1 airstrip?" And I said,

4TH MARINE DIVISION

The 4th was the first division to sail directly into battle from its base in the United States, seizing the twin islands of Roi-Namur in the Kwajalein atoll on February 1, 1944. Its capture of Saipan in the Mariana chain between June 15 and July 9, marked the first invasion of Japanese territory and provided a base for B-29 bomber strikes against Japan while simultaneously cutting off large numbers of her troops on island bases to the south. The 4th followed this operation by making an August 1 assault landing on nearby Tinian to provide for more bomber bases. The division's next target was Iwo Jima in February 1945, where it suffered murderous casualties but provided a vital airstrip from which fighter escorts could accompany the lumbering B-29s to their targets, and where bombers, either damaged or critically low on fuel, could land safely instead of ditching in the ocean.

"Yeah." And he come over and he grabbed me. He said was a P-51 pilot and he was out of gas and they said, "Well, you could take a look at Iwo. You're right there and the Seabees are supposed to have some kind of a dirt strip there." So then he came in. So he grabbed me and he said, "I would have been a dead duck if it hadn't been for that."

Those B-29s and Mustangs would come in and they were hard to handle on that clay strip, you know. They'd bounce and jump around and they'd have those extra gas tanks on, and a lotta times they were supposed to drop 'em in the ocean and there was just a little wire clip that they pulled the trigger and they were supposed to drop and sometimes they didn't drop. They'd come down and they'd really bounce hard the first trip and then they'd go up out of the way, and these tanks would fall off then and they'd come bouncing end over end down the strip.

You'd really be on your toes because [the fuel tanks] looked pretty small up in the plane but when they came bouncing down the strip, why, they were pretty good-sized tanks. I think the worst I saw was a B-29 that came in and belly-landed. It was sliding down the strip and caught on fire and it was just one big ball of fire and didn't get anybody out.

 Cyril J. O'Brien, Marine combat photographer, remembers the first flag-raising and fierce fighting on Iwo Jima.

I didn't hear much about Iwo Jima at all until probably shortly before it happened. I think they kept pretty much quiet because I guess if I learned about it as an enlisted man on Guam, then sure as heck the Japs would know about it, too. We had no idea what Iwo Jima was. We seemed to be cruising a hell of a long time and then suddenly we got up to Iwo Jima. My first impression of Iwo Jima was pandemonium, everything going on at once. My troopship pulled in very close to the shore, so close that you could actually sometimes see a firefight. I was on the ship itself when Herb, the photographer assigned to me, poked me and said, "Obie, look." I looked up at Suribachi [the famous volcanic mountain on Iwo] and I saw the flag.

It was the first flag, about ten-thirty in the morning. I had two impressions, one was erroneous and another opinion, which was very accurate. The first was, because I could see it myself, how [the flag] exemplified how efficient, how great these Marines were. I was fascinated that these Marines had done this already. We had hardly come ashore. And the second thing was the impression, which was

JACK LUCAS

the erroneous one, my God we won—that impression of victory when you saw the flag go up. But it wasn't the case because some of the worst fighting on Iwo Jima was down at Katano Point, Cushman's Pocket, the Amphitheater—all these things happened down that end of the island, remember. Suribachi of course got all the attention. They put me ashore with the Ninth Marines.

My goal coming ashore was to watch the Marines, find out what happened. I wrote, and every time I wrote I thought I was writing the greatest epic of the war—and usually I was right. The interesting thing is, you're so interested with what you were doing you sometimes almost forgot there was a war on.

I came ashore late. The beach was littered and there were the remains of amtracs turned upside down, shell cases, just the debris of war...mostly vehicles, vehicles that were broached or had been hit. Sometimes they were just torn apart but you realize that must not have been done by the surf. It had to have been done by a shell, which blew into pieces and there were direct hits with everybody killed.

The visual scene I saw of Iwo Jima when I first saw it: confusion, pandemonium, and courage. The courage I saw was these young men attacking bunkers, going in, and coming back and falling. And the other thing that impressed me was one of the instruments that

RIGHT: The first American flag raised on Mount Suribachi is wedged into the volcanic rock by survivors of E Company, 28th Marines' 3d platoon augmented by a squad from its mortar platoon. Corporal Charles Lindberg stands above and behind Private First Class James Michels in the foreground with a carbine; platoon commander Lieutenant Harold Shrier (who carried the flag) sits behind Michels, keeping an eye out in the opposite direction while Sergeant Henry Hansen (in cloth cap) and Private First Class Raymond Jacobs (standing to Hansen's right) work the flag into the rock. A firefight erupted immediately after this photo was taken, even as men cheered its raising and ships off the beach began to blare their horns.

At seeing the activity high up on the mountain, Navy Secretary James Forrestal turned to V Amphibious Corps Commander Lieutenant General Holland M. "Howlin' Mad" Smith and said "Holland, the raising of that flag on Suribachi means a Marine Corps for the next 500 years."

helped the war tremendously—flamethrowers. We used them, of course, as infantry, but the most compelling thing of all was to see these tank flamethrowers. They threw a blast of flame that seemed to me the length of a football field. The ridges were low and the flamethrower would come in and it would blast all the way along, searing all those inside of the cave. You know the pandemonium that they endured—these young and brave Japanese soldiers. Remember, they were soldiers the same as we were.

 Marine Jack Lucas was almost killed during the brutal combat on Iwo Jima.

We had a tank to come up and fire napalm into this pillbox. And we were firing on, I guess, several hundred Japanese on our side of the airstrip. Well, they had miles of underground tunnels. So they had underground tunnels linking all the pillboxes and they would come underground and come out into the trenches and that would give them some protection from direct fire. So we were firing at these Japanese in front of us when we ran into this one trench. The group leader jumps over in the other trench and there's Japs over there. He jumps on the back of one Japanese and immediately came back into ours.

It was later told to me there were eleven Japs in that trench. 'Course I didn't stop to count them myself and this is just information given to me later. I shot the first Jap in the head and the second one I could just see where it struck him right above the eye. And then my rifle jams and my buddies are firing too. But when the rifle jammed I looked down to my right, I could see two grenades. I didn't know whether they'd been there one second, two seconds, or three. So I knew I had to do something. If you see a grenade coming in, a lot of times, you can either catch it or grab it quick enough to throw it back at 'em. I immediately hollered "grenade" to alert them that they were in danger and I jammed one deep in the volcanic ash and went over with my rifle and grabbed the other one and put it under me.

RIGHT: After the initial flag-raising, a much larger flag was sent up the mountain so that the first could be sent back to the United States and preserved. A detail from E Company's 2d Platoon was sent up with the flag and within a few hours, the second raising was immortalized on film (right) and in a still photograph that would serve as the basis for the Marine Corps Monument in Washington, D.C. Both the 2d and 3d platoons suffered very heavy losses over the next several weeks of fighting. Three Marines in the second photo were killed in action, as was Sergeant William "Bill" Genaust who filmed the event.

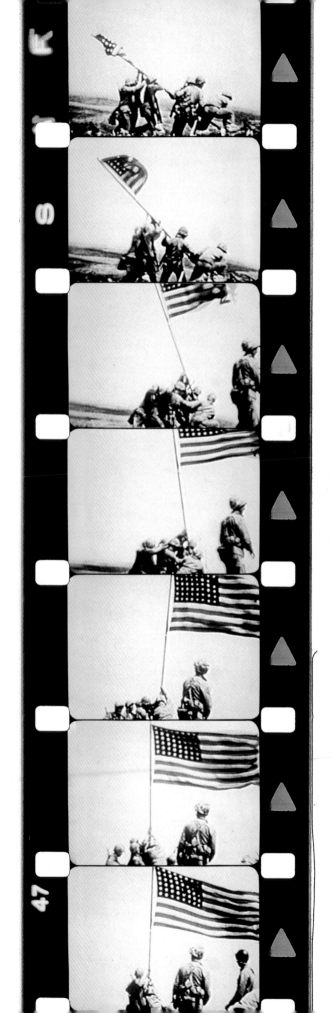

Fortunately, that one didn't go off—it was still in my hand—but the other one, it busted up my arm and got my chest and both shoulders and wounded me and also my right thigh. Some of it went up into my helmet and ricocheted down into my brain. I have about eight pieces of shrapnel in my brain; it blew my right eye and left eye out on my cheek and I was bleeding profusely from all the all these different holes in me. Even though it perforated my right lung, it still didn't knock me out. My mother later said, "I knew you were a hard-headed young man." But I survived the blow and had I been knocked out, I would have drowned in my own blood. And I was having a hard time breathing because of that.

I had to get rid of the blood so I could breathe. That was my worst problem at first. And then that numbness began to subside and all the pain racked my body. But my men had already gone on. They were still in the firefight after they'd left the trench. They

thought I was dead. The next outfit moving up noticed me moving the fingers on my left hand and they sent a corpsman over to medicate me. Injected morphine in my left arm and began to medicate all the different holes in me. By driving that grenade into the volcanic ash it blew a lot of volcanic ash into my wounds they helped coagulate a lot of my wounds. But I give more of the credit to God because I said at that time it wasn't for me to think about Mom and apple pie back home and, "Mom, will you save me?" I said, "God, will you save me, please save me God." And it seemed like the bleeding subsided from my wounds.

The corpsman was kneeling next to me and after he had medicated me and was waiting for the stretcher another Jap started to come out of the hole at the end of the trench. He killed that one. They [Navy hospital corpsmen] saved my life that day twice by being there for my wounds and giving me medication and then killing that Jap.

BELOW: Amid seeming chaos, supplies are laboriously hand-carried up the loose volcanic gravel of an Iwo Jima beach. The shoreline was under Japanese artillery fire for the first two days of the operation. The beached ship at right is a Landing Craft, Infantry (LCI), while those to its starboard are tank-landing ships (LSTs).

Bob Hope and the Troops

In 1944, Bob Hope took his intrepid band of entertainers on "The Pineapple Circuit." Throughout the summer and fall, they hopped from island to island across the South Pacific entertaining the soldiers, sailors, and Marines during more than 150 performances. It was an emotional and exhausting journey—and dangerous as well. On August 14, 1944, one of the engines on their PBY Catalina sputtered to a stop, and throwing their luggage out of the aircraft failed to lighten the aircraft enough to keep it airborne. The pilot made a forced landing near the small Australian town of Laurieton. A local fisherman, Allan "Bunny" Wallace, rescued the craft, crew, and passengers and took them ashore in his "schnapper boat." By the time the tour was all over, the little band had logged more than 30,000 miles. Plans were afoot for another tour of the Pacific when atom bombs were dropped on Hiroshima and Nagasaki.

Bob Hope: "Admiral Halsey's been very supportive of the show performing in combat areas. He promised to keep a supply of my blood type on hand, even if he had to kill the chicken himself."

LEFT: Bob Hope and his troupe exchange a few laughs with a small but "choice" audience of wounded soldiers being evacuated from Saipan on August 13, 1944. From the top, comedian Jerry "Pop Eyes" Colonna, singer Frances "I'm in the Mood for Love" Langford, guitarist Tony Romano, Hope, dancer Patty Thomas, and comedian Jack Pepper. (Above) Bob Hope joins the audience to heckle his troupe, and (below) tries to come up with a joke during a show in Munda.

ABOVE: War correspondent Ernie Pyle spends time with young Marines on a troop transport bound for the Okinawa invasion. Admired and respected by troops for his steadfast reporting of the common fighting-man, Pyle landed with the III Marine Amphibious Corps and took part in numerous patrols into Japanese territory, armed with a pocketful of pencils and a small stack of notepads. Pyle was later killed during an ambush on the Okinawan island of Ie Shima.

ICEBERG on Okinawa

The invasion of Okinawa, the main island in the Ryukyu island chain, was in many ways Iwo on a much larger scale. The Japanese objective was not simply to bleed the Americans, but to defeat them and throw them back into the sea. The Japanese Army, having failed to achieve a decisive battle in the Philippines, had decided to make the defense of Okinawa the "decisive battle" that would bring the Americans to their senses and buy time for Japanese diplomatic efforts. Perhaps a repeat of the slaughter at Iwo Jima on a more massive scale would keep the "barbarian" from Japan's sacred shores and leave its emperor on the throne.

General Simon B. Buckner, Jr. (who had commanded in the Aleutians), was chosen to lead the Tenth Army—augmented by the III Marine Amphibious Corps under Major General Roy S. Geiger. Eventually over half a million men, fought during Operation ICEBERG. Admiral Spruance would again command overall, but would essentially be limited to naval support once the troops were ashore. Spruance and Buckner had no idea what was in store for their soldiers, sailors, and Marines.

Lieutenant General Mitsuru Ushijima commanded the Japanese 32d Army on Okinawa. He was ably seconded by his brilliant operations officer Colonel Hiromichi Yahara. Yahara had convinced Ushijimi not to contest the beaches, but rather to withdraw into a series of fortified lines along the perpendicular coral mountain ridges that formed natural barriers across the southern part of the island. As at Iwo Jima and Peleliu, the goal was to force the Americans into a bloody battle of attrition against defensive lines well supported by artillery—a World War I-style battle. Despite losing his best division to reinforce Formosa, Ushijima still had about 100,000 men and over 1,000 kamikaze aircraft to commit to the battle.

The Americans' ground, air, and naval forces at Okinawa exceeded even those for Leyte Gulf, and would go down in history as the greatest seaborne invasion perhaps of all time. Over 180,000 men were landed in the first twenty-four hours. However, first blood went to the Japanese as the American carrier forces attempted their now-standard practice of neutralizing Japanese air power prior to the landing, beginning as early as March 1945. By the time Buckner's forces landed on D-Day April 1, 1945, Spruance already had four large carriers damaged by the new Japanese aerial suicide tactics and the aircraft carrier USS *Franklin* was so badly damaged she almost sank. However, the landing forces—embarked on over 1,200 ships—swarmed ashore and overran the northern half of the island quickly.

When Buckner's Army forces turned south, they ran into the first of the Japanese defensive lines and fierce resistance. The fighting now turned into a full-blown attrition battle

LEFT: Field glasses in hand, the commander of an M18 tank destroyer directs the fire of its 76mm gun in support of the 306th Infantry Regiment's May 11, 1945, attack against Chocolate Drop Hill on the Shuri Defense Line. Imperial forces on Chocolate Drop and the nearby Flattop Hill held out for more than a week against the 306th and another 77th Infantry Division regiment, the 307th. These were only two of the many defensive concentrations along the Shuri Line and its approaches that delayed the American advance on Okinawa between early April and May 21.

BELOW: Marines of the 8th Regimental Combat team seize Ibeya Island northwest of Okinawa on June 3, 1945, in order to ensure that it does not become a base for Japanese suicide boats.

on land and on sea. Ashore it was "cave warfare" against the Kakuza Ridge and then the even more formidable Shuri Line. The Japanese had planned a counteroffensive for the second week of April and damaged their defense in trying to execute it, thus losing critical manpower in needless assaults against the dug-in Americans with their superior firepower.

 One of the many unique capabilities the Americans fully exploited at Okinawa was the Army's highly skilled Nisei (Japanese) linguists, who were often first- and second-generation Japanese-Americans. Ben I. Yamamoto assigned to the 4th Marine Division remembers arriving on Okinawa.

I hit the beach on the fourth day and was greeted by a stack of dead Marines and a group of live ones sitting with blank stares. These gyrenes [Marines] have had it—cracked. They were so gung-ho on the transport, but two or three nights on the front lines broke them. This was not an encouraging start for me. We were assigned an area near the airstrip, told to dig in and wait for orders. The first night's mortar barrage was a nightmare, some shrapnel landing too close for comfort.

Another unnamed Nisei linguist remembers how their mastery of Okinawa's unique dialect proved useful during the battle.

The ability of most of our team members to speak the Okinawan dialect proved most helpful in interrogation of Japanese prisoners. This was especially valuable and effective in separating out the Japanese soldiers masquerading as Okinawan civilians. A few basic questions to them in the Okinawan dialect immediately unmasked their disguise. Very few Japanese soldiers could understand, much less speak, the dialect. They would be embarrassed when unmasked and, thereafter, would be in a more cooperative mood.

[The civilians] are cooperating very well. This morning we had quite a time inducing a crowd to come out of a cave. They said they had been told they would be tortured with needles. Now they seem happy to be safe—from the way they are chipping in to clean up rubbish, wash clothes, and make things livable. They are poor peasants for the most part—a pitiful lot who didn't expect this kind of treatment.

77TH INFANTRY DIVISION

Storming ashore on Guam in the Mariana Islands in July 21, 1944, the 77th Infantry division fought its way north to seize Mount Tenjo and effected a junction with the 3d Marine Division's beachhead. Resistance ended on August 8, and the 77th was unexpectedly sent to Leyte in the Philippines, where it fought up the east coast in December to seize Ormoc, then Valencia, and finally the key Libungao-Palompon road junction. Elements of the division made fifteen landings while securing Okinawa's outer islands between March 26 and 31, 1945. On April 16, 1945, it landed on Ie Shima, captured the airfield, and engaged in brief but bitter fights for "Bloody Ridge." Transferred to Okinawa, extremely heavy resistance slowed the 77th's progress to a crawl. The ruins of Shuri Castle were occupied in late May, and in June the division "sealed" countless Japanese cave positions during the final American drive.

The Japanese had decided to unleash the full fury of their kamikaze forces, both airplanes and suicide boats, against the American Fifth Fleet. These attacks (including a futile suicide sortie by the super battleship *Yamato*) strained the nerves and defenses of the American Navy to the breaking point. A British carrier task force, brought in to defend against the southern kamikazes out of Formosa, did well principally because their armored flight decks proved superior to the American carriers' unarmored decks for this kind of close-in fighting. In the north, the Americans invented modern combat direction doctrine as they formalized the use of picket destroyers and ship-controlled CAP to counter the northern kamikaze threat. However, the cost in lost lives and equipment was immense.

Navy Nurse Ann Bernatitus describes kamikaze attacks against her hospital ship, USS Relief (AH-1), during the invasion of Okinawa.

On April 1, we invaded Okinawa. The next day the *Relief* arrived along with the *Comfort* [AH-6]. At 6:10 a single-engine Japanese plane crossed her bow at about 5 miles, made a 10 degree turn, and approached the *Relief* and *Comfort* from bow on. The destroyer *Wickes* [DD-578], on picket duty off Okinawa, came to our rescue. As the enemy plane continued

BELOW: With the Shuri Line broken and abandoned, Imperial troops were forced deeper and deeper into Okinawa's southern wastes. These soldiers of the 7th Infantry Division, having survived thus far, cautiously scan the ridge ahead during the final days of the campaign. The bullet-scarred monolith providing them with a degree of protection is a Shishi, or "lion dog," which according to Okinawan mythology, guarded the countryside from evil spirits. Although the fighting was officially declared at an end on June 21, 1945, the Tenth Army commander, Lieutenant General Buckner, was killed by Japanese artillery fire near this spot only three days before that.

BELOW: Crewmen at port-side midships of the light cruiser USS *Phoenix* reflect the stress and anticipation of the kamikaze attacks as they strain to identify a plane flying overhead during the invasion of Mindoro in the central Philippines, December 18, 1944. This was a time of intense kamikaze attacks, as the expressions on the men's faces indicate. The large-barreled weapons trained skyward are 5-inch guns capable of engaging aircraft at great distances. The trio of light 20mm guns along the right are the cruiser's last line of defense, and the quad 40mm mount located high on the superstructure over-laps the other weapons' long and short ranges.

straight toward the *Relief*, the destroyer's gunners placed close bursts of antiaircraft fire so near as to rock the enemy's wings. This came just as the aircraft released a bomb, causing it to fall a few feet wide of the *Relief*. A few hours later, another enemy plane flew over for a few minutes but made no attack. During the day, the ship anchored off the invasion beach and deployed to sea at night, illuminated like a Christmas tree. On April 10, we went to Saipan with 556 casualties. On April 27, we went to Tinian with 613 casualties.

On April 19, the *Comfort* was attacked by a kamikaze with some loss of life. We alternated with the *Comfort* taking these patients wherever they were going. When we stopped retiring out to sea at night all lit up, we would stay where we were anchored—ready to pick up casualties. Every time the kamikazes would come, we would get the alarm over the loudspeaker. They would say, "Kamaretta red, smoke boat make smoke." And then this boat would fill the bay with white smoke so the kamikazes couldn't see.

Sonarman First Class Jack Gebhardt aboard the destroyer USS Pringle *remembers the fierce kamikaze attacks that finally sank his vessel off Okinawa.*

The *Pringle* sailed from Iwo Jima before the island was secured and went to Ulitihi Island to await the invasion of Okinawa on April 1, 1945. It seemed that every invasion was bigger as the war moved closer to Japan.

The invasion of Okinawa began with routine anti-submarine patrol, then providing antiaircraft defense as Japanese air raids started to intensify. The Japanese came in waves and sent everything at us. All attacks were now kamikazes and every type of aircraft was used, some barely able to fly. What a waste of human life as we shot them down. Once the airfield on Okinawa was secured, our Marine pilots began using it, but had a difficult time because everybody was so trigger-happy from the constant Japanese attacks.

The U.S. destroyer picket stations around Okinawa numbered about twenty-six ships

BELOW: An Okinawan leads a U.S. patrol and its Nisei (Japanese-American) linguist to a cave where Japanese stragglers are hiding, July 10, 1945. Between a tenth and a quarter of the island's 400,000 men, women, and children were dead by that time. Military government personnel were encouraged by the large number of survivors, and found that, after the Okinawans recovered from the astonishment that they weren't going to be executed, and received enough food and medical assistance to stabilize their individual situations, they immediately began to work industriously to get their small farms back in order as quickly as possible.

JACK GEBHARDT

positioned about 75 to 100 miles off the island. They were the "eyes" of the early warning system and the Japanese attacked them prior to every raid. The *Pringle* was assigned to Radar Picket Station No. 26 about 75 miles north by northwest of Okinawa with the destroyer USS *Hobson* [DD-464] and two landing craft. The *Hobson* had better radio equipment and acted as the lead ship. No one knew why the landing craft were along because they had very limited air defense capability and very slow, but we found out the purpose was to pick up survivors after a ship was sunk.

The first several days of picket duty were quiet, but on April 15, 1945, after being at battle stations for almost twenty-four hours, the Japanese attacked in great strength. They knew we had been awake all night fighting off small frequent air attacks and were exhausted. The main attack lasted all day and finally about dawn on April 16, 1945, the *Pringle* was attacked by a horde of Japanese planes. Some were shot down, but one Zeke [A6M single-engine fighter, also known as the Zero] got through our air defenses and crashed near number one stack, aft of the bridge and chart house, where I was stationed as a telephone talker during General Quarters. The plane flew over the starboard bow and passed 10 to 15 feet above where I was standing and crashed in a huge ball of fire.

When the two 500-pound bombs on the plane exploded, it seemed like the world ended as the chart house rumbled and years of dust crashed down from the overheads. I sensed the *Pringle* was severely damaged and tried to get off the bridge through the starboard door, but the door was jammed and [the] access ladder was blown away. I

People can do strange things when in a stressful circumstance. I put on my life jacket, the type that inflates with a rubber tube, and prepared to go over the side. But when crawling off the bridge I forgot my tin helmet so went back to the chart house to get it.

—Jack Gebhardt

managed to bend the door from the top and slide out onto the open bridge area. I looked toward the stern and the ship was a burning hulk with men stumbling dazed and bleeding from the flying debris, smoke, and flames. I looked forward and saw men going over the side. Just then someone yelled "Abandon Ship" and I saw a 40mm [antiaircraft] ammo magazine under the bridge on fire so I went to the starboard side of the bridge and worked my way down to the main deck.

The bridge splash shield was blown away, so I climbed down to the gun deck where I took off my shoes and hat and laid them neatly against the bulkhead as if I was coming back! People can do strange things when in a stressful circumstance. I put on my life jacket, the type that inflates with a rubber tube, and prepared to go over the side. But when crawling off the bridge I forgot my tin helmet so went back to the chart house to get it. While searching for my helmet I saw more men going overboard and without thinking dove into the water and swam away from the ship as fast as I could. I don't know how far I swam, but it seemed like several hundred yards before stopping to look back and see the Pringle engulfed in flames, broken in half, sinking amidships. The bow and stem were pointed sharply upward and I heard screams. It all happened in less than five

BELOW: On May 3, 1945, more than a month into the Okinawa invasion, Radar Picket Station No. 10 to the west of the island was made up of a pair of destroyers, the Little (DD-803) and Aaron Ward (DM-34), supported by LCM(R)-195 as well as three small "coffin bearer" LCS boats for additional fire support and rescue operations. During an hour-long assault by twenty-five aircraft at sundown, two "suiciders" hit Little, breaking her in half, and another struck LCM(R)-195, which blew up. The Aaron Ward, pictured here, shot down four, but was struck by six kamikazes, plus two 500-pound bombs that left her dead in the water, badly holed, and the entire ship aft of the forward superstructure smashed almost flat. It would later sail to the United States under its own power to receive major repairs.

Damaging strikes were made by kamikazes on numerous American battleships, such as the USS *Maryland* where sixty men were killed or wounded. Suicide pilots were instructed to aim for their relatively lightly armored decks or vulnerable nerve center—the bridge. The crew of the USS *Missouri*, however, experienced the extreme good fortune of having their single kamikaze strike occur along the thick armor belt protecting the ship's hull. As the photo at right shows, if the aircraft had come in higher, scores of sailors could have been killed in an instant. Instead, the damage—from what looked to surrounding ships to be a spectacular hit—was limited to some scorched paint on the starboard side and a 40 mm gun barrel (opposite) that was impaled by one of the kamikazi's machine guns blown free during the explosion. Below, the essentially undamaged *Missouri* sails serenely along, leaving behind it a pall of smoke to mark where a suicide aircraft smashed into its armored side.

minutes after the Japanese plane hit and *Pringle* disappeared.

When the ship sank, I rolled onto my back and floated high in case a depth charge went off, but there was no explosion, only the cries of wounded men and the continuing battle. I watched helplessly as the *Pringle* sank and could do nothing to save her. The Japanese planes circled overhead like a swarm of angry hornets to make sure *Pringle* was dead. I was in the water for only a short time when one of the stewards [attendants for the officers' wardroom], a large Filipino, cried for help. I didn't know the man, but swam to him to offer assistance. The man's muscles had cramped and he couldn't swim and had no life jacket so I gave him mine since I was a fairly good swimmer. I grabbed a piece of wreckage drifting by and remained in the water floating near the *Hobson* hoping she would pick me up, but the strong current swept me around the ship's stern and away from her.

I watched the *Hobson* put up an intense blanket of antiaircraft fire as the Japanese tried to strafe us in the water. They drove the Jap planes off and fired several 20mm [anti-aircraft] rounds into the water to chase off any sharks. When the attack finally ended, the landing craft moved in and picked us up. I had been in the water about seven to eight hours after the *Pringle* sank and the water was rough most of the time. To keep up my spirits and stay alert, I prayed, sang, and did anything to survive. Finally the landing craft crew threw a line to a raft holding our wounded, the line fell short so I swam for it and brought the line back to the raft.

We were pulled alongside the landing craft and a cargo net lowered to the raft so the wounded men could be brought aboard. The landing craft's crew opened their hearts with compassion, clothing, and food. I was given 32-inch waist pants which fit, but on *Pringle* just a few hours before I wore a 36-inch waist. A bottle of whisky was passed around and everyone took a big gulp. My hands shook as I drank and thought of my shipmates, sharks, fire, and terror of the last few hours. The sight of *Pringle* going under was still vivid in my mind.

The landing craft took us to a hospital ship at Okinawa for medical treatment and then transfer to the transport *Starlight* [AP-175], a troop ship bound for San Francisco. The casualties suffered by *Pringle* on April 16, 1945 were sixty-nine men killed and seventy wounded—some later died—from the attack. I felt lucky the ship sank quickly as more casualties could have resulted if the ship remained afloat to be a lingering target. To this day, I still remember the shipmates who didn't survive and can see *Pringle*'s final moment as a burning, broken hulk slipping beneath the water.

During the course of the two-month campaign, twenty-one ships were lost, sixty-six seriously damaged, and more than 10,000 sailors killed and wounded—the highest naval losses of the Pacific War. Ashore, the butcher bill was no less sobering, and a reflection of the horrors of total war—in addition to the annihilation of the 100,000-man Japanese garrison, the civilian population lost at least 80,000. American casualties ashore numbered almost 70,000 wounded, missing, or killed, including General Buckner, who was killed during the last days of the campaign.

Antiaircraft Defense

ABOVE: Shipyard workers make adjustments to the optical range finder of an armored Mark 37 gun director turret. An M4 radar antenna, integral to the director crew's control of the ship's long-range 5-inch gunfire, crowns it. "Kill" flags attributed to this director are painted on its sides, much as a pilot would have "kills" indicated on his aircraft.

RIGHT: The Essex carrier *Hornet*'s port stern quad 40mm antiaircraft mount is put through its paces during a spring 1945 training exercise. The Bofors, also mounted singly and in pairs, was capable of firing up to 120 rounds per minute per barrel (note the spent shell casings). It was a critical component of the fleet's air defense. Each 40mm mount operated in conjunction with a Mark 51 optical director (above right) nearby in its own "tub" or co-located with the mount. Before the appearance of the kamikaze, 20mm Oerlikon guns (opposite) were the principal killer of Japanese aircraft, but now lacked the power to break up a plunging "suicider.

BELOW: In the beginning, kamikaze attacks were organized on an ad hoc basis from Nichols Field, a former American airbase in the Philippines. On October 13, 1944, the aircraft carrier USS *Franklin* was apparently the first target of a kamikaze one week prior to official authorization of the thirteen-aircraft Shimpu Tokubetsu Kogekitai (Divine Wind Special Attack Corps) unit of volunteer suicide pilots. First blood was drawn on October 25–26, when a five-plane raid sank the small escort carrier *St. Louis* and damaged three similar ships. This prompted many more young fliers to volunteer. The *Langley* was struck on October 29 and on the following day, kamikazes damaged two fleet carriers—the *Belleau Wood* and *Franklin*, at center and right respectively—so severely that they had to be pulled back to the Ulithi anchorage for repairs. Within days, another large flattop fell victim, as did three more toward the end of November. This stunning disruption of carrier air power spelled the loss of ten Liberty ships and LSTs as well as six destroyer-type vessels during the opening days of the Leyte invasion, and had a pronounced effect on the conduct of the ground campaign.

PAUL W. TIBBETS

ABOVE: Colonel (later Brigadier General) Paul W. Tibbets, Jr. As commander of the 509th Composite Group, he was both the pilot and mission commander of the B-29 Superfortress that dropped the first atomic bomb on Hiroshima. Previously, Tibbets had commanded the 340th Bomb Squadron, 97th Heavy Bomb Group flying B-17 Flying Fortresses. On August 17, 1942, Tibbets piloted the lead bomber on the Eighth Air Force's first bombing mission against Nazi Germany.

Armageddon

Okinawa was a severe strategic defeat for the Japanese, especially the Imperial Army. However, the generals were not yet inclined to admit defeat to their emperor, who was desperately seeking a way to end the war and yet remain on the throne. The Japanese Army and Navy were encouraged by the results of the kamikaze campaign and had firm intelligence that the next American objective was the southern island of Kyushu. Surely another bloodbath would convince the Americans to back down from their unconditional surrender terms. Accordingly, they devised a combined kamikaze and ground campaign that would dwarf Okinawa in terms of the casualties it might inflict, including almost 7,000 aircraft carefully dispersed and hidden for the kamikaze attacks. All food on the island would be requisitioned for the Army and the civilian population would be employed as a last suicidal line of defense. The hope was that all Japanese on the island, military and civilian, would sell their lives dearly for the emperor.

On the other side, Okinawa forced the Americans to order incredible numbers of Purple Hearts for the upcoming invasions of Japan. Casualty estimates for the Kyushu operation and subsequent invasion of the Tokyo area on the island of Honshu amounted to over 720,000 "dead and evacuated wounded" for the Army and Army Air Corps alone, and it was at this point that two other factors came into play to end the horrific war Japan's aggression had provoked. The first factor was the successful test (TRINITY) of an atomic bomb by the Manhattan Project in New Mexico on July 16, 1945. As the preparations for the invasion of Japan proceeded apace, the remaining two atomic weapons produced were shipped to a special B-29 unit (the 509th Composite Group) located on Tinian. At the time, the use of these bombs was regarded as simply another weapon, albeit a very special one, in the strategic bombing campaign.

The other factor influencing the end of the Pacific War was Soviet Premier Joseph Stalin's promise to enter the war against the Japanese three months after the conclusion of hostilities in Europe. The Japanese diplomats, who were banking on a Soviet mediated peace, received a shock when their Soviet counterparts first repudiated their neutrality vis-à-vis Japan and then rejected all attempts by the Japanese to have the Soviets leverage their Western Allies to modify their demand for unconditional surrender.

By August, all of the pieces were in place. On August 6, 1945, a B-29 piloted by Colonel Paul W. Tibbets dropped the first atomic bomb on the port city of Hiroshima, killing tens of thousands instantly, with the toll quickly climbing to as many as 80,000 from residual blast and radiation deaths. Then, before midnight on August 8, the Soviets notified the Japanese that they were now at war, hostilities to commence the next day. Over the next few weeks, huge mechanized Soviet armies overran the critical Japanese puppet state of Manchukuo. Hours after the Soviets attacked, a second atomic bomb fell on the city of Nagasaki and another 35,000 Japanese were instantly incinerated.

Army Air Corps Colonel Paul W. Tibbets talks about the defenses for the B-29s of the 509th Composite (Bomber) Group used to drop the two atomic bombs.

At Alamogordo [New Mexico], they had all kinds of fighters. I had the B-29 experience and people to fly B-29s, so that's why we were sent there from Grand Island, Nebraska. By accident I learned that the fighters as we knew them, which included the Jap Zero and the German Messerschmitt, our P-47s, P-38s, and P-51s, could not do any more than make a single pass at the airplane if I could get about 5,000 more feet [of altitude] out of it. How do you get altitude? Sacrifice weight from something else. I said I learned it from accident because the B-29 equipped tactically with all the turrets and with all the armor plates and so on broke on us one day when we had a critical test to fly. I had this hulk, this B-29 with nothing. It was just a flying machine. It had nothing in it. I took that airplane to run the test and by not paying too close attention to what I was doing, the airplane from 25,000 feet kept drifting higher and higher and higher while we were conducting these tests. It turns out by unconsciously allowing this airplane to drift higher—because I'm busy watching the fighters—as we burned off fuel and got lighter and lighter the airplane kept going higher and higher. I found myself at 33,000 feet.

The fighters didn't have enough power and didn't have any maneuverability at that altitude. They could get up there, but they were staggering at that point. If they made a pass at us, they stood a chance by luck to hit us on one pass. But by the time they could recover, they were so far below us that, [with] the speed of the airplane at that altitude, there was no way they could catch us and climb back up, because their engines overheated and they just had to

chop everything off and descend. I recorded that in the back of my mind. There's the best defense I could get against fighters. I think when [General Curtis E.] LeMay first heard about it, he wanted to call the psychiatrist out to have my head examined, because the idea in those days was you pile on more armament. You don't take it off to defend yourself.

I had a discussion with the old man. [He asked,] "Why did you do this?" so forth and so on. I said, "Because I can fly higher and faster than they can. They can't touch me." That's the way that turned out. We stripped them [the B-29s. The 509th bombers only carried the twin .50 caliber guns and no armor]. I got 7,600 pounds of dead weight out of each one of those airplanes by stripping them. That 7,600 pounds translated into that additional altitude.

The fighters didn't have enough power and didn't have any maneuverability at [33,000 feet]. They could get up there, but they were staggering at that point. If they made a pass at us, they stood a chance by luck to hit us on one pass. But by the time they could recover, they were so far below us that,[with] the speed of the airplane at that altitude, there was no way they could catch us and climb back up, because their engines overheated and they just had to chop everything off and descend.

—Paul W. Tibbets

BELOW: The *Enola Gay*, pictured here in post-war livery at its Roswell, New Mexico, training base, was specially modified for its atom bomb mission. All internal armor plating in crew and key component areas was removed as were extraneous components, most gun turret housings, and ten machine guns, leaving the bomber with only a twin 50-cal stinger on its tail. The resultant savings in weight, however, made the aircraft virtually immune from all existing Japanese fighter aircraft. Other bombers in the 509th Composite Group, such as *Bocks Car*, which struck Nagasaki, were identically configured. The crew that dropped the atom bomb was specially chosen and had trained together for months before the actual mission, flying simulated flights with dummy weapons that weighed the same as the actual weapon. The *Enola Gay* is currently on display at the National Air and Space Museum's Udvar-Hazy Center, located at Dulles International Airport, Washington, D.C.

ABOVE: Paul Tibbets returning his ground crew's salute as he prepares to take off on the first atom bomb mission against Imperial Japan, August 6, 1945. Tibbets named his B-29 after his mother, Enola Gay.

Colonel Tibbets explains the use of barometric altimeters to fuse the atomic bomb detonation mechanisms, and the bombs themselves—the uranium bomb known as "Little Boy" and the plutonium bomb known as the "Fat Man."

What it was was the barometric deal. A little bit different than radar proximity. The firing mechanism was triggered by the baros [barometers]. As the bomb went down and reached a point—roughly they wanted to explode at 1,500 feet above the ground. That was a theoretically ideal place for that weapon to explode based on the blast effect they predicted. It would cover more area with more intense damage than any other altitude. Too high or too low it would get less effect. So that was the ideal altitude. We did an awful

lot of dropping at Wendover [Army Air Field in Utah] with practice shapes we called them, because they weren't a bomb. They were things that looked like a bomb. They were steel external cases, and they were weighted inside with basically cement. We had to develop an aerodynamic trajectory that we could predict the fall of that weapon. By being so high, releasing so far back with a certain amount of speed, we could say we could put it in a coffee cup. But this was not an easy task.

The Hiroshima bomb [Little Boy] was one of a kind only. It wasn't so difficult. The Fat Man [used on Nagasaki], that was the problem. It had to be fired at thirty-six points around the sphere simultaneously to crush it—implosion. What they [the Manhattan Project] were having trouble doing—they were having trouble getting the firing mechanism internally to fire all of them. They were Champion spark plugs by the way—an advertisement for Champion. They were trying to get each one of those spark plugs to fire at the same time. So this created a problem. The next thing was, the problem was to get the right type of baros [barometers] with the accuracy that they needed to detect the atmospheric conditions as the bomb came down and at that right point trigger it so that it would explode almost simultaneously at that point. In other words, 1,500 feet above the ground. This was the dilemma of trying to get those things to function exactly as they had to function. We worked on that longer than we worked on anything else. They could release a smoke charge from the airplane the minute the bomb left the airplane. The cameras would pick it up, and they could follow it all the way down.

The firing mechanism was electrical and the scientists were concerned that a radar impulse might trigger the bomb mechanism. They wanted to be sure nothing would interfere. We had to keep the bomb warm, too. We couldn't have it up there in that very cold atmosphere because, again, electrically speaking, when you freeze electrical wires you run into another problem. Freezing the baros you run into something else. We couldn't afford to have all of that happen. So we had to keep the bomb heated. [Lieutenant Jacob] Beser did both. He watched for the sweep of this thing, and he helped [Lieutenant] Morris Jeppson keep track of the temperature. He kept track of the temperature of the bomb riding in the bomb bay in that cold atmosphere. The fissionable material was installed after we were en route, had taken off, climbed up over the clouds, roughly 8,000 feet at night, and it was armed at that particular point. They did the same thing on the Fat Man on the Nagasaki mission. The performance of doing it was two different things because of the different type of bombs that you had. Both of them were made active after they were in the air. It was safe in the airplane. There was a split opinion on it. Some of the scientists said it would explode and so forth. I think [J. Robert] Oppenheimer said, "Yes, it will explode, but the only thing that is going to explode is the torpex. It's going to be a big bang, but you are not going to have a nuclear explosion. You are not going to have a critical mass because an explosion of that type could not compress that thing simultaneously." He said that was the secret to it. If you didn't get it all at the same time, you did not have a critical mass.

Colonel Tibbets described the final moments as the crew of the Enola Gay *navigated its final run to Hiroshima, and what happened when the bomb exploded.*

[Major Thomas W.] Ferebee [the bombardier] is looking through the optics on his bombsight. He's got the city way back. He said there is no doubt in his mind that he is looking right straight at Hiroshima. Then Dutch [Captain Theodore J. Van Kirk] comes up from the navigator's table in the back and stands basically right behind Ferebee between [Captain] Bob Lewis and me. He's got his maps, and he and Ferebee are looking. He even looked through Ferebee's bombsight because that was one of the things we wanted [for] verification. Lewis and I are looking, and we all see the same thing. Before he put the crosshairs on, he is looking to see, is that Hiroshima? The answer is, no doubt. Then the next thing Tom says, "I've got the aiming point"—a certain bridge. Of course, Lewis and I couldn't say anything about it. Van Kirk went up and he looked and said, "That's the aiming point." Such and such a bridge.

We were absolutely certain they had no antiaircraft that could do anything to us at that altitude. We knew that. The question was, could the fighter do it based on the experience at Alamogordo with the Zero fighter? The answer was no. They couldn't get within 5,000 feet of us. A Zero wasn't that good a performer. There were also three shock waves from the Hiroshima weapon. The first one was a good jolt. The second one was quite noticeable. The third one was only visible to the tail gunner. He could see it coming.

BELOW: The nuclear blast over Hiroshima, approximately fifteen seconds after detonation. U.S. leaders hoped that the sudden and unexpected use of atomic bombs would "shock" Imperial Japan into an early surrender and make a costly invasion of the Home Islands unnecessary.

Bob Caron [Staff Sergeant George R.] in the tail had his [goggles] on because he watched it [the bomb] explode. We were all issued them, including myself. To show you how naive I am, I didn't think so much about it. I had my goggles up on my forehead as we go in. I'm waiting for the autopilot to release after the bomb leaves the airplane and so forth. As it releases, I pulled my goggles down over my face and I'm blind. I can't see a damn thing. How am I going to fly an airplane around that tight turn? So I immediately pulled mine off and flew the airplane around this way. There was—and I was quite aware of—a brilliance in the airplane. Everybody else was wearing goggles except me, and I couldn't do it.

After the fact, we know it wasn't necessary because the only person that could look at that weapon was Bob Caron. He could have a direct look at it. What they didn't want was a direct stare at the explosion. I'm sure that would have had a blinding effect. Bob said, "That thing came through those welder's goggles like nobody's business." He said, "It just lit up like a house."

Simultaneously with that, I tasted it. When I was a kid and you went to the dentist, you had a cavity. What he did was he filled your tooth with a compound that was a mixture of silver and something else. Electrolysis. Because in those days we could be eating ice cream or something like that, you take a spoon and touch one of those damn things, and, goddamn, you jump because it was like a toothache hitting you. That happened. By the same token, every time you did that, it left a taste of lead in your mouth. This particular taste was referred to as a lead taste. I tasted that thing [the bomb] just as clear as could be.

 General LeMay discusses the use of the atomic bomb against Japan.

I guess I was one of many who didn't actually realize the explosive power and potential of the bomb. However, I agreed then with dropping, and still believe the decision to drop it was correct. The Manhattan [Project] scientists wanted to send out the plane with a fleet of B-29s. I figured it was better to send it out like a regular weather plane. While the war with Japan could have been won without dropping either of the two atomic bombs, I am certain in my own mind that they significantly shortened the war and, therefore, saved lives in the long run. We all wanted to end the war before an invasion of Japan became necessary.

 Colonel Tibbets and his crew were required to make an immediate vocal recording of their impressions of the blast.

There was a wire recorder in the airplane. The purpose of the wire recorder was for the Manhattan Project to have a record. What they wanted us to do was to express individually, one at a time, after the bomb had been dropped and we were out of the area and on our way back. They wanted each one of us to record our impressions as quick as we could. We did do that. The security guys the minute we got back got a hold of that wire recorder. It went to Leslie Groves [Major General Leslie R. Groves, the head of the Manhattan Project]. I have had several historians ask me, where is that thing? The answer is, I don't know because it went to Leslie Groves.

The Japanese diplomats argued for peace under the terms of the Allied Potsdam Declaration. The Japanese Army leadership, realizing their strategy for defending the beaches in Kyushu was hopeless if the Americans could obliterate their defenses, reluctantly "stepped aside" but did not openly endorse peace yet. The emperor recorded an address announcing the surrender to his people and explaining why it was necessary. However, it was touch and go prior to the recording's broadcast. Radical elements of the Japanese Guards Division in Tokyo attempted to find the recording, destroy it, and initiate a coup. However, troops loyal to the emperor suppressed this revolt and on August 15, the emperor broadcast an appeal to his people to "endure the unendurable."

INSET: The Japanese delegation aboard USS *Missouri* in Tokyo Bay for the surrender on September 2, 1945. The delegation included the signatories to the surrender document, Foreign Minister Mamoru Shigemitsu and General Yoshijiro Umezu of the Imperial General Headquarters, plus three representatives each from the Ministry of Foreign Affairs, the Imperial Navy, and the Imperial Army.

On September 2, 1945, General MacArthur received the surrender of the Japanese representatives aboard the battleship USS *Missouri* anchored in Tokyo Bay.

 Navy Pilot Clarence A. "Bill" Moore flying an F6F Hellcat shot down the final Axis aircraft of World War II on August 15, 1945.

We were operating off USS *Belleau Wood*, CVL-24. On the morning of August 15, we were all scrambled to go make a strike on Tokyo. Our efforts that day were to go to the electric works in Tokyo and destroy the final source of [electrical] power for the Tokyo area. We were up around 20,000 feet and climbing, getting into position to make our bombing run and so forth, but we were flying cover for bombers that were in the flight. We were in sight of our target—it was still early in the morning—when we heard, "All planes, all planes. Now hear this. This is the admiral. An armistice has been declared. All planes return to their bases."

Needless to say, there was chaos in the air. We all had 500-pound bombs under our wings, we had rockets, and we had a full load of ammunition for six 50-caliber machine guns. Our planes had three guns on each wing. When the armistice announcement came over the air, I believe every pilot dropped all of his bombs and jettisoned all of his rockets; it looked like the Fourth of July. It's an amazing thing that someone didn't actually get killed in that particular episode.

But we were all so thrilled and excited! We had no order, no rank or anything of the sort, and we had to return to the ship. Normally, in flight, we attempted to fly in some kind of order, but on this particular morning during the return to our ship, we all had to get there on our own, because

we couldn't find our buddies. Our flights were all broken up. We all did, finally, get down. Our particular flight was down on the deck and we had relaxed for just a few minutes, when all of a sudden we heard, over the speaker, that Flight Ten of the Second Wing Division was to go aloft and fly cover for the fleet. We'd been down only about half an hour or an hour, when we [were] ordered to resume flight, which we did. We climbed to around 10,000 feet. But it was kind of a monotonous day. We figured everybody was having a grand time onboard the ship, and here we were having to fly cover for what we thought was no particular reason. After all, the armistice had been declared.

Not long after we'd reached our cruising altitude, we received word from the command center that there was a "bogey" [unidentified aircraft] approaching at 12,000 feet and headed right toward the fleet. We were ordered to scramble and find and destroy. We all did everything we could to gain altitude so we could come in from above. And we were able to do just that. It just so happened, I guess, that I had the liveliest plane of the bunch, so I was able to get to the site of the target first. The target turned out to be a Japanese Judy [Yokosuka D4Y1 dive-bomber], which intended to make a kamikaze attack on our fleet. And of course the target, I'm sure, was the carrier.

So we were able to get into position. I was able to get into position and above the Judy. I dropped down behind the Judy and surprised him; I was able to hit the plane with a full burst of four guns, two on each side. At that particular point, he burst into flames and exploded. That, purely and simply, is what happened. It wasn't until 1990 that I learned that that airplane—that Judy I shot down— was the last [Japanese] airplane shot down in World War II.

🎙 *Nurse Bernatitus remembers the end of the war and subsequent operations to retrieve the POWs, including her Medical Corps comrades from Bataan.*

In July we left Saipan [aboard USS *Relief*] for San Pedro Bay, Leyte, and served as a fleet base hospital in the Philippines until the end of the war. August 15 was V-J Day [the day victory over Japan was celebrated, though Japan formally surrendered on September 2, 1945] and that was a day! We had just gone up on deck for a movie when it was announced. And that bay lit up that night like you've never seen. The sky was bright, everybody firing something or another. It was beautiful. I remember standing at the rail with somebody. The person said, "Well, maybe now we can go home." And I said, "No, I don't think so. I think we have to go get the war prisoners first." I was still thinking about Dr. Carey Smith and Dr. Claude Fraley [who had been captured in 1942 when the Philippines fell]. So, sure enough, that's what we got orders for.

So on the twenty-eighth [August] we were enroute via Okinawa for Dairen, Manchuria, to pick up the prisoners of war. We were escorted by the destroyer escort *McNulty* [DE-581] and the *Eugene E. Elmore* [DE-686]. We picked up a Chinese man and woman. The next day the *Relief* was guided past ten floating mines. However, one crew member of the *McNulty* was injured by shrapnel and transferred to the *Relief*, but he died. At 9:18, we docked with no help from anybody.

The POWs had to come down to the docks from Mukden by train, but the Japanese had blown up the rails. And so there were food drops to the men. So, they didn't look too bad. So many of [those] 753 people we brought out were the ones who started [as] the American defenders of Bataan and Corregidor. I packed a box for Dr. Fraley and Dr. Smith—candy bars and oranges, and I don't know what else—for the doctor to take back to them. It was not till the eleventh [September] that the prisoners came aboard, 753 of them. That was really something. First of all, music was blaring from the ship and everything was all lighted up. Well, they didn't let them come right aboard. They had to be deloused first— fumigated and then given showers.

They came aboard at 8:50 p.m. I remember the supply officer who was in charge of food, came to me and said that the senior medical officer was going to give them sand-

CHARLES MCVAY

ABOVE: Captain Charles B. McVay, III, the last commanding officer of the heavy cruiser USS *Indianapolis*. McVay, loved and respected by his crew, was made the scapegoat for the ship's sinking by the Navy. He later committed suicide.

OPPOSITE, TOP: A July 1942 photo of mess attendants aboard the *Indianapolis* who had volunteered for additional duty as gunners. Captain Edward W. Hanson, the ship's commanding officer at that time, is the second officer from the right beside steward William Henry. The men are in battle dress and some are wearing World War I style helmets.

OPPOSITE, BOTTOM: A close-up view of the cruiser's forward superstructure and 8-inch, triple-gun turrets from off the port side, taken on December 7, 1944, at the Mare Island Navy Yard, California. The *Indianapolis* had just completed an overhaul, and was one of the few American warships at that time to have a completely modern suite of antiaircraft weapons. White outlines mark recent alterations to the ship. Note the new Mark 33 gun director atop her open bridge, 20mm and quad 40mm gun mounts, as well as the 8-inch projectiles behind her No. 2 turret.

wiches and I said, "Listen, if you can't give them a steak dinner and ice cream or something, we ought to be ashamed of ourselves." They would stand in line waiting from one meal to the next and they ate bread. God, they ate bread! The men were up on the SOQ (Sick Officers' Quarters). The galley was in the middle and my office was to the left of it. Because all the bread and butter were on my desk, they reached in to get bread and butter, then with their trays they would go through the galley to load up, and then go out to their bunks.

Captain Charles B. McVay, III, USN, Commanding Officer of USS Indianapolis *(CA-35) recalls the ship's sinking by a Japanese submarine after delivering the components for the first atomic bomb to the island of Tinian in the Marianas Islands.*

On about July 12, I got orders which indicated that we had to perform some special mission, so that we knew that we would not be able to take our usual refresher course [for the latest tactics, such as antisubmarine maneuvers] on the West Coast, but had been told we would receive that in the forward area. I was informed...that when we were ready for sea on 16 July, we would proceed as fast as possible to the forward area. On Sunday, the fifteenth of July, about noon, we were at Hunters Point [Naval Shipyard] and they put on us what we now know was the atomic bomb. We sailed from San Francisco, 0800 the morning of sixteenth July. We ran into a little rough weather outside the Golden Gate, so the

first day we only made 28 knots. When we arrived in Pearl [Harbor], we had established a new [transit speed] record. We made the trip in seventy-four and a half hours. When I arrived at Pearl, I knew the approximate date that I had to get out to the Marianas. We made [our] sustained speed without any difficulty so that we arrived in Tinian the morning of July 26 and unloaded the material and the bomb which was later dropped over Hiroshima.

We left Tinian immediately upon unloading and went to Guam, where we arrived the next morning and went through the usual antiaircraft practice. We replenished ammunition, stores, and fuel and left Guam Saturday morning at about 0930. We were given a routing from Port Director, Guam, and a speed which we were told to maintain except under conditions where we thought we had to make a greater speed in order to avoid either navigational or other obstructions. We had no incidents whatsoever. We passed an LST [Landing Ship Tank] headed toward Leyte, as we were also, on Sunday, and talked to them. They were north of us and they were preparing to go further north in order to get out of our area to do some antiaircraft shooting. My instructions from Guam called for me to make an SOA [speed over-all] of 15.7 knots and to arrive at Leyte at 1100 Tuesday, July 31.

On Sunday night, the twenty-ninth of July, we had been zigzagging [evasive movement, making the vessel a difficult target for torpedoes fired from submarines] up until dark. We did not zigzag thereafter. We had intermittent moonlight, so I am told, but it was dark from about 2330 until sometime earlier the next

At approximately five minutes after midnight [on July 30], I was thrown from my emergency cabin bunk on the bridge by a very violent explosion followed shortly thereafter by another explosion. I went to the bridge and noticed, in my emergency cabin and chart house, that there was quite a bit of acrid white smoke. I couldn't see anything.

—Charles B. McVay, III

morning. At approximately five minutes after midnight [on July 30], I was thrown from my emergency cabin bunk on the bridge by a very violent explosion, followed shortly thereafter by another explosion. I went to the bridge and noticed, in my emergency cabin and chart house, that there was quite a bit of acrid white smoke. I couldn't see anything. I got out on the bridge. The same conditions existed out there. I asked the Officer of the Deck [senior officer on duty] if he had had any reports. He said "No, sir. I have lost all communications, I have tried to stop the engines. I don't know whether the order has ever gotten through to the engine room."

So we had no communications whatsoever. Our engine room telegraph [device used to communicate speed changes from the command bridge to the engine room] was electrical, that was out; sound powered phones were out; all communications were out forward. As I went back into my cabin to

RESTRICTED

> **I knew from past experience that we had had in Okinawa, since we had our bloodbath, you never had to pass the word for anybody to man the general quarters station [battle station] or get on topside when something was wrong. The ship and crew sense it.**
>
> **—Charles B. McVay, III**

get my shoes and some clothes, I ran into the damage control officer, Lieutenant Commander [Kyle C.] "Casey" Moore, who had the mid-watch [midnight to 4 a.m.] on the bridge as a supervisory watch. He had gone down at the first hit and came back up on the bridge and told me that we were going down rapidly by the head [sinking bow-first], and wanted to know if I desired to pass the word to abandon ship. I told him "No." We had only about a three-degree list. We had been through a hit before, we were able to control it quite easily and in my own mind I was not at all perturbed. Within another two or three minutes the executive officer came up, Commander [Joseph A.] Flynn, and said, "We are definitely going down and I suggest that we abandon ship." Well, knowing Flynn and having utter regard for his ability, I then said, "Pass the word to abandon ship." As I had this word passed, I turned to the Officer of the Deck. This had to be passed verbally, [and] the man on watch, the boatswain's mate, had to go below.

Two people did go below and the word was passed. However, I knew from past experience that we had had in Okinawa, since we had our bloodbath, you never had to pass the word for anybody to man the general quarters station [battle station] or get on topside when something was wrong. The ship and crew sense it. They come to their stations immediately. So I am sure that everybody who could get up topside was up topside before we ever passed the word. Then I turned to the Officer of the Deck, Lieutenant [John Irwin] Orr, and said, "I have been unable to determine whether the distress message, which I told the navigator to check on, has ever gotten out."

I had asked Commander [Johns Hopkins] Janney, the navigator, when I first went on the bridge to make certain that he got a message out. He went down below and that was the last I saw of him. So knowing that it was absolutely essential that someone be notified where we were, since we were unescorted, I felt that was the most important thing to know at this moment and told the Officer of the Deck I was going to Radio Room One, below the bridge, to find out for myself if this message had gotten out. Also, I wanted to take a look at a part of the main deck that some people had said had split near number one stack. I could not yet visualize why we were going down by the head.

Nobody had given me any report that we were other than just badly damaged. I passed through the chart house and picked up in my emergency cabin a kapok life preserver, which I put on and stepped out on the after-side of the bridge and Captain [Edwin M.] Crouch, who was a passenger and who had been sleeping in my cabin, said, "Charley, have you got a spare life preserver?" I said, "Yes, I have. I've got a pneumatic life preserver," and I stepped back into my cabin and picked this up and handed it to, I believe, a seaman quartermaster by the name of Harrison and asked him to blow this up for Captain Crouch. I then stepped to the ladder on the bridge, which leads down to the signal bridge, and as I put my foot on the first rung [of the ladder], the ship took a 25-degree list to starboard.

People started to slide by and I went down to the signal bridge. As I reached that platform, she went to about 40 or 45 degrees [of list]. I managed to get to the ladder leading from the signal bridge to the port [left] side of the communications deck. As I reached the communications deck, she [the ship] seemed to be steadied at around 60 [degrees of list]. There were some youngsters there that were jumping over the side and I got to the lifeline on the communications deck and yelled at these boys to not jump over the side unless they had life jackets, or to go back by the stack that was just behind me and cut down the life raft—or the floater net rather—and throw that over the side before they jumped.

Within another few seconds the ship listed to 90 degrees and I jumped to the forecastle deck and pulled myself up on the side and started to walk aft [the ship was on her side and the captain was able to walk toward the rear on the ship's side]. She apparently stayed in this position for some time, at least long enough for me to walk from abreast the bridge to approximately No. 3 turret on the after deck, at that point I was sucked off into the water by what I believe was a wave caused by the bow going down rather rapidly, because I found myself in the water and looked above me and the screws [propellers]—port screws—which by this time had been stopped, were directly overhead.

I immediately thought, "Well, this is the end of me," and turned around and immediately swam away from the descending screws. Within a few seconds, I felt hot oil and water brush over the back of my neck and looked around and heard a swish and the ship was gone. The sea at this time was rather confused. There had been storms up north and I was buffeted about quite a bit. We had a long, heavy, groundswell, the wind was from the southwest and force about two. We could still see nothing. It was still dark and I could hear people yelling for help.

The rest of the story: Out of a crew of more than 1,100 men, about 850 made it off the *Indianapolis*. However, their ordeal had only just begun. Because of the secrecy of the mission, and an almost criminal breakdown in communications, the fact that the ship had been sunk went unnoticed for three days until she failed to arrive at her destination in the Philippines. There were only three small life rafts and Captain McVay ordered them lashed together. He thought that the twenty-five to thirty men with these rafts were the only survivors (the sinking had occurred at night) and the wind blew the rafts and Captain McVay in the opposite direction of the current, which carried the majority of the floating crew (of whom the captain was unaware) in the opposite direction. During this time, the swimming survivors endured the horrendous conditions of floating in the open ocean fighting thirst, hunger, exhaustion, a scorching sun, heat, and, worst of all, the voracious sharks of the Philippine Sea. By the time the Navy realized the ship had gone down and found the survivors— on the rafts and in the sea—only 318 men remained. After the war, McVay was unfairly found negligent and court-martialed, although his sentence was later remitted and he was restored to duty. He committed suicide in 1968. In 2000, Congress absolved him of all blame, principally due to the efforts of the surviving crew members and their families (including his own).

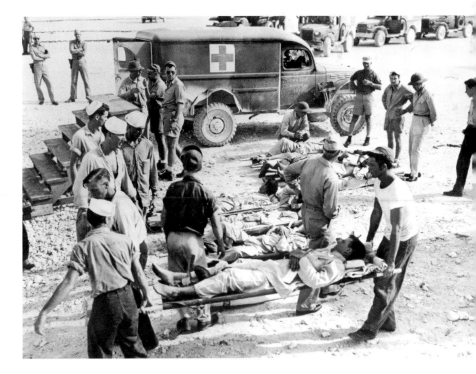

BELOW: *Indianapolis* survivors en route to a hospital following their rescue, in a photograph released on August 14, 1945. The ambulance in the background is marked "U.S.N. Base Hospital No. 20," which was located on Peleliu. These men endured one of the most horrific ordeals of the war and were among the relatively few lucky survivors from a crew of more than 1,100. They floated in the open sea in only lifejackets and were subjected to gut-wrenching thirst, heat, and—worst of all—voracious shark attacks.

Purple Hearts and the Invasion of Japan

In the midst of the bloody fighting on Okinawa, the newly sworn-in president, Harry S. Truman, received a warning that the planned invasion of Japan could cost as many as 500,000 to 1,000,000 American lives. The document containing this estimate, "Memorandum on Ending the Japanese War," was one of a series of papers written by former President Herbert Hoover, at Truman's request, in May 1945.

BELOW: American casualties await transportation to a hospital ship during the fighting in the Pacific.

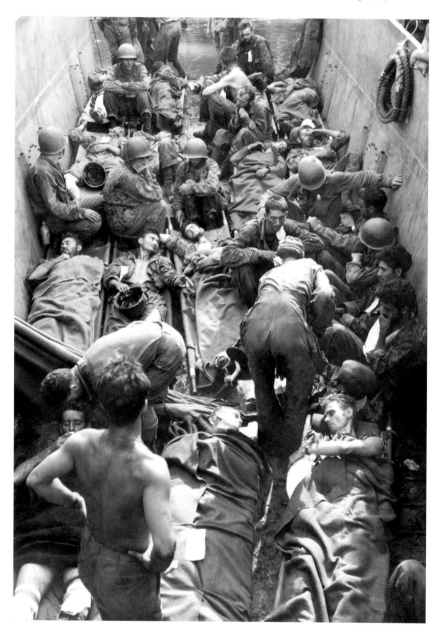

Hoover had been receiving regular briefings from War Department intelligence officers, and although his memorandum is well known, most historians assumed that Truman solicited it purely as a courtesy to Hoover and Secretary of War Henry L. Stimson, who had earlier been Hoover's secretary of state. As it turns out, Truman had a much higher opinion of Hoover than did the historians.

Recently discovered documents show that Truman forwarded the memorandum to his manpower czar, Fred M. Vinson, director of the Office of War Mobilization and Reconversion. Vinson had no quarrel with the casualty estimate, and suggesting that Hoover's paper be shown to Stimson, acting Secretary of State Joseph C. Grew, and former Secretary of State Cordell Hull. Truman sent copies of the memo to all three men, asking each for a written analysis of it and summoning Grew and Stimson to a meeting to discuss their analyses with him.

Stimson wrote: "We shall in my opinion have to go through a more bitter finish fight than in Germany...." Truman also met with Admiral William D. Leahy on the matter. In addition to serving as the president's White House chief of staff, the admiral was his personal representative on the Joint Chiefs of Staff and acted as unofficial chairman at their meetings. Leahy sent a memorandum stamped URGENT to the other JCS members, as well as to Stimson and Secretary of the Navy James Forrestal, saying that the president wanted a meeting to discuss "the losses in dead and wounded that will result from an invasion of Japan proper," and he stated unequivocally: "It is his intention to make his decision on the campaign with the purpose of economizing to the maximum extent possible in the loss of American lives."

At the June 18, 1945, meeting all the participants agreed that an invasion of the Home Islands would be extremely costly—but that it was essential for the defeat of Imperial Japan. Stimson said he "agreed with the plan proposed by the Joint Chiefs of Staff as being the best thing to do, but he still hoped for some fruitful accomplishment through other means." Those other means ranged from

FIFTH MARINE DIVISION

increased political pressure brought to bear through a display of Allied unanimity at the imminent Potsdam Conference to the as-yet-untested atomic weapons that might "shock" the Japanese into surrender. As for Truman, he stated that he "was clear on the situation now and was quite sure that the Joint Chiefs of Staff should proceed" but expressed the hope "that there was a possibility of preventing an Okinawa from one end of Japan to the other."

The invasion plan, code-named DOWN-FALL, contained four major components. First would come Operation OLYMPIC. An area the size of Connecticut on Japan's southernmost island of Kyushu would be seized by the end of 1945 by the U.S. Sixth Army for the construction of airbases and ship anchorages. Excluding replacements sent during the lengthy campaign,

three-quarters of a million American soldiers and Marines would be initially involved in OLYMPIC —nearly three times the number that invaded Okinawa.

Next, would come an even larger assault in the spring of 1946, Operation CORONET involving over a million and a quarter troops, to be landed within striking distance of Tokyo itself, on the island of Honshu. As it was envisioned, the U.S. First and Eighth Armies would undertake this mission and battle the bulk of the several-million-strong Imperial Army.

The third component would be a continuation of the second as Tokyo was surrounded and thus cut off from Japanese reinforcements before the summer monsoons. The U.S. Tenth Army would join the fray as well as contingents of Australian, British, and Canadian forces.

ABOVE: One of the U.S. Marine Corps cemeteries on Iwo Jima, where the 21,000-man garrison inflicted 28,666 American casualties. Marine and Navy casualties: killed in action: 4,917; died of wounds: 1,401; missing, presumed dead: 494; wounded in action: 19,198; combat fatigue casualties not returned to action: 2,648.

Finally, if the Japanese had not yet surrendered, Tokyo would be taken in brutal block-by-block fighting, while other U.S. forces, principally from the Sixth and Tenth Armies, seized areas of continued Japanese resistance.

When the war came to its sudden and unexpected end, the U.S. First Army and Eighth Air Force were in the midst of their long journey from Europe to the Pacific to reinforce General Douglas MacArthur's invasion armada. The First Army had already fought its way across France and into the heart of Nazi Germany, while the Eighth Air Force had pummeled the Reich from England.

With luck and hard fighting, Truman believed the brutal business of subjugating Japan might be completed by the end of 1946, if much of the remaining country could be induced to surrender—but there were no illusions about the potential costs. As early as the summer of 1944, Joint Chiefs of Staff planners had cautiously estimated the price of this endeavor to be "half a million American lives and many times that number in wounded," because of the willingness of Japanese soldiers to stubbornly fight to the death.

A half-century after the war, some historians would pick up much smaller casualty projections made for specific parts of the opening assault to "prove" that the number of dead and wounded would not have been nearly so dreadful. But the fact of the matter was that casualty numbers were already climbing to record levels as the fighting grew closer to Japan at Iwo Jima and Okinawa, and as the Navy fought off kamikaze suicide aircraft at sea. And there is no more clear an example of this than the massive production of Purple Heart medals given to American troops wounded in battle and to the families of those killed in action. When representatives of Imperial Japan signed surrender documents aboard the battleship *Missouri* in Tokyo Bay, some 500,000 Purple Hearts became the most welcome "war surplus" of all.

The cost to the Imperial Army and Navy by war's end had already been staggering and, in Japan itself, nearly 300,000 Japanese civilians had lost their lives during B-29 incendiary bombings—with more than six million rendered homeless—even before the atomic bombs were dropped. A July 1945 War Department document grimly predicted: "We shall probably have to kill at least five to ten million Japanese [and] this might cost us between 1.7 and four million casualties, including 400,000 to 800,000 killed."

Some civilian elements in the Japanese government had come to a similar conclusion and were determined to try to find a way to end the war before the U.S. invasion was launched. Unfortunately, the fanatical military was in firm control of the government, and Japanese moderates had to tread gingerly for fear of arrest or assassination. It was the hope of Truman and his senior advisors that the tremendous shock of the few nuclear weapons available would stampede the Japanese into a quick capitulation. In the end, this is precisely what happened—but not before a coup attempt nearly blocked Emperor Hirohito's surrender announcement. World War II ended on September 2, 1945, instead of late 1946 or even 1947.

As for the Purple Heart medals minted for the anticipated invasion, while all the other implements of war—from bullets, to aircraft carriers, to tent pegs—had long since been used up or scrapped, the 500,000 Purple Hearts continued to be distributed, and roughly 120,000 were still available at the turn of the century after the Korean and Vietnam wars. Refurbished in the late 1980s and intermingled with small quantities more recently produced, they continue to be awarded to American service personnel. Said one veteran who learned for the first time that he had received a medal minted for his grandfather's generation: "I will never look at my Purple Heart the same way again."

SELECTED BIBLIOGRAPHY

Asada, Sadao. *From Mahan to Pearl Harbor: The Imperial Japanese Navy and the United States.* Annapolis: Naval Institute Press, 2006.

Baer, George W. *100 Years of Sea Power: The U.S. Navy, 1890–1990.* Stanford, CA: Stanford University Press, 1994.

Bergerud, Eric M. *Touched by Fire: The Land War in the South Pacific.* Viking, 1994.
_____. *Fire in the Sky: The Air War in the South Pacific.* Viking, 1996.

Dower, John W. *War Without Mercy.* New York: Pantheon Books, 1986.

Drea, Edward J. *In the Service of the Emperor: Essays on the Imperial Japanese Army.* Lincoln: University of Nebraska Press, 1998.
_____. *MacArthur's ULTRA: Codebreaking and the War Against Japan, 1942-1945.* Lawrence, KS: University of Kansas Press, 1992.

Farago, Ladislas. *The Broken Seal.* New York: Random House, 1967.

Hornfischer, James D. *The Last Stand of the Tin Can Sailors.* New York: Random House, 2004.

Kent, Molly. *USS Arizona's Last Band: The History of U.S. Navy Band Number 22.* Kansas City: Silent Song Publishing, 1996.

King, Ernest J. *U.S. Navy at War: 1941–1945, Official Reports to the Secretary of the Navy.* Washington: U.S. Government Printing Office, 1946.

Lundstrom, John B. *Black Shoe Carrier Admiral: Frank Jack Fletcher at Coral Sea, Midway, and Guadalcanal.* Annapolis: Naval Institute Press, 2006.
_____. *The First Team and the Guadalcanal Campaign: Naval Fighter Combat from August to November 1942.* Annapolis, MD: Naval Institute Press, 1994.

McNaughton, James C. *Nisei Linguists: Japanese Americans in the Military Intelligence Service during World War II.* Washington, D.C.: Department of the Army, 2006.

Miller, Donald L. *D-Days in the Pacific.* New York: Simon and Schuster, 2005.

Morison, Samuel Eliot. *The Two-Ocean War: A Short History of the United States Navy in the Second World War.* Boston: Little, Brown & Co., 1963.

Naval Historical Center website: http://www.history.navy.mil/faqs/faq87-3.htm, accessed 10/01/2007.

Parshall, Jon and Anthony Tully. *Shattered Sword: The Untold Story of the Battle of Midway.* Washington: Potomac Books, 2005.

Peattie, Mark R. *Sunburst: The Rise of Japanese Naval Air Power, 1909 – 1941.* Annapolis, MD: Naval Institute Press, 2001.

Reynolds, Clark G. *The Fast Carriers: The Forging of an Air Navy.* New York, NY: McGraw-Hill, 1968.

Sledge, Eugene B. *With the Old Breed: At Peleliu and Okinawa.* Oxford: Oxford University Press, 1990.

Spector, Ronald. *Eagle Against the Sun.* NY: Vintage Books, 1985.

Ugaki, Admiral Matome. *Fading Victory: The diary of Admiral Matome Ugaki 1941-1945,* Trans. Masataka Chihaya, with D.M. Goldstein and K.V. Dillon. Pittsburgh: University of Pittsburgh Press, 1991.

The United States Marine Corps. FMFRP 12-34: History of U.S. Marine Corps Operations in World War II. Washington: Government Printing Office, 2000.

Willmott, H.P. *The Battle of Leyte Gulf: The Last Fleet Action.* Bloomington: Indiana University Press, 2005.

Series:
Naval History Magazine, series.
United States Naval Institute Proceedings, series.
U.S. Army in World War II, The War in the Pacific, series.
Marines in World War II Commemorative Series.

Thanks also to kind efforts and access to their oral history databases by:
The Air Force Historical Research Center
The Naval Historical Center
The United States Naval Institute
The Combined Arms Research Library, Fort Leavenworth, KS

INDEX

Note: Page numbers in *italics* refer to either illustrations or captions.

Langford, Frances, *239*
Langley, 251
Lanphier, Thomas G., Jr., 144–45
Layton, Edwin T., 144
LCIs, *238*
LCM(3)s, *214*
LCP(L) boats, *92–94, 110*
LCVP boats, *92–94*, 230, *231*
Leahy, William D., 264
Leckie, Robert, 204
Lee, Willis, 116, 224
LeMay, Curtis, 228–29, *228–29*, 253, 257
Leuthen, Joseph, 111
Lewis, Bob, 255
Lexington, 22, *24*, *66*, 67–69, *68*, 76, 79, *142*, *161*, *189*
Leyte Gulf, Battle of, 207–15, 224–25
Leyte Island, 201
Lindberg, Charles, *236*
Lindbergh, Charles, *186*, 186–87
Lipes, Wheeler B., 40–41, *176*, 176–77
Lisianski Island, 71
Little, *247*
Lockwood, Charles A., Jr., 176, *178*
logistics, 198–99
Lomax, Vincent, 37
London Naval Treaty, 14
Long Island, 135
Loomis, H. F., *20*
Los Negros Island, 180, *181*
LSTs, *215*, *238*
Lucas, Jack, 230, 231, *236*, 237–38
Lutjens, Paul R., 125, 127
Luzon Island, 23, 201, 216, *222*
Lynd, William E., 132–33

M
M3 Stuart light tanks, *127*, 129
M4A2 Sherman tanks, *5*, *7*, *165*, 167, *214*
M5 Stuart light tanks, *184–85*
M8 Howitzer Motor Carriages, *184–85*
MacArthur, Douglas, *56*, 67
    defense of Philippines, 40, 42, 47–48
    evacuated from Philippines, 54, *116*
    invasion of Philippines, 180, 182–84, 197, 200–202,
        207, 214, 215, 219, 224, *257*, *258*, 266
    as SPT commander, 61, 93–97, *94*, 109, 125, 127, 131,
        139–40, 149, 151, 159, 173, *178*, *180*, 187, 188
    war preparations, 21–22
Macdonald, Charles H., 186
Maghakian, Victor, 195–96
MAGIC intercepts, 20–21
Makin Island, 161, 164, 166–67, 171, 176, *187*
Malaysia, 24–25
Manchuria (Manchukuo), 8, 10, 14, *14*, 204, 258
Manhattan Project, 252, 254, 257
Manila Bay, *221*
Mao Zedong, 10
March, H. A., *148*
Marco Polo bridge incident, *14*, 15, *105*
Mariana Islands, 161, 171, 180, 184, 188–92, 194–97,
    234, 242
Marshall, George C., 54, 61, 120, 227
Marshall, S. L. A., 167, 169
Marshall Islands, 44, 45–46, 161, 167, 169–73
Maryland, *30*, *33*, *162*, *248*
Mason, Charles Perry, 149
Matsumura, Heita, *28–29*
Maui, *21*
Maury, *121*
Maya, *106–7*, *208*
McCain, John, 109, 136, *136*, 225
McClusky, Clarence Wade, 75, *79*

McColm, George, *23*
McColm, J. E., *23*
McFarland, 117
McGuire, Thomas, *186*
McMorris, Charles H., 131
McNab, Alexander, 129
McNulty, 258
McVay, Charles B., III, *260*, 260–63
Medendorp, Alfred, 124–25
Melhorn, Charles, 116, *116*, 118
Meyer, Cord, Jr., 173
Michels, James, *236*
Midway Island, 22, 64, 67, *70*, 70–82, 84, 86–88, 90
Mikawa, Gunichi, *104*, 105
Mikuma, *60–62*, *88–89*
Miles, Sam, 102
Miller, Danforth P., 115, 133
Miller, Joe, 186
Miller, P. J., *186–87*
Mills, Archie, *24*, 71, *71*
Milne Bay, Battle of, *95*, 95–96
Mindanao Island, 202, 217
Minneapolis, *66*, 119, *119*
Missouri, *16–17*, *248*, 257, *259*, 266
Mitscher, Marc A., *63*, 189–92
Mobile Fleet (Japan), 188–89, *190*
Mongolia, *105*
Moore, Clarence A. "Bill," 257–58
Moore, Kyle C. "Casey," 262
Moore, Raymond A., 73
Moore, Thomas, *176*
Moosbrugger, Frederick, *138–40*
Morotai, 187, 202, *203*, 214
Morton, Dudley, *178–79*
Mucci, Henry A., *216*
Mukden incident, 14
Munda, *96*, 149–51, *151*, 155, *160*, *239*
Musashi, 14, *15*, 207, *208*, 224, *225*
Musser, Francis, 71
Myoko, *106–7*, *208*

N
Nadzab Airfield, *125*
Nagano, Osami, 70, 76–78, *208*
Nagasaki, Japan, 255
Nagato, *208*
Nagumo, Chuichi, 19, 29, 71–72, 77–78, 190
Nakagawa, Kunio, 205
Namur, 169–73, *234*
Nanking, Rape of, 10, 15
Neches, 46
Negishi, Asao, *28–29*
Nevada, *30–31*, 34
New Britain, *96*, 102, *143*, 153, 159–60, 180
New Georgia, *151*, *152*, 160
New Guinea, 59, 76, 94–96, 124–27, 129–37, 139, 149,
    153–54, 159–60, 180, 182–84, 186–87
New Jersey, *141*, 219
New Orleans, 119, *121*
Newman, Oliver P., 184
Niagara, *21*
Nickerson, Herman, 101
Nimitz, Chester W., 12, 59, *59*, 61, 66–67, 70, 76, 78,
    93–94, *94*, *111*, 116, 118, *124*, 131, 132–33, 136, 139,
    144, 149, 153–54, 161, 167, 172–73, *180*, 188, 197,
    201, 202–5, 207, 224–25
Nishimura, Shoji, 206–7, 225
Nittsu Maru, *179*
Noemfoor Island, 187
Nomura, Kichisaburo, 18–19, *19*, 20, 21
North Carolina, 191
Northampton, 119

Northern Force (Japanese), 207–8
Noyes, Leigh, *104*

O
Oba, Sakae, *9*
O'Brien, Cyril J., 196, *235*, 235–37
Oda, Kensaku, 129
Odell, Robert H., 126–27, 129
Oglala, *21*, *28–29*
O'Hare, Edward "Butch," 79
O'Kane, Richard H., *179*, *191*
Okinawa, 9, 102, 166, 171, 201, 220, *226–28*, 240, *241–43*,
    242–43, 245–47, 249, 252, 266
Oklahoma, *21*, *28–29*, 30, 33, 36
Okumiya, Masatake, 88, 90
Oldendorf, Jesse, 207–8
Operation A-GO, 188
Operation AL, 76, 78
Operation CARTWHEEL, 140, 142–51, 153–57, 159–60
Operation CORONET, 265
Operation FLINTLOCK, *168–69*
Operation GALVANIC, 162
Operation ICEBERG, 240, 242–43, 245–47, 249
Operation MI, 76
Operation MO, 66, 76
Operation OLYMPIC, 265
Operation RECKLESS, 182
Operation STALEMATE, *202*
Operation WATCHTOWER, 93
Oppenheimer, J. Robert, 255
"Orange" war plans, 8, 44, 139
Orr, John Irwin, 262
OS2U-3 Kingfisher floatplane, *30*, *34*, *191*, *218*
"Oscar" fighters. *See* Ki-43 "Oscar" fighters
Owens, James C., 73
Ozawa, Jisaburo, 188, 189–91, 208, 224, 225

P
P-38 Lightning fighters, 110, *111*, 115, 142, 143, *143*, 144,
    145–49, 156–57, *157*, 186, *186*
P-39 Airacobra fighters, 135, *135*, 137, 140, 142, *187*
P-40 Kittyhawk fighters, *96*
P-40 Warhawk fighters, *187*
P-47 Thunderbolt fighters, *147*, *187*
P-51 Mustang fighters, *187*, 234–35
Pack, William, *134–35*
Panay, 15
Parker, Alva, 149
Patch, Alexander M., 124
PBY-5 Catalina flying boats, *24*, *25*, *34*, 70, 71, 135
Pearl Harbor, 8, 10, *12–13*, 16, 17–25, *21*, *28–34*, 29, *33–38*,
    36–39, 59
Pederson, Norman, *134–35*
Peleliu, 102, *200–203*, 202–5
Pennsylvania, *28–29*, 33, *199*
Pensacola, 74, 119, *120–21*
Pepper, Jack, *239*
Percival, Arthur E., 24–25, 58–59, 258
Perry, Matthew C., *258*
Perth, 58–59, 59
"Pete" seaplanes. *See* F1M2 "Pete" seaplanes
Philippine Division, 42
Philippine Scouts, *23*, 42
Philippine Sea, Battle of the, 191–92, 194–97
Philippines, The
    American defense of, 22–23, 40–43, *40–43*, 47–49,
        47–52, 54–57, *57*
    American recapture of, 166, 181, 201–5, 207–19, *222*,
        224–25, 242, *244*
    American rule in, 8, 10, 17
    Japanese attack, 25
    war preparations in, 21–22, 29

PHOTO CREDITS

Front Jacket Photographs: ©Bettmann/Corbis; ©W. Eugene Smith/Time Life Pictures/Getty Images (inset)

Back Cover Photograph: U.S. Army Heritage and Education Center

AP Photo: pp. 50, 112 (bottom), 223 (top), 240; ©US Navy Photo: p. 193 (top)

Courtesy of Australian War Memorial: pp. 95 (top), 96, 143

Author's Collection: pp. 14 (top), 17, 19, 42 (patch), 47, 52, 66-67, 71 (top), 79 (patch), 85 (bottom), 94, 95 (bottom), 103, 108 (patch), 124, 125, 126, 127, 128-129, 130, 134 (top), 147, 150, 152, 154, 167, 168-169, 174-175, 181 (patch), 183, 184 (patch), 214, 215, 217 (patch), 222, 223 (bottom), 226-227, 234 (patch), 238, 241 (top), 242 (patch), 243, 245, 253, 257, 258, 264

Corbis: pp. 9, 18 (right), 25, 35, 57, 68, 109 (bottom), 114 (top right), 116 (bottom), 117, 135, 137, 144 (top inset), 153, 155, 156, 158 (bottom), 161, 162, 163 (inset), 165, 166, 170, 171, 181, 185, 189, 192 (top), 194, 197 (bottom), 205, 228, 250 (top right), 252, 256, 265; ©Bettmann: pp. 1, 11, 18 (bottom), 20, 34, 41 (right), 49 (inset), 53, 54-55, 134 (bottom), 136, 143, 163, 173, 216, 221, 224, 239, 260; ©Jack Fields: pp. 6-7; ©Hulton-Deutsch Collection: pp. 185 (top), 188, 221 (inset); ©Fenno Jacobs: p. 148; ©Charles Kerlee: p. 196; ©Wayne Miller: p. 149; ©Museum of Flight: p. 158 (top); ©Amos Nachom: pp. 2-3; ©Seattle Post-Intelligencer Collection; Museum of History and Industry: p. 53 (inset); ©Tom Shafer/ Bettmann: p. 217; ©Pfc. John J. Smith: p. 204; ©Edward Steichen: p. 142; ©Stanley Troutman/Bettmann: pp. 200-201; ©Underwood & Underwood: p. 14 (bottom)

Courtesy of Sadao Asada: p. 28 (Japanese postage stamp)

Courtesy of Perry Dahl: pp. 111 (top), 157

Courtesy of Molly Kent from *USS* Arizona's *Last Band: The History of U.S. Navy Band Number* 22: pp. 12-13

Courtesy of John Kuehn: p. 198

Courtesy of Admiral Larson Collection/www.usspringle.org: p. 218

Courtesy of Richard Marin from the publication: *War of Our Fathers*: endpapers

Courtesy of Kevin McGuiness: p. 108 (patch)

Courtesy of Jon Parshall: pp. 26-27

Courtesy of Jim Sandalier: pp. 218 (inset), 246 (inset)

Courtesy of Kevin Ullrich: pp. 266

Ernest Arroyo Collection: pp. 32-33

The Forbes Collection, New York. ©All Rights Reserved: p. 31 (inset)

Getty Images: ©HO/AFP: p. 30; ©Hulton Archive: p. 122 (top right); ©Keystone: pp. 92-93; ©National Archives: pp. 30-31; ©W. Eugene Smith/Time Life Pictures: p. 195; ©Time Life Pictures/US Marine Corps: p. 105; US Navy Photo/Time Life Pictures: pp. 88-89, 193 (bottom)

Granger Collection: p. 76 (top inset)

Library of Congress: pp. 108 (top left), 132, 138-139, 154 (left)

The MacArthur Memorial Organization: pp. 51, 56

Marine Corps University, Quantico, VA: Research Center Archives: pp. 203, 236; flag raising film footage courtesy of Visual Information Repository: p. 237

Marine Corps Heritage Center, Quantico, VA: pp. 164, 165 (top)

Museum of World War II: p. 145

National Geographic Map Collection: pp. 86-87

National Museum of the United States Air Force: pp. 63 (insets), 64 (bottom inset), 147 (inset), 186, 187, 229, 254, 255

Naval Historical Center: pp. 15, 16, 18 (top & left), 21, 24, 25, 28-29, 37, 38-39, 40, 41 (left), 42, 44-45 (top inset), 46 (inset), 58, 59, 60-61, 62, 63, 64-65, 66, 69, 70, 71 (bottom), 72, 73, 74, 75, 76 (bottom inset), 77, 78 (inset), 79, 80, 81, 82, 83, 84, 85 (top), 89 (inset), 91, 97, 98-99, 100, 101, 104, 106-107, 113, 115, 116 (inset), 118, 119, 120-121, 122 (top inset), 122-123, 131, 133, 141 (bottom right), 144 (bottom inset), 148 (top left), 178-179, 180, 190, 191, 192 (bottom), 199, 202, 206 (top), 208, 209, 210, 211, 212, 213, 219, 220 (inset), 225, 230, 235, 241 (bottom), 244, 246-247, 250 (top left and bottom), 251, 257 (inset), 261, 263

U.S. Army Signal Corps: p. 69 (left)

U.S. Army Heritage Museum: pp. 102 (patch), 166 (patch), 171 (patch), 234 (patch), 242 (patch)

U.S. Army Military History Institute: pp. 12-13 (top), 22, 23, 151, 160, 184, 231, 232, 233

U.S. Marine Corps: pp. 45 (bottom inset), 48, 98, 100 (inset), 107, 110, 111, 112 (top), 114 (top left), 164, 165 (top), 197 (top), 205 (top), 235 (top), 236 (top), 242

U. S. National Archives: pp. 36 (bottom), 43, 109 (top), 140, 146, 159, 172, 173 (top), 177, 248 (bottom)

U. S. Naval Institute: pp. 141 (bottom left), 206 (bottom), 248 (top), 249

U. S. Navy: pp. 88-89, 122 (top left)

U. S. Navy Submarine Force Museum: p. 176

USS *Arizona* Memorial: pp. 33, 36 (top)

Wisconsin Maritime Museum Collection: p. 141 (top)